ADVANCE PRAISE FOR

What Does Somebody Have to Do to Get a Job Around Here?

by Cynthia Shapiro

"Cynthia Shapiro puts you on the inside track to getting the job of your dreams—without the nightmares. If you want to compete with confidence, this is the only job-search book you need."

—Lois P. Frankel, Ph.D.,
author of *Nice Girls Don't Get the Corner Office* and *See Jane Lead*

"Startling! This edgy, eye-opening book tells it like it is and reveals surprising secrets that will help you land the job of your dreams. It's the best investment you can make on behalf of your career."

—Sam Horn,
author of *POP!: Stand Out in Any Crowd*

"You can't get on the fast track if you can't get in the door. This book shares the hidden snares and insider secrets that will give job seekers the edge they've been looking for."

—Anne Fisher,
"Ask Annie" columnist, CNNMoney.com and author of *If My Career's on the Fast Track, Where Do I Get a Road Map?*

"Cynthia's insights into the job-search process are invaluable. Whether you are just starting out or a seasoned professional, her insider tips will show you how to supercharge your job search and get the jobs you want."

—Penelope Trunk,
columnist for *The Boston Globe* and Yahoo! Finance, and author of *Brazen Careerist: The New Rules for Success*

"Applying for a job is the most important game you will ever play, but employers keep the rules secret. Shapiro reveals how hiring decisions are really made, and gives you the map you need to get through this minefield safely."

—Lewis Maltby,
President, National Workrights Institute

"There's nothing like insider secrets to give you an edge over the competition, and when it comes to getting the top jobs, Cynthia Shapiro knows her stuff! This book will change the way you view job searching forever. Stop settling for less and go for the best!"

—Barbara Stanny,
author of *Secrets of Six-Figure Women*

"Think job hunting is all about résumés, skills, and experiences? Think again. Ex–human resources executive Cynthia Shapiro pulls back the curtain to reveal the secret hiring practices of corporate America and tells you everything you need to know about beating hiring managers at their own game. Don't be left wondering why you didn't get the job—before you send out another résumé, read this book!"

—Michelle Goodman,
author of *The Anti 9-to-5 Guide: Practical Career Advice for Women Who Think Outside the Cube*

What Does Somebody Have to Do to Get a Job Around Here?

ALSO *by* CYNTHIA SHAPIRO

Corporate Confidential: 50 Secrets Your Company Doesn't Want You to Know—And What to Do About Them

What Does Somebody Have to Do to Get a Job Around Here?

44 INSIDER SECRETS
THAT WILL GET YOU HIRED

Cynthia Shapiro, MBA, ELC, PHR

St. Martin's Griffin New York

 Printed in the United States of America. For information, address St. Martin's Press, 175 Fifth Avenue, New York, N.Y. 10010.

www.stmartins.com

ISBN-13: 978-0-312-37334-4
ISBN-10: 0-312-37334-1

10 9 8 7 6 5 4 3

This book is lovingly dedicated to two very giving people:

my husband, Kevin Shapiro, whose unwavering support led to the realization of this book as well as *Corporate Confidential,* as well as the joyous fulfillment of my lifelong dream, my mission, and consulting services that are now helping people around the world;

and

my mom, Barbara Siegmund, who gave me the world and taught me that I could do anything I put my heart to.

Just look at what love can do.

CONTENTS

ACKNOWLEDGMENTS

SO MANY WONDERFUL AND TALENTED PEOPLE HAVE come together to bring this book to fruition. I am eternally grateful to each and every one of you!

I am so thankful to all those who courageously gave their stories and time, sharing their personal experiences for this book. I was not able to use all the stories collected, but I greatly appreciate each and every one of you who were so willing to share your touching, victorious, and sometimes heartbreaking experiences. Your stories will help countless readers. Thank you.

A loving thank-you to my husband, Kevin, who generously allowed me to pursue this dream and has courageously supported me every step of the way. Kevin, thank you doesn't even begin to cover it. You are a truly amazing and supportive partner, friend, and husband.

And of course my fabulous agent, Jessica Faust. Thank you so much for your tireless efforts, your insights, and your support. It's so fantastic to work with someone I have complete and total trust in! You're wonderful.

Next are the talented and hardworking people at St. Martin's Press. I will always be grateful to St. Martin's for giving me the opportunity to publish these books. And a special thank-you to my editor, Sheila Curry Oakes, and her assistant, Alyse Diamond, for the marvelous editing, guidance, encouragement, and support.

A very heartfelt thank-you to George Conley for his higher understanding and crystal clarity, ensuring that both the message and I stayed on track and in balance. You are such a blessing in my life and the lives of others!

To my family and friends who read manuscripts, provided much-appreciated suggestions, shared positive thoughts, and sustained me during the writing and crafting process, I thank each and every one of you!

A huge thank-you to my mom, Barbara Siegmund, for being such a loving and supportive presence in all I do. To my sister Nancy Ward, for her insights, assistance, and support. To Deb Freng, for her tremendous support and friendship, and for selflessly giving her time and expertise when this project really needed it. To Christine Corday and Brie Schwartz, who constantly pour love into my life—I feel it every day. To Michelle Fisher for her last-minute, much-appreciated, and brilliant editing, rearranging, and title crafting.

This has been quite a journey, and each of you who've touched my life is part of the gift this book brings to those who read it. I will always feel blessed to have been surrounded by such exceptionally talented, loving, and generous individuals. I am so grateful. Thank you!

INTRODUCTION

CRACKING THE HIRING CODE

WE ALL FIND OURSELVES WONDERING WHAT GOES ON behind the closed doors of the hiring managers. What is this mysterious group thinking? What are their secret criteria?

Don't you wish you had a crystal ball to look into the minds of these powerful corporate gatekeepers and find out what they're looking for? What their idea of a top candidate really is, really looks like?

Now you will. Your crystal ball is here.

This book is the first to take job seekers behind the closed doors of hiring managers, providing a true, uncensored, and sometimes even shocking look at their processes and systems. For the first time you will see their hidden agendas, secret discriminations, fears, and motivations. It's all here. You will finally know exactly what these people are trained to look for, say, screen out, and recommend for hire. You will learn the common traps and pitfalls most job candidates accidentally fall into that knock them out of the running. And you'll learn why no company and no interviewer will ever tell you what you did wrong that cost you the job you wanted.

You will learn how to get past online résumé screeners, psychological assessments, and underhanded tactics so you will stand out among the overwhelming competition for top jobs. You will finally understand the true nature of the system and how to work it to your advantage.

This is not the standard "corporate-approved" job search guide providing generic advice ensuring you'll look and sound like everyone else applying for the job. It will take you deep on the inside, where no hiring manager wants you to go. It will give you an unveiled glimpse into the real world of corporate selection and the hidden realms of the key decision makers, so you'll know exactly what to do at each step of the process to stand out from the crowd as the star candidate.

Recently, I had a client who had not been able to find a job after nine months of frustrated searching. He was about to lose his house and couldn't figure out why he kept getting calls and interviews but no offers. He was highly skilled, very personable, and overall an extremely desirable candidate but had not been able to get past the initial interview process. As this happened to him repeatedly, he had become more and more despondent. Little did he know it was a matter of changing one simple thing. In less than an hour we suddenly had our hands on the problem and turned it around. It was one of those things that nobody talks about and you won't find in any other job search book. He could immediately see it would make all the difference, and as the clouds mentally parted for him he asked me, "Why haven't I heard this anywhere before?"

The sad truth is, most of what you truly need to know in your job search is currently known only to the hiring insiders and is protected as "top-secret" information within companies. It is hidden away in secrecy because companies don't want you to have the power in the interview process. That scares them. If you knew you could manipulate the entire interview process, then companies would no longer have the upper hand. Then you would be screening them instead of the other way around.

With his very next interview my client had a top-tier job offer. Nine months of rejection and frustration for lack of one bit of insider information. What worked for him was Secret 32, just one of the secrets I share in this book. There are forty-four insider secrets collected here to help you remove those unfair barriers, supercharge your job search process, maximize your income potential, and get those multiple job offers rolling in.

To increase your chances of getting any job you desire, nothing is more powerful than insider information from someone who has been deep in the hiring trenches. As a former human-resources executive and hiring manager, I've hired people at all stages from entry level to Chief Operating Officer. I've trained human-resources departments and taught companies the very same underhanded and intimidating strategies I describe here. I've been involved in hiring searches from small start-ups to large corporations, and I'll tell you that they are all looking for employees using the same basic criteria: things they will never tell you, things they feel are critical to their survival. There is no leeway. One move on the wrong side of the invisible line they've set will land your résumé in the trash (a.k.a. the "I'll keep your résumé on file" drawer). But it no longer has to be that way. I've seen firsthand the underhanded, unfair, and grueling tactics used by hiring managers and I'm ready to share all their best-kept secrets.

Being able to recognize and get past the tactics of these powerful corporate gatekeepers can mean the difference between getting the job of your dreams and getting the disheartening form letter saying "thanks but no thanks."

I know exactly what companies are looking for in those teetering stacks of résumés, and I can tell you how to get yours on top. I know why they ask you trick questions during interviews, and I know exactly what they're screening for. I know what secret discriminations and hiring criteria are lurking within the hiring process and how to keep them from impacting your success. I know how to push the magic buttons to get the highest possible salary and greatest benefit package. In addition, I know the powerful secrets to looking like the newest company star within the first ninety days. Now you will, too.

Whether you find yourself suddenly out of work, a recent graduate looking for your first job, or simply unhappy with your current situation and looking for something new, these insider secrets will give you a huge lead over the competition.

Prepare yourself. You are about to understand the interview and hiring process from an entirely different viewpoint. You are about to become the one in charge of the process. In this book, nothing is considered taboo, nothing held back, no holds barred. This is the real deal on how top candidates are screened and hired all across America from the biggest corporate giants to the smallest mom-and-pop operations. The real system is not always politically correct, is often unfair, and sometimes is not even legal. But if you learn how this secret system works, you'll know how to sail through the interview process and become the top candidate for any job. You will never have to stress over answering trick questions correctly, explaining that gap in your employment history, handling a termination on your record, or looking like the top candidate any company would be proud to hire on the spot.

You will never look at a job search the same way again, and the overly powerful corporate gatekeepers won't be able to stand in the way of your dreams once you know all their best-kept secrets.

1

YOU ARE BEING ELIMINATED

DO YOU THINK THE HIRING PROCESS IS ONE OF SCREENing and interviewing applicants to determine the best fit for a job opening?

It's not. Not anymore.

In the last several years, what used to be a standard process of candidate consideration and placement has changed dramatically, and not in your favor.

The new tactics employed by today's hiring mangers are enough to make us all yearn for the days when sweaty palms and nervous interview answers were the worst of our worries. Most people have felt a shift in our hiring practices but can't quite pinpoint why things feel so much more stressful than they used to. It's not your imagination.

If it seems tougher out there than it used to be, that's because it is. Interviewing and hiring has gone from being a merely stressful process to a full-scale gauntlet that most candidates are finding themselves unprepared for.

The new hiring and interviewing practices have morphed into a barrage of trick questions, hidden discriminations, psychological traps, secret criteria, and unfair barriers that are actually designed to make you fall apart during the process. Some are even designed to make you eliminate yourself.

The real question is not why things feel so much more stressful; it's how are people handling what's going on out there. Sadly, many are not handling the job market well at all. Today, according to reported data from the Bureau of Labor Statistics, as many as 37 percent of America's unemployed have been without work for up to six months or more. That's the highest percentage in twenty years. Right now, for every job opening in the United States there are three unemployed workers waiting to take it. To make matters worse, it's estimated that only 1 percent of résumés are effective enough to make it to an interview and almost 95 percent of all interviews will end with unreturned phone calls or the dreaded form letter. In the midst of all this, there is no way for candidates to find out the real reason that they didn't make it. That is, until now. It is imperative that candidates learn how to read the signs, get the insider secrets, and protect themselves in this new hiring environment.

This chapter will give you an unparalleled glimpse into the true motivations of hiring managers, what they're up against, and what tactics they've been trained to use to get what the company wants. You'll learn how closet discriminations, secret criteria, and interviewer tactics play a part in the candidate screening process and how to protect yourself so you can move forward.

I will not be discussing some of the more obvious aspects of résumé and interview preparation you may have seen or read elsewhere. I am going where no other job seeker guide has dared to go before—into the taboo aspects of the job search process and into the world the hiring managers don't want you to see. You will uncover where their best-kept secrets are hidden and finally achieve a unique and powerful advantage in the hiring process.

I'm going to show you how to work the system from an insider's perspective so you'll never have to worry about what's expected, what they really want to hear, what to avoid, or how to look like their top candidate. Some of these secrets are indicative of issues that cannot be changed but are still critically important to understand. Many secrets represent issues absolutely within your control, so you can use this information to make the decisions that are best for you throughout the process.

It's time to learn the truth about what candidates today are truly up against.

INSIDER SECRET 1
You're not being hired; you're being excluded.

"I HAD ALL THE QUALIFICATIONS THEY WERE LOOKING FOR. This would be such a perfect fit. Why didn't I get a phone call?"

"I'm the one with exactly what they said they were looking for. Why couldn't they see that?"

We'd all like to think that hiring managers are paid solely to look for the perfect fit for each position. Don't they read every résumé and cover letter, actively looking for anything that might signify a good match? If you have the right qualifications, you'll certainly be up for consideration, right? As many of you may have already guessed, that's not how the process really works.

Imagine instead teetering stacks of résumés, directors and vice presidents screaming at harried hiring managers to hire for that open position "or else," and the phone ringing off the hook with unwanted calls from candidates wanting to know "the status of my résumé." Hiring managers don't exactly have a leisurely job and don't have the time or energy to care about your résumé or your desire to work for the company the way you'd like them to. Everyone who submits a résumé wants to work there, and that means hiring managers are squeezed from all sides. They are pressured to make placements as soon as possible, but the people hired have to be the perfect candidates with all the right skills, have to be a good fit with the manager and team, and above all have to be a safe bet for success, or that hiring manager could soon find him- or herself out of a job.

And what if the manager for the position is doing the hiring rather than someone from human resources? That can be even worse. A busy manager leading a team and meeting deadlines has even less time to deal with résumés and interviews, no matter how much he or she wants or needs that position filled.

So what does all this mean? It means that when you submit your résumé, you aren't being considered for hire. From the first moment the process starts to the very end, you are being excluded from hire. There's a big difference.

Those in charge of hiring for a company are not like recruiters. They aren't trying to find the best fit. They are not looking to place you in a position. They are looking to eliminate 98 percent of the candidates as quickly as possible.

It's a common misconception that the hiring process is one of inclusion, carefully looking at each candidate to find the right match. The harsh truth is that until you have an offer letter in hand, you are in a system of elimination. Thinking the opposite will hurt your chances for making it to that coveted 2 percent.

Today's candidate-screening process consists of a brutal three-phase elimination that begins as soon as you submit your résumé. Most hiring managers don't have the time or resources to go through every résumé carefully looking for qualifications that match the position. In fact, they most likely aren't even reading them. They are scanning and quickly separating résumés into piles labeled "maybe" and "no."

The typical hiring manager spends only three seconds on your résumé. That's it, three seconds. That means if it doesn't stand out immediately, it's in the "no" pile before the hiring manager has finished a sip of his coffee. Some résumés don't even get that three-second courtesy. If the cover letter is too long or seems boring, the hiring manager may not even bother to look at your résumé. That also goes for résumé submissions that are several pages long. Unless you're applying for a high-level executive position, résumés that are longer than one page may not be considered at all.

That's if your résumé even gets to a real person. Having a total stranger do a quick scan on your résumé to decide your future is actually the best-case scenario. Many companies now use scanning software tools that look for certain key words to determine if you're a viable candidate. If you don't have enough of those secret key words, your résumé will never be seen by a human being. It will be screened out as soon as you hit that "submit" button on the company's online résumé submission site.

The truth is: It's estimated that only 1 percent of résumés capture the attention of a busy hiring manager. The rest end up in the "no" pile. And none ever come back from that pile.

I know this sounds brutal, but you have to understand that résumé screening is quite tedious. It's not that hiring managers don't care; it's just that after the first hundred résumés, every submission starts to look the same and their instinct to narrow the field kicks in. Thus the fast and furious exclusion process begins.

If you craft your résumé imagining it will be carefully screened and analyzed by everyone who reads it, burying your key attributes in the details of your entire career history, you'll ensure that it looks like everyone else's résumé in the pile and you won't have a chance of standing out in the crowd.

What if you get a phone call? You know, the one that says the company you'd love to work for likes your résumé and wants to ask you some questions or determine your availability for an in-person interview. This would certainly mean you're moving up, right? You'll be included now, right? Well, sort of. It is definitely an accomplishment when you can escape the stack of résumés and graduate to the level of a phone call, but it's not time to let your guard down. You will be moving up, but you will also be moving into phase two, a much tougher aspect of the elimination process.

Most people believe that if they've managed to get that coveted phone call from the hiring manager, they're in. They're now being actively considered. Well maybe, but only if they survive this next phase of the elimination process that more than half of participants won't. This introductory phone call is known in human-resources and recruiting circles as "the phone screening." And it's called that for a reason.

Phone screening is not designed to get to know you and is not focused on hearing more about your skills. It's designed to look for secret red flags that will remove you from consideration before money and time are spent on a face-to-face interview. In fact, if you don't know what they're specifically looking for, you will find out that these phone screenings are often the last time you hear from the company. The phone screening is so heavily fraught with trick questions and traps that there's less than a 50 percent chance a candidate who gets one of these calls will move on to an actual interview.

If you're one of the lucky few to survive the first few elimination phases and move on to an interview, certainly you'll be close to being considered for hire, right? Sorry, not yet. You can certainly feel very proud that you've made it this far, out of the stacks of literally hundreds of hopeful résumés. But you will still be in that process of heavy elimination. In fact, you'll be in phase three. The person or people interviewing you won't be looking for reasons to make you an offer. They will be actively looking for reasons to show you the door.

Companies simply have too much at stake every time they hire someone. So, instead of looking for the best candidates, they will be much more concerned with actively looking for any red flags or danger signs that this hire may not work out. They do this because an unsuccessful hire can cost the company a great deal of money and time in both removal and replacement. Depending on the industry, a company can spend as much as 150 man-hours on hiring-related tasks and cost-per-hire can be as high as almost half a new employee's first-year salary. The fear of making a hiring mistake that could cost the company double its hiring costs or become a contested removal creating a legal liability has morphed the hiring process into the gauntlet we see today. And the interview itself has the highest stakes in the process.

Once you've made it to an interview, the company believes you have the skills and talent to do the job. That's the good news. The bad news? They will be screening for other things in this face-to-face meeting, secret things. They will be looking for company fit, appearance, personality, and, yes, danger signs that can best be discovered while talking to someone in person. No company will admit to this, but they all do it. The interview is an in-person high-stakes elimination process filled with trick questions, personality profiling, Internet screenings, background checks, and even psychological testing: "The last time you took illegal drugs at work, did it adversely affect your performance? True or false." (Yes, that's a question on an actual employment test!)

Again, this is all designed to eliminate potentially undesirable candidates so the hiring manager can determine the safest bet for hire. Because a hiring manger's job is on the line with every recommendation for hire, the safest bet is the one who will receive the offer, not necessarily the one with the best qualifications. Explains quite a bit, doesn't it?

This is what you're truly up against in the process. You will be actively eliminated right up until you get a formal offer in writing from the company. If you approach the process thinking that they are looking for all the reasons they should hire you, you won't be at the top of your game and you won't be able to stand out from the crowd of other hopefuls.

If I've scared you with all this talk of exclusion, elimination, and your résumé in the trash bin, don't worry. These are all things that can easily be overcome if you know the insider secrets I'm about to share with you. I'll give you all the best insider tips on how to create a résumé that goes right to the top of the pile, how to protect yourself in that initial phone screening, and exactly how to work the interview system to your advantage for survival and success. I'll give you the secrets to get around each of these elimination processes so you'll find yourself way ahead of the standard pack of hopefuls.

First, a few more secrets about what you're truly up against in this process and a closer look at the secret criteria companies are using against you. . . .

INSIDER SECRET 2
You don't fit their secret criteria.

MOST PEOPLE WHO SUBMIT FOR OPEN POSITIONS HAVE THE skills, talent, and qualifications to get the job. But they won't. Why would a candidate who matches exactly what the company is looking for not get a chance at the opportunity? There's clearly something else going on in the selection process that's excluding you from the jobs you desire. **The truth is: Skills and talent won't get you the job**. When a company has several candidates with equal skill sets, something else comes into play, something secret and unique to each company. The number one hidden factor in the exclusion of qualified candidates is a company's secret criteria.

Every single company, whether tiny or gigantic, has its own set of secret screening criteria that it requires its hiring personnel to follow. These criteria are never written down anywhere and go way beyond the standard requirements for the position. Some are things you've heard about such as: We don't hire anyone with a prior termination, or who doesn't have at least three stellar references. But there are many others that we don't hear about such as: We don't hire anyone who has been out of work longer than three months, has not worked for one of our competitors, or doesn't appear to match our company's ideal image. Then there are the ones that a company never wants you to find out about: We don't hire anyone of a certain religion, ethnicity, background, appearance, lifestyle, health level, or parental status. That final tier in the secret criteria list is largely based on the personal preferences of the key decision makers at each company, and often these criteria fall squarely into the realm of discrimination.

Yes, discrimination during the hiring and interview process is illegal, but companies still do it every day. How do they get around the laws designed to protect us? By making it part of their secret criteria that's never written down and never openly discussed.

Most job candidates know it's illegal to discriminate against them for reasons based on age, gender, ethnicity, sexual orientation, religion, disabilities, marital status, or medical issues, so they feel comfortable sharing these issues during the hiring process. I've heard countless times: "What does it matter if I tell them what religion I am or that I'm a recovering cancer patient? They aren't allowed to discriminate, right?" Yes, that's true; they aren't legally allowed to discriminate or exclude you because of these things, but they do. This type of information regularly causes candidates to be secretly eliminated from consideration. The company will never tell you the real reason that you weren't offered the position and won't even openly talk about it themselves. You'll be given the standard lines as to why the job went to someone else, such as "Your skills weren't the ideal match for the position" or "We decided to go in a different direction." Maybe you won't get any explanation at all.

It's important to understand that anything you choose to share with a potential employer, whether in a formal interview scenario or informal chat, may be used against you.

There's always a written and public list of qualifications for each position. Those will match the requirements of the law exactly: "Equal Opportunity Employer" and "all candidates considered." They are all prominently displayed in a job posting and on the walls of a hiring manager's office. But what is legally or ethically required doesn't always match what's really going on behind the scenes.

Behind closed doors, many companies are willing to do whatever it takes to get the perfect profile they desire. A CEO will walk into a hiring manager's office and say something like "Make sure the next person we hire is a black female so we can get our affirmative action numbers up." Or "We have too many working parents here who traipse off to soccer games during deadlines, so make sure the next person you hire doesn't have any kids." Or even "We've had too many people going out on medical leave this year and it has really hurt us, so make sure the next person you hire is in excellent health." For obvious reasons, these kinds of criteria will never have a paper trail and will never be openly spoken about. Everything from physical characteristics to health and marital status is secretly screened for. From long legs for the new vice president's assistant, to an attractive male to head up the marketing department whom potential clients will find appealing, to an older woman to work with the executive who has a jealous wife, you name it, it's been secretly specified and screened for, and no hiring manager will ever admit to it.

"Jason" was in the final stages for a job offer when he happened to mention that he wouldn't be able to start work until his responsibilities with the local gay pride parade were completed. He had agreed to manage certain aspects of this detailed parade and wanted to delay his start date until those requirements were complete. He didn't think anything of it, and the interviewer didn't say anything to show that this could be an issue.

Jason was therefore shocked when, instead of the offer that was promised to arrive via fax the very next morning, he received a dry "no thank you" letter. When he called the interviewer (whom he had met with several times in person and who had always been highly responsive during the hiring process), he got no response. No phone calls were returned, and even his e-mail inquiries met with no reply.

He later discovered that the president of the company was a religious individual who had issues with the local gay community. Jason had been told on several occasions that he was the top candidate for the job, and during the last meeting a full offer had been discussed and negotiations had taken place, with a start date determined. All that was left in the process was the formal offer to be faxed over and signed. Jason realized what had happened to his new job, but it was too late. No discrimination could be proven because nothing was done in writing and it became an issue of "who verbally said what when."

In the end, Jason may not have wanted to work for a company whose president supported such discriminatory behavior, but this was his dream job, and he would never have intentionally jeopardized such a prized opportunity. Had he a better understanding of the levels of discrimination that can go on behind closed doors within the hiring processes of Corporate America, he could have better protected his dream job. His only mistake was assuming that because the law protects against discrimination, his disclosure of involvement in gay pride would have no bearing on a job offer. Living in a city that was accepting of his lifestyle had numbed him to unfortunate and necessary cautions.

It's important to understand that candidates are regularly screened out based on criteria that have nothing to do with skills or talent but have everything to do with preferences. There are some companies that make a concerted effort not to tread on illegality, trying very hard to create genuinely fair and equal hiring practices. However, many companies are not so careful.

"Dan" had been through several interviews with a firm that was his first choice to join. He was extremely well qualified and was now meeting with a high-level executive for his final interview before the ultimate decision was to be made. To Dan's shock, at the end of this interview the executive said, "Well, you really are the perfect candidate. If you only had boobs, there would be an offer letter in your hands right now." He did not get the job.

He was understandably outraged and even attempted to file a discrimination claim. But the executive denied the conversation had ever taken place and pointed to a particular skill in the job description Dan didn't have that suddenly became the "deciding factor" in the decision-making process.

This is one of the more blatant examples of the secret criteria at work, and chances are you will never encounter an executive or hiring manager dense enough to come right out and say something like what was said to Dan (unless the executive really enjoys inviting potential lawsuits). In Dan's case, he was able to count himself lucky that the company exposed its true nature before he started working there and he was able to move on to work for a company that didn't employ such distasteful tactics. But in most cases, when secret criteria discrimination occurs, the response Jason received is the norm—sudden uninterest followed by the cold shoulder. The truth is: Once it's determined that a candidate doesn't fit within a company's secret hiring criteria, the opportunity is closed, and it's not coming back.

Whether the screening specifications include illegal discriminatory practices or not, in every hiring and interview scenario there will always be some form of unwritten screening process.

Countless jobs have been lost due to a lack of understanding that this level of screening occurs every day, and it is imperative we learn how to protect ourselves. The law cannot do it for us. (These steps to protection will be discussed in detail in chapter 3.)

Don't make the mistake of believing the law will protect you during a discriminatory event. It cannot. Companies have become very skilled at putting their secret criteria deep underground where it's not easily seen and no proof or paper trail exists. If a company wants their next executive to have boobs, they will make sure that's what they get, even if that kind of screening is illegal. If a company wants to screen out a certain group, ethnicity, or status, it will do it.

If you find that you are suddenly out of the running for a job you are well qualified for, most likely you've run up against one of these secret criteria discriminations. And unfortunately, that opportunity is now over for you.

The next logical question is "Why?" Why have hiring practices become so harsh, secretive, discriminatory, and unforgiving? That's in Secret 3. . . .

INSIDER SECRET 3
You only get one shot.

AT EVERY POINT ALONG THE WAY, YOU ARE BEING SCRUTINIZED and judged within an unforgiving system. The stakes are high and you only get one shot at each phase of the process. One three-second shot at wowing them with your résumé, one phone screening, and usually only one interview with each key member of the group. Why such scrutiny with no room for error?

Because companies are running scared. It's expensive and risky to hire a new person. And they've got the added factor of bringing an unknown into the company dynamic. There is more at stake than you realize. Just one imprudent hire can cost, at the very least, money and, at the most, the momentum and positive attitude of an entire team. A company also knows it runs the risk of letting in a potentially litigious individual who doesn't have the best interest of the company at heart. Or someone who is just pretending to be an ideal employee only to cause great grief and managerial headaches once employed. Companies know it's much easier to get someone hired than to get a bad placement removed.

Companies have all experienced the horror stories of employees who are hired only to immediately go on workers' comp or disability leave or to trump up a lawsuit that threatens the company's profits for the year. They've also experienced hiring an employee with seemingly great promise who turns negative almost immediately after being hired and takes an entire department down in the process. All too soon a positive and well-motivated team is complaining about everything from management style to compensation and no work is being done.

These risks are in the back of a hiring manager's mind throughout the entire interview and screening process. The severity of the screening process is based on fear: fear of making a bad recommendation for hire that will cost the company time, money, and productivity; a bad recommendation that could lead to the end of the hiring manager's job as well. There really is no leeway for the hiring managers.

A hiring manager knows that candidates will put on their best act as a prime employee throughout the process. They'll try to look their best, say the right things, hide undesirable issues from their past, and say what they think the interviewer wants to hear. Hiring managers know it's relatively easy to act like the perfect candidate for an hour or two. So they are trained to scrutinize everything so closely that they read "potential danger" into everything they see and hear from an applicant.

You may be an ideal candidate, with no intent to harm or take advantage of your potential new employer, but the hiring manager does not know that. So any red flag raised, whether accidental or even inaccurate, will stop the process immediately.

In this high-stakes game, you will only get one shot at each phase of the process. There won't be any "He didn't do very well in the phone screening, but maybe he'll do better in the interview." **The truth is: Once you've hit a snag in the process, you are immediately moved into the "no" pile.** And you will never get a truthful explanation as to why.

During this intense screening process, they won't ever allude to the fact that you've just made a critical mistake. In fact, they may even encourage you to say more now that you're on a roll, and make you feel like this disclosure won't be an issue in the decision-making process. They won't ever want you to know that you've made a mistake that could cost you the job. Why? That's in Secret 4. . . .

INSIDER SECRET 4
No one will tell you when you've made a mistake.

SHOULDN'T SOMEONE TELL YOU WHEN YOU'VE JUST MADE A mistake that cost you the job you wanted? Wouldn't that be a nice thing to do, at least for future reference? It would. But I wouldn't count on seeing it happen any time soon.

In fact, a company representative will never tell you what happened that landed your résumé or interview on the "outs."

No one will tell you that your résumé wasn't up to par; it will simply land in the trash and you'll never get a phone call. No one will tell you that you said something that scared the interviewer during a phone screen; you'll just never be able to get that person on the phone again. And no one will tell you if you did or said something wrong during your interview; you'll just get that dreaded form letter weeks later, if you get anything at all.

Which all leads, again, to the inevitable question of "Why?" Why do companies treat their candidates this way?

"Karen" had submitted her résumé to an interesting company on the recommendation of a friend who worked there. She was called immediately after submitting her résumé and then had a very successful in-person interview with the head of the department. Karen was feeling better and better about this opportunity as the process progressed and began to imagine herself happily working there. As she met with others through a series of interviews, she was soon notified that her references had been contacted and that there was just one last meeting before an offer would be made. The human-resources person asked Karen about potential start dates and told her what the offer would consist of in compensation and benefits. Karen showed up for her final interview in high spirits. She met with each member of the team she'd be working with, was shown where her office would be, where her parking spot would be, and was given a tour of the entire facility. She was even given the book of employee benefits information to take home and peruse while waiting for the formal offer to arrive. When she e-mailed in her thank-you note to the key person who had organized the meetings throughout the day, Karen was told that an offer would be arriving within the next few days.

But when she received a rather thin envelope with the company's letterhead on it, she became suspicious. Shouldn't an offer be a little thicker than this? It wasn't an offer. It was an insultingly brief letter thanking her for her time and letting her know that they had determined her "skills may not be the best overall fit for the current needs of the position at this time." When she e-mailed the head of the department to ask what had happened, she got no response.

Think a company wouldn't be allowed to get away with this kind of behavior? They can, and they do. It happens to candidates every day, candidates who accidentally say or do something that spooks the company into dropping the offer. **The truth is: Until a formal written offer has been extended and signed, you are still in the screening process.** Even this late in the process, any red flags can cause a company to pull their verbally "promised" offer and exchange it for the form letter.

Ever wonder why so many companies send that dreaded form letter? That horrible little piece of paper that blandly states you are no longer a candidate and then adds insult to injury by saying they'll keep your résumé on file for future opportunities and they wish you well in your job search.

It says nothing of any value to a job seeker. And they do that for a very specific reason.

The truth is: They aren't allowed to give you any information whatsoever about why you weren't hired. Any information they disclose about the actual decision-making process could open the company to a potential lawsuit. No hiring manager will risk his or her job for that. It's a much more defensible position to say "Your skills don't match the position" or "We've decided to go in a different direction" or some other such company line. Those lines are rarely the truth.

A hiring manager or other company representative will never tell you that you mentioned money too many times, or that they were worried about the upcoming surgery you casually mentioned, or that you didn't have the right "look" they wanted, or that one of the interviewers thought you were a little bit negative in your answers. This kind of honest disclosure could cause a prior candidate to run straight to a lawyer. And even if that candidate didn't have a strong case, it would take time and money that the company doesn't want to spend to fight it. All companies know that even one lawsuit threat could pull them off their game or even cost their profits for the year. It's something companies are very afraid of and won't risk.

The truth is: Most companies are more afraid of being sued or having their secret hiring criteria made public than they are of lying to a candidate.

If they took the time to call you on the phone or interview you in person, you had the skills they were looking for. Your skills matched the position when you were called, so what happened? Secret criteria, interviewing tricks, and screening happened.

If you get one of these letters or, worse yet, get nothing at all and suddenly can't get anyone to return your phone calls, chances are you activated one of the secret elimination flags or hit a snare you weren't even aware existed. You stepped on the wrong side of the invisible line even for a moment. And there will be no second chance.

People are called or interviewed because the hiring manager thinks they're a good match, but people are excluded from continuing in the process because of red flags and secret criteria they don't know about.

Don't make the mistake of believing that just because no one has told you that you aren't interviewing well, or are doing or saying something that's costing you opportunities, that everything is fine. If you aren't getting calls after qualified résumé submissions and aren't getting offers after interviewing, things are not fine.

The truth is: Because companies are unable or unwilling to tell candidates when they've done something wrong, most candidates are unknowingly carrying multiple mistake patterns throughout the job search process that continue to cost them one opportunity after another.

No company will tell you the truth about how you're doing in the process, so candidates don't know what to fix or improve, let alone that there *is* something that needs fixing.

If you aren't getting the responses you'd like from your job search, you need to look for the hidden mistake patterns that could be costing you jobs. . . .

INSIDER SECRET 5
Hidden patterns cost you jobs.

"MARK" HAD BEEN GOING ON JOB INTERVIEWS FOR OVER A year. He'd always had trouble finding a job when he needed one, and this time had proven to be no exception. He had begun to wonder if he was blacklisted within his industry. How could it be that someone with his qualifications would find it so hard to turn an interview into an offer? He assumed that someone in his employment past must be giving bad references or saying negative things about him, but that wasn't the case. After checking, we found that his references were saying wonderful things about him. What was really going on was that Mark was carrying a mistake pattern that had accidentally cost him job after job. His only mistake? Answering two common questions in a way that was raising a red flag for interviewers.

The two questions were: Why such a long job search? And why did you leave your previous employer?

When asked why he'd been out of work so long, he never wanted an interviewer to think it was because he was doing something wrong or not a good catch, so he would talk about how bad the economy seemed to be and how difficult it was for everyone to find a job in the industry these days.

When asked why he'd left his former employer, he didn't want it to seem like he'd done anything wrong, so he talked about how unhappy he was there, how unfair the boss was, how bad the work environment was, and how he wanted to find something better, where he'd be happier. These seem like pretty harmless answers, don't they?

Mark had no idea now negative these comments made him seem in the eyes of an interviewer. But no interviewer ever told Mark what was wrong. The interviewer would simply end the interview and move on to the next candidate, leaving Mark without any helpful information for his next interview opportunity.

No one ever told Mark that talking about his previous workplace or boss in a negative way would make him look like an unsuccessful or unlucky hire. And no one ever told him that complaining about a bad job market would have the same effect. Hiring managers know there's always a high demand for good candidates no matter the state of the economy or market. Mark would have done much better talking about getting some additional credentials, doing some personal projects, looking for just the right job during this period. Anything other than complaining about how tough it was to get a job or commenting negatively on his previous employment circumstances. Once he discovered what he'd been doing wrong, he was able to easily correct his answers. He soon received two job offers in a row and was able to leverage the two against each other to achieve a nice jump in salary. He was amazed to find that what had been plaguing his job search his entire career was suddenly no longer an issue with one small correction.

"Maria" was looking for a job that paid at least $60,000 per year. She had no interest in considering anything less than that. She had determined that amount was what she needed to pay her bills and didn't want to waste anyone's time if that wasn't going to be the compensation offered. So she made her salary requirement known on cover letters and during phone screenings. But she began to wonder why she never got any callbacks. She was puzzled.

What no one ever told her was that stating her compensation requirements up front made it look like money was all she cared about. That kind of thing makes interviewers nervous and tends to knock candidates out of the running. Maria was shocked to hear this. She thought she was doing these companies and interviewers a favor by not wasting anyone's time. What she didn't realize was the name of the game is to move through the hiring process until you reach the point where you can negotiate these kinds of things from a solid foundation.

Even when a company tries to corner you by directly asking for your "desired salary" during an initial interview or requiring you state your "compensation requirements" in a cover letter, don't bite the hook. In these situations it's always best to state what you're currently making and say that you are flexible and open to consider any offer. This leaves you with a solid foundation for effective negotiation down the line without knocking you out of the running. (More on the secret to negotiating top dollar in Secret 28.)

Once I taught Maria the right way to go after the money she was looking to make, her next interview turned into an offer. An offer that not only met her monetary goal but also ended up being $10,000 more than the top compensation level specified in the job ad.

These are just two stories, but these kinds of simple mistake patterns cost people the jobs they desire every day. A hidden mistake pattern can knock a candidate out of the running the moment they submit their résumé, with one wrong word during a phone screening, or with an inappropriate story during an in-person interview. That's all it takes for an opportunity to turn into a dead end.

Even though I've been telling you the harsh truth about the current hiring processes you're about to go up against, you don't need to have a single sleepless night worrying about it. I'll show you how to protect yourself by telling you precisely what these hiring managers are screening for at every stage of the process. We'll be going through each of the most prevalent mistake patterns in the following chapters, how to neutralize each one, and how to turn them to your highest advantage in the job search process.

This is what you're truly up against. Now I'll show you the secrets and insider tips that will turn it all in your favor.

Are you ready? Here we go.

YOU ARE BEING ELIMINATED KEY POINTS TO REMEMBER

SECRET 1: YOU'RE NOT BEING HIRED. You are actively being excluded from hire. Understanding that this process is one of elimination rather than inclusion will help you stay at the top of your game and help you differentiate yourself from the competition at each step of the process. As you move up, you are not being included; you are moving through more stringent processes of elimination.

SECRET 2: YOU'RE BEING SCREENED OUT. The truth is, even though it is unethical, unfair, or illegal, companies are eliminating and discriminating against candidates for a wide variety of reasons: age, gender, ethnicity, marital status, sexual preference, looks, social standing, even parenthood.

SECRET 3: NO SECOND CHANCES. The current system is one that does not allow for second chances. If your résumé is not in the best format, if you don't know what to say when they surprise you with a phone call, or if you make a mistake during the in-person interview, that opportunity will be over and it's not coming back. There are no second chances.

SECRET 4: WHAT MISTAKE? No interviewer and no company will ever tell you when you've made a mistake that cost you the offer. It's too much of a risk. That means most candidates are carrying multiple mistake patterns throughout their job search that cost them job after job, without ever being told.

SECRET 5: WHAT'S HIDING IN YOUR JOB SEARCH? If you aren't getting a high level of responses for the résumés you're sending out or you aren't getting offers after interviewing, chances are you're carrying one of the common mistake patterns no company will tell you about.

2

STOP PLAYING RÉSUMÉ ROULETTE

SHOULD I INCLUDE AN OBJECTIVE? WHICH OF THESE ten résumé formats I found online should I use? What do I do with that big employment gap? What should I put when they ask for a degree and I don't have one? How will they know I'm the best candidate unless I put everything on my résumé? How do I get past those online résumé screeners?

How do I get my résumé to stand out?

Every time you play this résumé guessing game, you are gambling with your career. You are throwing your career opportunities onto the spinning roulette wheel with worse than a 1 in 40 chance you'll get a phone call, crossing your fingers that it will land in your favor.

"Sarah's" résumé had always been her friend. She felt confident about it and had always had good responses with it. But not anymore. She had taken a job with a company that seemed incredibly promising, but things had unexpectedly gone badly and within only six months she was looking again. The résumé she'd once had such confidence in now seemed to have a big blemish on it, and as the months continued to creep by with no offers she began to hate her résumé. She was tired of having to explain in every interview what had happened at this particular company and why they'd let her go after only six months. It seemed like that one item was now overshadowing everything else, all her wonderful experience and otherwise solid track record. But what could she do? She thought about taking that job off her résumé, but if a potential employer checked up on her previous work history, wouldn't they find out about the omission?

"Kyle" was very frustrated with his résumé. He was just starting out in his career and had worked for only one company so far. It had been a solid experience, but it was looking rather lonely on his résumé. The rest of his experience consisted of internships while in school and the jobs he'd taken to get through school. He'd been looking for a new job for almost a year and wasn't getting any calls. He realized he needed something to make his résumé stand out. How could these people possibly see how wonderful he was by looking at one piece of paper? As he became more and more frustrated, he realized he would have to step it up a notch; he would have to get creative. He would make them notice him. The next time he submitted his résumé to a company he really wanted to work for, he would hire someone to deliver it by singing telegram. He wrote the song himself highlighting all his best qualities as a candidate. This would certainly be something they couldn't ignore.

"Andy's" résumé was the product of a lot of hard work. He'd been studying how to create the perfect résumé and cover letter. He had read no fewer than five books on writing a winning résumé and was very proud of his creation. He posted it on the Internet and was sending out at least ten a week for promising-looking jobs. But so far, he hadn't received one phone call. What was going on here?

Résumé creation and submission may indeed be the most frustrating part of the entire process. But what most don't realize and no company will tell you, there is so much more to effective résumé creation and submission than we've been told. Unfortunately, these three people were making very common mistakes in their approach, mistakes that were costing them opportunities.

There are only two reasons that a résumé submitted for a qualified position wouldn't result in a phone call. Either the individual submitting it didn't know how to grab the attention of the hiring manager the right way or he or she made a common mistake in résumé creation or submission that immediately landed it in the "no" pile.

Résumé submission is not the mystery "they" would like you to believe. Hiring managers know exactly what types of résumés go to the top of the pile and exactly what types fall to the bottom. **The truth is: Résumés have a success formula that has been kept secret from job seekers.** The reason hiring managers don't make this information public is because it makes their job easier. If a candidate submits a top-level résumé, it signals that this is a top-level candidate. They don't want job seekers finding out what a hiring manager is truly looking for, because they don't want you to employ these insider tips like a formula. It's a test that allows a busy hiring manager to go through a résumé pile much more quickly. Those who are truly worth considering as serious candidates will have the top-tier résumés.

The reason you don't get a phone call for every résumé you submit is because you are guessing at what these hiring managers are looking for instead of knowing. There is no reason that a qualified submission wouldn't get a call for every single résumé sent out. But it requires thinking about your résumé in a new way.

A résumé is not something that just happens as you move through your career. And it's not something that's crafted only when looking for a job. How you choose to craft and submit your résumé may be more important than what the résumé actually says. There is a way to work the system to give you the best shot against the competition without resorting to desperate and counterproductive measures like singing telegrams.

Most candidates take their résumé quite seriously, but there are always those who don't. Either these hapless candidates don't understand the importance the résumé carries in creating future opportunities, or the résumé creation and submission process has become such a mystery that they've become overwhelmed and have simply stopped trying. These people throw their résumé together and send it out, letting the chips fall where they may. And shockingly enough, these candidates may actually get a phone call if they send out enough résumés, but they are also losing countless opportunities along the way they'll never know about. Opportunities that could have held that candidate's dream job.

Your résumé starts the entire job search process; it is the one and only emissary that will go into the company you'd like to work for. It stands between you and any job you'd love to have. It is arguably the most important piece of paper you will generate in your lifetime. It holds your future earning power, opportunities, and livelihood in its two-dimensional grasp. Your résumé is the key that opens the gates to your promised land—or closes them. Treating it like any other piece of paper is hazardous to your career.

The truth is: If you are sending out a sub-par résumé or you don't know how to get noticed the right way, there is no point in sending your résumé out. Most candidates mistakenly believe they can always send another résumé to the same company later on, but that's not the case. Sure you can submit, but if the company has seen you before, you will be discarded yet again. Unless you know the secrets to making this all-important résumé-screening process work in your favor, your résumé submissions may be doing you more harm than good. If you've been sending out résumés and getting form letters or nothing in return, you need to rethink your strategy.

In this chapter, I'll show you the secrets to creating and managing a top résumé, navigating potentially damaging new trends in résumé screening, avoiding secret pitfalls, and getting attention the right way. In this game, you only get one spin, one chance, with each company, and I'll show you how to make it land in your favor every time.

INSIDER SECRET 6
Your résumé is headed for the trash.

YOU HAVE THE EXPERIENCE, YOU KNOW THE INS AND OUTS OF the job you're going for, and you've read a few guides on how to write a résumé. You created an objective, made sure your contact information was correct, tried to sum up all your skills and experience in a few pages, then sent it off with your fingers crossed. Think that will do the trick? Ninety-nine percent of the time, the answer will be "no."

In fact, it's estimated that only 1 percent of traditional résumés are actually effective. That means in a typical stack of one hundred résumés sitting on a hiring manager's desk, only one may get the coveted phone call to schedule an interview. The rest will end up in a dusty file drawer until the law allows for them to be discarded, never to be looked at again.

Not a glorious end for a document that represents all you have to show for your hard work throughout your career. And not an illustrious beginning for your new job search.

Hiring managers are so inundated with résumés that from the very beginning of the submission process your résumé is headed for the trash unless you can craft it in a way that captures and holds their attention in three seconds or less.

The truth is that a résumé holds a powerful opportunity for candidates that very few understand how to take full advantage of. It shouldn't be treated as a list of positions and duties; it's not a chronological history. It's an advertisement.

It's up to you to make your advertisement worthy of an immediate phone call, or it will end up with all the other advertising junk mail that crosses the hiring manager's desk.

Your résumé is your one chance to put an ad for yourself in front of the decision makers and convince them you have something special, something different from others in the stack. What is your ad saying? "I'm the one you've been looking for" or "I'm just like all the others in this stack; keep looking"?

At the end of the day, your résumé is all you have to show for all your years of hard work and career building. It is the most important key to getting you in the door of the companies you want to work for. In many situations the way it's crafted is more important than your actual accomplishments.

Many job seekers believe a résumé "just happens," but it must be actively managed to get you the top opportunities each time you look to make a move. There are specific things to avoid throughout your career that can spell disaster for your résumé, as well as certain things that should never be mentioned. I'll show you how to turn your résumé from a boring biography into a dynamic billboard that will grab a potential employer within the three-second scan.

It's true that most résumés require a set format, but within that format there is a great deal of leeway you can use to stand out as the top candidate. The most effective résumés aren't documents containing all your experience and work history; they are carefully crafted full-page ads directly targeted to a hiring manager.

Just like most of the products we see advertised around us every day, we are persuaded to purchase or try out the ones that capture our attention. Like it or not, you are a product, presenting yourself for consideration. Only one will be chosen, and that one will have the most compelling presentation within the sea of submissions. Just like a résumé, most of the product advertising that surrounds us takes place in a two-dimensional medium, with a never-ending barrage of competition. Your résumé will either compel a hiring manager to pick up the phone and call you immediately or be passed by in search of something more interesting. It all depends on how captivating your personal advertising is.

Here are the secrets to creating a top résumé advertisement that will stand out in the crowd:

GIMMICKS HAVE LIMITS. With so much riding on your résumé and the need to make yours stand out from the crowd, it is understandable that many people resort to the land of gimmicks, especially when it's for an opportunity you consider to be your dream job.

It's important to clarify at this point that when I say your résumé needs to show something special and different from others in the stack, I mean in style, tone, and formatting. Under no circumstances should you resort to printing your résumé on pink polka-dot paper, dressing up like a gorilla with balloons to hand-deliver it, or wrapping it around an expensive bottle of champagne (all of which I've personally experienced).

An industrious individual in Seattle paid for a bus billboard to notify the city that he was looking for a job in a particular industry. He did get in the newspaper, but he didn't get a job. Another candidate sent a homing pigeon to a hiring manager. The pigeon was to be released if the company was interested, at which point it would fly back to the candidate's home, signaling that the company wanted to move forward with discussions. But the pigeon never came back.

All of these types of gimmicks will definitely get you attention and make you stand out from the other candidates. Unfortunately, it will be the wrong kind of attention. From a hiring manager's point of view, a qualified candidate with confidence in his or her abilities doesn't need to resort to these tactics. Qualified and confident candidates know their résumé can stand on its own, and they let it. So unfortunately, even the most interesting gimmick can make you look as though you lack confidence. It also makes it very difficult for a hiring manager to recommend the "pink résumé girl," "gorilla guy," or "billboard man" to move up to the next level in the hiring process without incurring laughter and side glances from coworkers.

The idea is to present a clean and confident résumé that will go through the system on its own merits. It should grab a hiring manager's attention based on its confident style and tone, not because it is the loudest or craziest presentation. Remember, you have to be the "safe bet" for a hiring manager to feel comfortable recommending you. Trust me, knowing how to make your experience and true potential shine in a résumé is all you need to stand out from the crowd.

IT'S A BILLBOARD, NOT A BOOK. Just as a well-crafted billboard can grab your attention and make you remember it as you speed by on the freeway, your résumé needs to do the same thing in that standard three-second scan from a hiring manager. Most people treat their résumé like a biography, crammed full of all their experience and work history details. But if you do that, what will stand out in that quick scan? Can you guarantee it will be what you want it to be? If you treat it like the billboard it is, you'll be able to format your experience so that all the important information can stand out in those few seconds.

Have you ever wondered why everyone tells you to keep your résumé to one page? It's not some cruel joke on job seekers; it's to help you craft something that can stand out during the short scan it will receive. It's because a multipage résumé looks too overwhelming to a tired hiring manager. And because putting down too much of your experience can make it seem as though you lack confidence and feel compelled to overexplain. It weakens your position.

The hiring manager is your potential consumer. Like all advertisers, your goal is to stand out from the competition, emphasize your best selling points and features, and get the consumer to feel comfortable enough to make a purchase—or, in this case, recommend you for hire. So with this in mind, put yourself in the hiring manager's shoes for a moment. With your busy lifestyle and all the things competing for your attention in a day, do you read several-page advertisements or do billboards capture your attention more often? Most of us will read a billboard that grabs our attention, and most of us can remember it days or even weeks later. This is not the case with several-page ads.

A hiring manager is bombarded by people wanting a job all day long. The best way to stand out is to be respectful of the hiring manager's time and the overwhelming nature of his job. It's the short, confident submissions that will stand out most in his world. It's not about telling the hiring manager all about you; at this stage it's about enticing him to *find out* more about you. If your résumé is not an enticing advertisement, it will be lost in the stacks.

So, how do you create an enticing résumé billboard? The same way advertisers do. They boil all the critical information down to the most intriguing bits of information that will capture the attention of the consumer in the quickest and most effective fashion. All extraneous information is cut out. To grab attention there is a lot of white space, and all the key information is designed to stand out at a glance.

One of the tricks to getting your résumé down to one page is allowing the job titles you've held to speak for themselves. Most of your experience and talent is rolled up into the job titles you've worked under. You wouldn't have been given those titles if you hadn't earned them, and you wouldn't have kept them if you hadn't done good work. So you don't need more than two or three bulleted points of accomplishments under each job listing. Make sure your titles and company names stand out in a quick, easy scan. To test your résumé, give it to a friend for three seconds and then ask him or her what stood out most that can be remembered. If it's not your three most important points you want a hiring manager to focus on, then you need to reformat. Here's a format that's quite effective:

WORK EXPERIENCE

Company Name **Job Title** *Dates*

- Responsible for . . . [general statement explaining your position]
- [Key accomplishment listed here, i.e.: Improved productivity by 20% and customer satisfaction ratings by 40% by implementing new ordering and tracking system for entire department]
- [Key accomplishment listed here]

The reason for formatting your titles centered down the middle is so they all stand out in a quick scan. You need to tell the reader where to go for the most important information. So, if you center your name at the top, you set a precedent that all-important key information will be down the middle. If you put your name off to the side (which I don't recommend, since this tends to looks like it lacks confidence), then you are telling the reader all your key information will be on that side of the page.

If you glance at your résumé and the first things that stand out to you are your headings, like "Work Experience" or "Education," then you need new formatting. You need to identify your key information, such as company names and titles held, then direct your reader to scan right to those items.

Now, what goes in the bulleted points? Most candidates make the mistake of putting down a laundry list of all the things they were required to do on a daily basis as part of their job. Boring.

Would you buy a vacuum that said it sucked up dirt, or one that sucked up 10 percent more dirt than the competition while operating 30 percent more quietly?

Make sure you emphasize your biggest accomplishments and most impressive qualities as a candidate rather than creating a list of daily duties and responsibilities. Most of the things people choose to put down on their résumé are already implied in their job title. Don't fall into that trap. That is wasting space. Instead, put in your most impressive accomplishments, promotions you received, numbers that can qualify your contributions like *$x* money brought in, a 20 percent increase in new clients, or a 10 percent increase in productivity directly attributed to something you did. If you must put in responsibilities, put in a general listing of key responsibilities not implied by your job title and make it your first bulleted point, followed by your accomplishments. Make sure the items you choose to put on your résumé/billboard make you stand out as a candidate. The standard laundry list format will make your résumé seem bland. Putting in accomplishments rather than duties will make your information jump off the page. Any hiring manager will know that there were day-to-day duties to perform related to your job and you wouldn't have kept that job if you hadn't fulfilled them satisfactorily. Those don't need to be listed.

Don't worry if this approach makes it feel as though you've left lots of important things off your résumé. Do you think billboards tell you everything you need to know about a product? Not likely, but that's not the intent. The intent is to get people interested as they speed by. Your résumé should do the same thing.

Remember, this résumé is intended to whet the reader's appetite for more. It should be designed to inspire the hiring manager to grab the phone and call you to get more information. If you put in too many complete details, hiring managers will feel they already know all there is to know about your experience and will start making assumptions. Believe me, you don't want them to do that. Those kinds of assumptions will rarely do you justice. The assumptions gleaned from a two-dimensional piece of paper, no matter how expertly crafted, will never be able to accurately represent the kind of employee you truly are. That can only be done in person, and that's what you're trying to get to—the in-person interview.

WHAT'S YOUR OBJECTIVE? So many universities, Career Development Centers, and outdated résumé books still teach that a résumé should have an objective. The problem with objectives is that they make you appear too narrowly focused, tend to be awkward, and don't usually add anything to the résumé itself. **The truth is: Objectives are passé for those very reasons and including one will immediately signal to hiring managers that this is not a professional-level, contemporary presentation.**

Using the cover letter for stating your career objectives, tailored to each opportunity, will be much more effective and will save you space on your now-one-page résumé billboard. But where the objective used to live on your résumé now provides a wonderful opportunity to differentiate yourself from all other candidates.

Instead of a dry two-line objective, try putting in an executive summary highlighting your years of experience, all your best qualities, and what differentiates you as a candidate: hardworking, responsible, well organized, great at team building. Qualities don't ever work well under job titles—that area should be reserved for specific accomplishments only—but qualities are very effective when highlighted all together in a summary introduction to your résumé.

Another reason for listing your qualities and summarizing your experience is that many company sites no longer allow you to submit a cover letter with your résumé. This summary will then take the place of your cover letter and make sure your best features are highlighted for the reader. It puts all your best assets right up front so a busy hiring manager won't miss them, and sets the tone for how you'd like the reader to view your experience. A well-crafted summary can be a lifesaver for people who have had multiple jobs in a variety of industries because it allows them to present a cohesive career path. You don't ever want to leave a busy hiring manager to determine what kind of focus your career has had or what you have to offer. Put it right up front.

This powerful and brief summary should be a solid advertising pitch about you and all you have to offer to this potential employer. You want it to be so strong that readers will be enticed to call immediately even if this is the only thing they read on your résumé. I like putting this summary (without any title heading) centered under the name and address for maximum impact. Centering again sets up the reader's eye to follow all the most important information down the center of the page. The rest of your information should be anchored on the left side of the page as always. But now what stands out down the center is your name, the summary highlighting best qualities and points of differentiation, then your job titles. This is a powerful résumé when you scan it. And that should be your only objective.

GO FOR THE CALL. It's always much easier to sell youself over the phone or in person than it is on a two-dimensional piece of paper. If you try to make your résumé say everything about you, you will seem as two-dimensional as the paper it's on. Leaving out details and alluding to interesting topics of discussion will make you appear too dynamic to fit on the page, and that's what will lead to a phone call. The secret is you don't want to go for the highly detailed biographical résumé; you want to get the call.

Candidates who make the mistake of trying to explain everything on paper are the ones who usually look boring or insecure and are screened out. Those who use the opportunity of a résumé submission to whet the appetite of the hiring manager, crafting their résumé more like an advertisement speaking to their special skills, qualities, and accomplishments, are the ones who go to the next level.

CONSISTENCY IS CALMING. Résumés are much easier to read and scan if they have a consistent format such as bulleted points, similarly sized paragraphs, and traditional fonts. Be sure you use the same format for each job listing. To visually lead the reader through your most important information, try putting the most bulleted points under your most recent position, then decreasing the number for previous positions. For example, your current position would have three bulleted points with responsibilities and accomplishments listed, the next few would have only two, and the rest would get one.

Don't go for crazy fonts, lots of boldface, or underlining. It will look too busy and be disruptive to the eye, detracting from your message. The cleaner the look, the more your qualifications will stand out, and the more confident your résumé will look. If you want to emphasize one aspect, like job titles, then just boldface or underline those, nothing else.

Try using active words at the beginning of each bullet-point description of your achievements. It doesn't matter whether you pick past or present tense, as long as you stick with it all the way through. I personally like active words such as "managing," "creating," and "handling." Make sure you don't use the same one twice under any given job title. Stay away from the common trap of using present tense for your current job, then switching to past tense for previous jobs. This breaks the continuity of your résumé and will break the flow for the reader.

WOULD YOU LIKE AN UPDATE WITH THAT? People tend to add on new experiences to their résumé history without going back and updating previous employment. When you're first starting out, any experience in the work world can be included to fill out your résumé, but once you've moved on to get some real experience, you should let entry jobs like flipping burgers to get through college slide off. In fact, you want to get into the habit of going through your entire résumé each time you add something new. Look to make sure you've only listed accomplishments from previous jobs that are currently relevant to the new level you've achieved. Many things you were rightfully proud of in your first or second job may not serve you at this point in your career if they're being featured front and center on your résumé. Leaving things like that on your résumé will weaken your message.

THERE'S NO "I" IN "RÉSUMÉ." Always write your résumé in the third person. It may seem like a small detail, but many résumé guides gloss over this point, and it can have a huge impact on the reader. A first-person résumé will weaken the message, while a third-person voice will give you a celebrity press-release feel that will draw the reader in.

There's no need to actually refer to yourself in the third person; that would work against you and seem silly. But you do want to craft the résumé in an actively absent third-person style. For example: Rather than saying "Stephen was responsible for handling all customer service calls" or "I was responsible for . . . ," you'd say: "Responsible for handling all customer service calls."

If this seems difficult, try imagining you're writing an objective advertisement for someone else with your experience, separating yourself from the fact that it's your résumé. This will help you objectively pull out your differentiating qualities and accomplishments to highlight. Distancing yourself as much as possible from your own experience will help you create the most compelling third-person résumé. Your opportunity to write in the first person comes in the cover letter only.

MANAGE YOUR MARKETING. Your résumé is the primary marketing/advertising tool for your entire career. Hiring managers, in all their varied forms, are your target market. This résumé, a.k.a. a one-page advertisement for the amazing product known as "you," is the emissary you will send out to each opportunity. As your primary marketing tool, it must be managed as carefully as a marketing campaign for your business.

One of the most common traps candidates fall into is believing that résumés "just happen." You take the jobs that come your way, and then, "oops," you have to write a new résumé. So you put the new information at the top of the list and send it out. A haphazardly planned résumé represents a haphazard marketing plan and will guarantee spotty results.

A résumé should be carefully managed and crafted so that it supports your career goals and objectives going forward. At the end of each experience, how that job looks on your résumé will determine a large portion of your future opportunities. For example, if your desire is to become a vice president one day, you should take jobs that will make your résumé look like you are solidly on that track. Your résumé should play into your decision-making process while helping to craft your career path. It's not just a list of positions held; it tells a story and shows your track.

If you are thinking of taking that job that pays the same but has a lower title than the one you held previously, you may want to think again. Taking that position will look like a backward step on your résumé and could derail you from continuing on the career track you were hoping for. Anything on a résumé that appears to show a backward move will be a huge red flag to the next interviewer. Questions like "Couldn't this person get any other job?" or "Was there an issue or problem that led to a backslide?" will come to mind, and that kind of red flag will be all it takes to remove you from consideration for the next set of opportunities.

Most of us don't think about our résumés until we have to write one, but if you make it part of your ongoing decision-making process, you can move much more smoothly in the direction you desire instead of running into unplanned obstacles along the way.

Now, if you found you really wanted the job that might appear to be a backward step on your résumé, realizing the potential issues that will arise can help you negotiate for what's most important—namely, keeping the same title or getting one the next level up so you show a consistent rise (no matter how small) in your career path and opportunities. Depending on the overall goals and objectives for your career, that change in title could be much more important than the salary you get for that position.

Now if you find yourself looking woefully at what you now realize could be construed as a haphazard résumé, don't fret. Establishing a solid-looking career track that matches your future intentions can be accomplished at any time during your career with some thoughtful planning. Grouping all your industry-relevant experience together on your résumé (even if it's not chronological) to highlight your future intentions can be quite effective. It's also important to know that the most recent jobs listed on your résumé are what will illustrate your career track intentions to a hiring manager. Now that you know the importance of having your résumé support where you'd like to go in the future, rather than looking like an account of where you've been, you can make the necessary changes. You can be more aware of what to emphasize on your current résumé and what choices should be next on your career path to reinforce those intentions. Make sure going forward that you bring your résumé into the mix when making career decisions.

MIND THE GAP. Most candidates already know that gaps in employment must be carefully managed, but many have no idea how to do this effectively. If you have a gap in your employment history, you need to create a reason for it that puts that gap in as positive a light as possible. The idea is to make it look intentional rather than an unfortunate bout with unemployment.

You should never address unemployment directly on your résumé (that will weaken your advertisement's effectiveness), but knowing that it will look like a red flag to a hiring manager, you may want to address it in your cover letter. Any positive reasons will do: You were spending time looking for just the right position, getting additional education, even taking that trip you've always wanted to take. Anything other than "I just haven't been able to find a job," "I needed some time off after that horrible problem with my last boss that led to my termination," or "I was in rehab, but I'm better now." Anything that puts you in a positive light is what you want to focus on.

Sometimes gaps just happen and there is nothing you can do about it. Coming up with a positive statement and explanation that you can present when confronted with the inevitable questions from a hiring manager will help you move forward. But having to explain away a gap is never the ideal situation, and the best protection for your résumé is to avoid the gaps altogether. Sometimes you won't get the chance to explain, or the company may be excluding anyone with a gap due to their secret criteria. **The plain truth is: If you find yourself in the middle of a gap, the longer you've been out of work the less desirable you will appear to a potential employer.**

It's better to carefully craft your résumé by finding your next job while still employed. This strategy protects you. Not only is it easier to find a job when you have one (because it makes you appear more desirable to potential employers); it can also help you get higher offers because the new company knows they have to make it financially worth your while to leave your current position. So if the writing's on the wall and you see that you could potentially be out of a job in the near future, start looking right away so you can make as seamless a transition as possible and avoid the gap.

It's important to know that you can't hurt your career by getting another job offer. If your company really wants you to stay, they will make a counteroffer to keep you. They may even realize they'll have to start treating you better or the competition will steal you away.

WATCH YOUR DATES. Short dates on your résumé must be carefully managed. If you have dates showing a job lasting only 3–12 months followed by a period of job searching, this will be a huge red flag. This is usually interpreted by the hiring manager as a firing or other mishap that led to the job not working out.

Sometimes short dates simply can't be avoided, but you will need to come up with a statement that creates a positive explanation for each one. Just like explaining a gap, the more positive the better. Something like: "While working at the company, I had the chance to learn about *x* industry, and I decided that was where my interests truly lie." (Make sure it's the industry you're currently interviewing for.) Whatever the real reason for this short date is for you to work out. What must be presented throughout the job search process is the most positive reason you can possibly come up with to explain this early separation.

Many know that short dates should be avoided if possible, but some take it too far. You don't need to turn down a good job offer just because you don't feel you've been at your current company long enough. Short dates on your résumé won't be a problem if you're moving seamlessly from one company to another. They only become a problem if there's a gap of unemployment in between. Companies know that sought-after people are always being "stolen" and enticed to go to the next company, and they expect sought-after candidates to show a history of shorter dates. A period of two years with each company is not a problem if there are seamless transitions.

In fact, having dates on your résumé that show too many years with the same company can actually work against you in today's job market. Rather than the previous image of loyalty and stability, those who stay too long at a company run the risk of being seen as inflexible and potentially unable to adapt to a new situation with ease. If you have more than 8–10 years with the same company, you begin to fall into this range. I'm not saying you should jump to another company if you are happy where you are, but you should know that having one company on your résumé for all your years of experience will not be as enticing to hiring managers as it once was.

Your résumé is not just a piece of paper; it is the key to achieving your career goals. With careful crafting and management and by treating your résumé like a dynamic marketing tool rather than a dry biography, your résumé will go straight to the top of the pile—instead of the bottom of a trash can.

INSIDER SECRET 7

You CAN lie on your résumé.

WHEN THERE'S A JOB YOU REALLY WANT, AN EXPERIENCE or a degree you wish you had, it can be tempting to think about doing it—you know—lying. One little lie on a résumé couldn't hurt, right? "Oh, I really, really want this job. If only I could say I was a . . ."

We all wish we could omit things that aren't in our best interest or even include something perhaps slightly misleading that will help our chances. Certain lies will get you caught immediately and should never be attempted, while others can actually be helpful in the process. I will tell you exactly what they are and how to use them to your advantage.

First, the lies that you should never try to get away with. They are far too easy to spot, to check, and they will land your résumé immediately in the trash.

- Titles
- Dates
- Compensation
- Education
- Companies

Did you know that your titles held and dates of employment are usually the only things a hiring manager knows he or she can absolutely check with a previous employer? All other information may not be easily accessible.

Today, when hiring managers call to check up on you with a previous employer, they know they will most likely only be able to get what insiders call rank, file, and serial number. In other words, your titles held, your dates of employment, your responsibilities, and sometimes your compensation. That's it. That's all they know for sure they can get. (More about this particular secret and its ramifications on the job search process in the next chapter.)

Because these few items are so easy to verify, coupled with the fact that they are usually the only information hiring managers know they can get, those items take on magnified importance in the minds of the hiring managers. Any discrepancies in these areas, even accidental, will take you right out of the running.

Education is another point on the résumé that is quite easy to check. Because so many people have tried to lie about it in the past (it is still the number one choice for fudging on a résumé), it is one of the main targets for checking.

And of course, saying you worked for a company that you did not work for is a major no-no. This is a pretty big fib by a desperate individual trying to make his or her résumé look beefier, but I've seen it done many times. This is simply too easy to check. One phone call will mark the end of your chances, and a fib that size could even land you on a blacklist for that industry.

The main idea behind a safe and helpful lie on your résumé versus a damaging one is: Your experience is *yours*. That means you can take off anything you think would be damaging to your forward momentum or opportunities. If you put it on your résumé, it is up for scrutiny and will be checked. But if you leave something off, there will be very little to check, nothing to explain.

Many candidates believe that if you've had a bad-luck work experience, you still have to put it on your résumé. You don't. In many cases it might be best to take it off entirely. For example, if you had a short-date experience with a company of 3–6 months that ended in a misunderstanding, firing, or other unpleasant experience that you're tired of trying to explain in interviews, you may choose to pull it off your résumé.

Now, your next question should be "Wouldn't that leave the dreaded gap on my résumé?" Yes. But leaving a gap in dates is better than trying to explain a termination or bad experience. When you're being considered during a hiring process, you don't want to have to explain any bad-luck issues in your working past. You are under such intense scrutiny that even if you have justifications or explanations or weren't even at fault, a hiring manager will shut you out "just in case." It might be better to explain that time as an extended period of job searching for just the right position, earning additional education or certifications, or even taking an extended vacation. Anything would be better than a bad job with a bad boss who might say bad things about you, should a potential employer call for a reference.

I was recently helping a client with his résumé and saw he had listed under one of his job descriptions that he'd been passed over for a promotion he'd worked five months to achieve. When I asked him about this interesting disclosure on a résumé, he said it was part of his job history, a big event in his experience with the company. He felt it would be dishonest not to include it.

Another résumé I saw indicated how the individual separated from every job, including firings. She felt it would be more accurate to disclose this information. This is not a good idea! Anyone would admire that level of honesty, but again, we are talking about your résumé as an advertising tool. That is what your résumé truly is, whether you want it to be or not. That level of honesty belongs in your personal and private information; it is for you to learn from in your career, but it does not need to be featured front and center on your résumé. The hiring process simply does not require or support that level of honesty. Would you buy a vacuum that featured in its advertising that it had a brief recall? Or that the company had worked very hard to win "Vacuum of the

Year" but only came in second? That is all part of the vacuum company's history. But as consumers with lots of competition to choose from, we make purchases based on the way products are presented. If the company wants us to purchase their vacuum, they will present all the best attributes of their product, not all the details of its history.

It's important to remember at all times that your résumé is a marketing tool. You have the right to emphasize the very best aspects of your experiences. Even in the interest of résumé accuracy, you do not need to include things that put you in a negative light. There may be a few not-so-great things in your work past, but every last thing you've done in your career does not have to be listed on your résumé. Use your discretion to include the things you believe will put you in the best light.

INSIDER SECRET 8
A computer is deciding your job prospects.

AS IF COMPUTERS HAVEN'T MEDDLED ENOUGH IN OUR already-complicated lives, there's a new twist to the résumé-screening process we now have to worry about.

Did you know that many busy departments are using special scanning software to pick out the top candidates?

Does that scare you? It should.

It means that if you don't have the exact words on your cover letter and résumé that match what they've set their software to scan for, no human being will ever see your résumé. It will be dumped into an electronic file slush folder.

But how can we get around this software? We couldn't possibly know what they're looking for in each position, right? Wrong.

The way this system usually works is through a series of

programmed key words. Each résumé submission is automatically scanned to find the best match. This system is designed to save time and weed out the submissions that do not match the company's specified criteria. If your résumé doesn't match a predetermined number of key factors, it will never make it out of the system. So, the next logical question is: How do you find out what those key factors are for each position?

The secret is: To save time, hiring managers either plan out the key words they want to scan for while they are writing the job posting or have someone in IT program in the key words for the scan off the job posting they've just created.

This job posting is the key. Go through it and find what you consider to be the main key words that most closely match your qualities and qualifications and then pepper those exact words throughout your cover letter and résumé. Using exactly the same key words will help keep you within the parameters of the scan. If the job posting says they're looking for someone who is "passionate about customer service," write in your cover letter or résumé executive summary that you are "passionate about customer service."

If they say they require a bachelor's degree and you don't have one, you can still count on the fact that this requirement will be part of the scanning process, so you may want to find a way to include it. For example, you could put in the cover letter something like "Even though I do not have a bachelor's degree, I have seven years' experience in this industry and have achieved two promotions during that time, which were directly attributed to my industry knowledge." However you need to do it, getting those key words in there is critical to the survival of your résumé.

Don't worry about being too blatant or obvious; this is about survival and getting your résumé through the barrier so an actual person will see it. Chances are hiring managers won't have the original job posting in front of them as they scan through the résumés, so it most likely won't stand out as a blatant copying of the ad. But even if it does, you have achieved your goal: A human being is looking at it. Your résumé is in play. It's not sitting in a dead-end computer file somewhere in cyber-land.

Now, for those of you who've known about this résumé software and have been coming up with ingenious ways to counteract it, a word of caution: They're on to you. As brilliant as many of the new ways are to beat the system, companies have figured most of them out, and the software can be easily programmed to disqualify you for using them. Tricks like putting key words in white type so they aren't seen when the résumé is printed but will be caught by the key-word software aren't a good idea. Neither is the genius black line within a résumé that's actually made up of super-tiny key words all strung together. The scanning software can easily be told to eliminate any submissions with white type or that have any fonts smaller than ten point. It's as easy as that.

It's true that some scanners are programmed to put résumés that have the most key words at the top of the pile. Filling your résumé with hundreds of key words to make that happen may get you in the door, but it won't get you the job. Even if you get to the top of the résumé scanner pile, you will not get the phone call unless you have the actual experience on your résumé to back it up. And you will most likely stand out as someone trying to trick the system, which will not help your image as a serious candidate.

All résumés that have the main key words will make it through, so you don't need to resort to these types of gimmicks. It's much better to put your key words front and center, such as in your cover letter and your new summary at the top of the résumé (where your objective used to be). This summary becomes the perfect place to add in those key words along with the highlights of your overall qualifications and best qualities.

This not only makes you look like a solid candidate; it has an added bonus. If the particular company you're approaching does not use this dreaded software but goes through the stacks the old-fashioned way, your putting the key words front and center will make you naturally stand out as an ideal match for the position.

You'll never know whether your résumé will go through software screening or be sitting in an old-fashioned pile on someone's desk, so you need a strategy that's best for both in order to have the highest chance for consideration.

INSIDER SECRET 9
You can be an "internal recommendation" or just look like one.

WE ALL WISH WE COULD HAVE THAT COVETED INTERNAL recommendation for our résumé. You know, the CEO of the company you want to work for plays golf with a friend of your brother-in-law's uncle and has agreed to hand-carry your résumé to the head of human resources. But most of us don't have a network that carries us that far, so what can we do? You can fake it. I'll show you how to get that celebrity status and hand-carried effect with a phone call and a postage stamp.

First, make sure your résumé gets into the stack in a timely fashion; there may be some sort of deadline or time crunch you don't know about. Send it in immediately as requested (by e-mail or fax).

If you don't get a response within two weeks, it's time to get some names. Call the company and find out who the hiring manager is for the position, making sure you get the correct spelling and job title. If it's a larger company, you can try getting the name of the head of the department with the open position.

Print your cover letter and résumé on high-quality white 100 percent cotton or linen paper and mail it the old-fashioned way to the name you were provided. If you can't get any names out of reception, try going on the company Web site and taking a name closely related to your position or the department itself. If the only name you can get your hands on is the CEO, go for it.

Handwrite the envelope and mark it "private and confidential" at the bottom. That way the receptionist or assistant won't open it before this key individual sees it. Letters marked that way are rarely opened by anyone other than the person to whom they're directly addressed. This gives you several advantages:

> **Advantage 1:** Your résumé gets in front of a key decision maker. (It doesn't matter for how long, because no other résumés are likely to have the same benefit.)
>
> **Advantage 2:** It will most likely be hand-carried from that person's office into the hiring manager's in-box, thus giving it the appearance of an internal recommendation.
>
> **Advantage 3:** Even if your nice 100 percent cotton hand-mailed résumé ends up in the same huge stack of résumés, it will stand out from the others. It will not feel like all the other faxes and e-mails that were printed on the same office paper. It will have texture and weight and will even be folded differently.
>
> **Advantage 4:** Psychologically, when we're holding the paper we're reading, things that are printed on high-quality paper seem to have more substance. This feeling often translates into what we're reading, making the résumé feel more important.

Don't worry that you now have two résumés in the stack; that often happens with internal recommendations. And if it's a stack of hundreds of résumés (which is typical, depending on the position), the person scanning through that stack probably won't remember seeing your résumé previously, but your name will seem familiar, giving you the potential for that celebrity factor.

This insider trick can also help you get around those online forms so many companies require you to fill out for consideration. Go ahead and fill them out, but as one client of mine so eloquently stated, "Those forms do nothing but ensure you will look just like everyone else." So after you've submitted your bland form for consideration, get moving to find the right name to mail your résumé to. Don't worry if the standard company line is that they "don't accept those types of submissions"; just go ahead and mail it in. If nothing else, it will make your name look familiar as the hiring manager scans through all the submissions that look the same. If all goes well, you will have the only hand-carried quality paper résumé for the job in the hiring manager's in-box—a good position to be in.

Most people try to have their résumé stand out from the crowd by calling the hiring manager to confirm he or she has received their résumé. This is a big and very common mistake. A résumé submission is not like sending a fax to a business client requiring a courtesy follow-up phone call to make sure it was received. Calling to check on your résumé will actually hurt your chances and lower your standing as a candidate. The standing rule of thumb is: Don't ever call to follow up. It's actually better to send in a second résumé a few weeks later than to call to see if they received the first one. If you're a busy hiring manager, it's easy to resent the constant barrage of candidates calling and interrupting your day to see if you've received their résumé and to ask if you're "reading it right now." Hiring managers hate this and it will severely hurt your chances, not to mention make you appear too desperate to be a serious candidate. If you haven't heard anything and aren't sure if your résumé was received, try using this "internal recommendation" trick and sending in another copy of your submission using a different avenue. (For example: If the first one was faxed in, then mail in the second one.)

When all is said and done, the very best way to look like an internal recommendation is to actually find one. If you are able to contact a friend, university alumnus, Internet buddy, mild acquaintance, or friend of a distant relative who works for the company you're interested in, don't hesitate to contact that individual and see if you can get an "in." Be fearless; you may be surprised at what can happen. A colleague of mine once met someone in line for theater tickets who later tracked her down and asked her to submit his résumé. He got the job.

A hand-carried résumé really is golden and is worth going after. But if you aren't lucky enough to have any latent connections with someone on the inside, this insider tip will get you halfway there.

INSIDER SECRET 10
Cover letters can cause immediate exclusion.

THINK COVER LETTERS AREN'T IMPORTANT? THAT THEY'RE just a cover sheet for your résumé? They are now more important than ever. In fact, having the wrong format and tone for your cover letter or skipping it altogether may cause a hiring manager to not read your résumé at all. **The truth is: Many hiring managers look at the cover letter to decide if the attached résumé is worthy of their time.** If the cover letter is boring, seems to lack confidence, or is too long, your résumé could land in the "no" pile without anyone reading it.

What's worse than that? Almost 80 percent of résumé submissions have ineffective, inappropriate cover letters.

Many of us have been taught to use a cover letter as an example of how well we can write a formal business letter. We've been taught it should be as formal in tone and feeling as the résumé itself. We've been taught wrong.

That was the ideal strategy a decade or so ago and many institutions are still teaching it, but those types of cover letters will do nothing but ensure your invisibility within the teetering stacks of résumés. Long cover letters are also viewed as less confident than a short note and can make it seem as though the candidate feels the need to overexplain something.

The most effective cover letters today are short, powerful, and enticing. Yes, like an advertisement. A cover letter can be a few short paragraphs in an e-mail with your résumé attached or a brief note on the cover page of a fax. It should stay between 200 and 250 words. And truthfully, that's all a busy hiring manager will be willing to read.

In the overwhelming masses of paper that come across a hiring manager's desk every day, only short, enticing notes have any chance of being read. Longer, more formal cover letters seem too overwhelming and can result in instant elimination.

Your cover letter is a fantastic opportunity to shine and stand out. Although a résumé must conform to certain parameters, focus on certain points, and be written in the third person, a cover letter need not. It can be filled with excitement, allowing you to state all your best qualities and create a positive feeling in the readers to set the right tone enticing them to read that attached résumé.

It also provides a wonderful opportunity to showcase the aspects of your experience that most closely match the requirements for the position. Rather than going through the exhausting task of tailoring each résumé you send out to each position, you can let the cover letter do all that work.

Here's a particularly effective six-part cover letter formula you can follow.

Cover Letter Formula Part 1: Make sure the tone of the letter is upbeat, confident, positive, and filled with enthusiasm—don't apologize for anything!

Cover Letter Formula Part 2: State the position you are submitting your résumé for.

Cover Letter Formula Part 3: State where you're currently working and how many years of experience you have.

Cover Letter Formula Part 4: Put in at least three key words from the job description that closely match your experience or best qualities that you'd like to highlight.

Cover Letter Formula Part 5: Say what you have a "proven ability for" or are "known for" that makes you stand out as a candidate.

Cover Letter Formula Part 6: Close with a positive statement linking your experience to the stated needs and qualifications of the position.

This should all be brief, short, punchy, and confident, setting a strong and positive tone for the résumé read.

For example:

> *I was excited to see your recent posting for a* Marketing Coordinator *position on* Craigslist. *I'm currently a Marketing Assistant with H&M Marketing Group here in Columbus. I have four years' experience in* target marketing, direct mail, *and* account coordination, *with a* B.S. in Marketing *from Columbus University. I am* passionate about customer service, *am known as a* creative problem solver, *and take pride in my* strong team-building skills.

I have a proven ability to go above and beyond to achieve the highest possible results for both clients and team members.

I've recently been involved in a new product launch that closely matches the product needs you described in the job posting and I'd love the opportunity to speak with you about it further.

Looking forward to speaking with you,

Edward Edison
555-555-1212

The underlined words were pulled directly from the job posting to create the image of an ideal match while relating "Ed's" résumé to the requirements of the position itself. *(This underlining was done to help clarify the example given, but you should never underline anything in your cover letter.)*

Now, there are a few things you should stay away from that can weaken your message. It's always best to stay away from statements that sound too desperate, such as "Thank you so much for taking the time to consider my résumé" or "I know I don't have the qualifications you're looking for, but I would love the chance to speak to you in person about how I can benefit your organization." It makes it sound like you are unworthy of the hiring manager's attention and time. The name of the game in an effective cover letter and résumé submission is confidence. If you don't appear fully confident, the hiring manager will assume there's a reason for it and move on to the next candidate. If you don't feel confident, fake it. At least *sound* confident so that others will have confidence in you.

It's also best to stay away from blatantly off-base statements like "This position is a perfect fit for me and my experience." Hiring managers tend to bristle at this kind of statement because from their point of view, no one could make that determination from a simple advertisement or job posting. That kind of statement can only be made after an interview. It is better to confidently state your experience and qualifications and that you're looking forward to speaking in person. Let the hiring manager make the determination based on your confidence, enthusiasm, and background that you are a "perfect fit" for the position.

To state another well known rule of effective advertising: Don't say it; be it. In other words, don't say you're the best candidate for the job; instead highlight the skills and experience in your background that will make the readers come to that conclusion on their own.

If you decide to send in a résumé and cover letter for a position you do not have the qualifications for, don't apologize or draw attention to it. Simply state confidently what you *do* have to offer and leave off the position title you're submitting for. If there is an opening that fits your experience level, the hiring manager will put you in the right slot.

The shorter the cover letter, the better the chance it will be read, and the more confident you will appear. And it's always good to include your phone number on the cover letter just in case it gets separated from your résumé.

One more thing—don't use "Dear Sir or Madam" when you don't have the name of the person you are submitting to. That greeting alone should tell you that you're using the wrong format for a casual, grab-their-attention cover letter. Just put "RE: the [job title] position advertised in *The Wall Street Journal*" at the top and jump right into your punchy and enthusiastic note. "Dear . . ." really only works when you have the person's name, and I usually recommend you save it until after you've met in person.

It's important to know that you don't ever need a formal format when submitting an e-mail or fax cover letter. Where things get a bit more formal is when you use the trick to look like an internal recommendation and mail in an old-fashioned résumé. You will want to use the same enthusiastic, short, and confident approach to the cover letter as you would for your more casual e-mail/fax submissions, but put it in a more formal format with date and business address at the top. In addition, when you snail-mail in a résumé you should always sign your name on the cover letter; otherwise it looks unfinished.

No matter what submission format you choose, no matter whom it's going to, remember the rule of confidence. If you've decided to mail your résumé and cover letter directly to the CEO, don't start your cover letter with "You don't know me, but . . ." Just jump right in there and write the letter as though it is already in front of your intended reader, the hiring manager. You don't have to explain why you're writing to the CEO just because his or her name is at the top. It will look more confident if you write it as though anyone could read it, whether it's the CEO or the hiring manager. Remember, you aren't trying to get the CEO on your side, although that can happen; you're simply trying to get hand-carried into the stack. The more confident you appear, even if it means ignoring the fact that you're breaking the rules a little and writing to someone who has better things to do than look over your résumé, the more successful you will be.

INSIDER SECRET 11
The Internet is working against you.

ANYTHING YOU CHOOSE TO PUT ON THE INTERNET—WEB pages, blog postings, or personal photos—is considered public domain. What does that mean to your job search? It means that all those things you thought were private are all part of the hiring process now.

Many people continue to mistakenly believe that what you personally post on the Net, having nothing to do with work, is private and will have no effect on your career prospects. However, this mistaken belief has proven itself dangerous and damaging time and time again.

The very act of putting information on the Internet means you are choosing a public forum for your expressions. There is a very important legal distinction between private and public. Private is what you do in your own home not intended for anyone else to see. But the moment you put an ad in the newspaper, post something on the World Wide Web, or otherwise move your personal views out into the streets, you are choosing to share them in a public forum and are subject to those entanglements. Don't make the common mistake of thinking that just because you make a public expression on your own time, away from work, unrelated to work, it is off-limits or in any way considered private. It's not.

If you choose to post something on the Internet, not only will hiring managers find it; they will also use it against you in the job search process. The Internet is now considered fair game in decision-making processes, and sharing things openly on the Web can get your résumé discarded.

"Janice" couldn't get a job. She was getting calls and interviews, and she knew people were checking her references, but no job. She was becoming frustrated and contacted me to examine her overall approach. From her interviewing skills to her résumé, everything seemed in order. In fact, she looked like a great catch whom any company would love to hire. The next step was to check the Internet. I explained to her that hiring managers were now routinely conducting Internet searches on candidates to see what might pop up. Sometimes this is done when references are checked, but more and more it's being done before the initial phone call is made.

Janice was sure there was nothing on there that could be a problem. But when we Googled her name, something quite unexpected came up, right at the top of the list—a series of sexy pictures she had posted many years ago when she was single and looking to spice up her dating life. She hadn't been single for several years now but had never bothered to take the pictures off the Internet. What had been happening was that every time hiring managers Googled her name, they were faced with beautiful pictures that unfortunately made their candidate look like a weekend porn star. Not a safe bet for a recommendation for hire. Once she had the images taken off the Internet, she started getting offers at the end of her job interviews.

A survey conducted by ExecuNet recently showed that 35 percent of recruiters reported eliminating a candidate because of something found online. Among the reasons stated were misstated academic qualifications, odd personal habits, legal proceedings against a former employer, and inappropriate postings. There should be nothing available on the Internet (that has your real name on it) unless it showcases your alignment with the company you'd like to work for or the industry you are looking to continue employment within. This is key for your overall job search image.

Even people who know the importance of managing their Web presence can get caught in other online snares that seem harmless—like blogging. The problem with blogging is, it usually inspires the sharing of open and honest opinions. If your opinions run contrary to the values or products of the industry or company you'd like to work for someday, you are harming your job prospects.

Let's say you'd like to work in the beauty industry and feel that blogging about your favorite beauty products would be a good "in." What happens if you post something negative about a product that belongs to the company now looking to hire you? What if you recommend a favorite product only to discover that the competition is now hiring for your dream job? When they read your postings (and they will), do you think they'll hire you? Not likely. Even if you were the top candidate for the job, a public display showing a lack of support for their products or open support for a competitor will be an automatic "out." These casual well intended blog postings have just limited your career opportunities in the industry you were hoping to join.

Sometimes the problem isn't what you've put in the Web but what others have posted.

A client came to me after experiencing tremendous difficulty over several months turning his interviews into offers. He would get very close to offers being made only to be met with what seemed like an abrupt slamming of doors. After looking at all the factors that could be causing this, we checked his name on the Internet, and what came up shocked both of us. His name popped up in a series of blogs with tirade after tirade on the evils of Corporate America, publicly bashing several companies by name. However, it wasn't him. He unfortunately shared the same name as this outspoken Internet blogger, and his career opportunities were clearly suffering for it. But the fix was a simple one. We separated their Internet presence so hiring managers could easily tell the difference between the two. My client had a different middle name from the outspoken blogger, so we prominently displayed his middle name on his résumé. He also crafted his own career-related Web page to create an Internet presence that supported his career goals. So now when his full name is punched into a search engine (hiring managers tend to search your name exactly as it appears on your résumé), what pops up is something that helps his job search, highlighting him as a great catch, while distancing him from the blog ranter.

What is your Internet presence saying to potential employers right now? If you don't know, you'd better find out quick. And if you're actively job-searching, you will want to keep a sharp eye on your Internet presence. (The resource section at the back of this book provides tools to help you do this.)

And certainly don't forget about e-mail addresses. Yes, one should always be listed on your résumé, but this is not a place to get creative. Something as seemingly small and personal as an e-mail address removes candidates from consideration all the time.

Putting an e-mail address on your résumé like "asskicker2," "swingersnkeggers," "bigboobalicious," or even "oldmoney" may not send quite the right message. (Yes, those are real e-mail addresses I've seen on actual résumés!)

E-mail addresses say a lot about you, like it or not. Anything that depicts you as a potential hell-raiser, is sexual in nature, sounds like you're a trust funder who really doesn't need or want a job, or suggests some sort of alter-ego lifestyle must be avoided. Even better, get yourself a free e-mail address that shows your alignment with the position or industry you're applying for like "MarketingMan" or "AmyTheAccountant." I know it's a bit more on the boring side, but it will help maintain your résumé image without scaring away a hiring manager.

So, is there any way to make the Internet work for you in your job search? Absolutely. This new focus on the Internet in job searching provides a wonderful opportunity to showcase things that you can't put on a résumé, adding depth to your candidacy. You know they're going to check, so why not craft your Internet presence to give you the upper hand in the hiring process? If you belong to the many online communities out there like LinkedIn, MySpace, Facebook, or Friendster, use them to craft pages and showcase images that make you look like an ideal candidate, that show you in action on the job, that highlight successful projects you've worked on that you know hiring managers would be interested in. Many people believe hiring managers don't care about those sites, but they have been known to create secret accounts on communities like these to conduct searches on potential employees.

If there are things on the Net that aren't flattering to your job search and that you're unable to remove, create your own career-friendly Web site and ask others to link to it so it will rank higher than those you don't want hiring managers to see.

Be mindful and careful about what goes on the Net. Once

it's out there it can be quite difficult, if not impossible, to remove. At the very least, if you find you simply must participate in an incendiary blog or expose company injustices, *please* don't use your real name. And if you have to have pictures of yourself strewn throughout the Internet, make sure they aren't the kind of photos that would make your boss blush if he or she stumbled across them.

INSIDER SECRET 12
Professional references are useless.

REFERENCE CHECKING USED TO BE AS EASY AS CALLING A previous employer or manager listed on an employee's application form. Not anymore. Those references won't give hiring managers what they're really looking for.

In fact, reference checking has become a very sore subject within internal human-resources and hiring circles. They don't talk about it much with outsiders, but this subject has become the focus of detailed articles, focus groups, seminars, forums, and legislation across the country.

What's going on is that changes in reference laws have essentially tied everyone's hands. Employers no longer feel safe giving any kind of detailed information on past employees, and hiring managers are finding it very difficult to get any useful information on the people they're considering for hire.

Why is all this happening? Many current laws are so strict that employers can be sued if they say the wrong thing about a previous employee.

Because of the nature of current laws, most employers feel safe giving very basic information but do not feel safe providing any sort of commentary or opinion on their previous employees. For example, all companies feel safe verifying that a previous employee worked there from *x* date to *x* date, what job title was held, whom he reported to, what his basic responsibilities were. But they are treading on dangerous ground to say something like "He was such a sloppy worker," "We were all happy to see him go," or even "He was the best worker we ever had." That would be considered commentary. The safest stance within the current laws is to treat all employee references exactly the same.

These laws have become so restrictive that they've actually become counterproductive, and many states have passed reference immunity laws in the hopes that employers will feel safer giving additional information. But this continues to be a legally treacherous issue that causes most companies to choose the safest route possible. That means only sharing information that will have the least chance of resulting in potential legal complications for the company. Namely, the standard rank, file, and serial number.

What does all this mean to you? It means that your once informational and helpful professional references, those previous bosses you've listed on your application form for the potential employer to contact, are now largely useless for any actual information. It means that a hiring manager checking your standard professional references will most often be faced with a bland verification of job title held, dates of employment, possibly responsibilities, and sometimes compensation. That's it.

If you think your previous boss can be a little more forthcoming as a reference, you're wrong. In recent years, many companies have changed their reference policies to a strict requirement that if anyone calls for a reference, it must be routed to human resources or to an outside designated contractor who provides all reference information. This shift is intended to avoid the potential legal risk of having a boss say the wrong thing while giving a reference and expose the company to a potential lawsuit. This means your previous boss may be prevented from giving any useful information about you, under penalty of severe disciplinary action and even termination.

Obviously, this very well kept secret within hiring circles can be strategically used to your advantage (more about that in Secret 31), but as a résumé tool it poses a wonderful opportunity for you to stand out from the crowd.

Allowing the standard professional references to speak for you will do very little and certainly won't help you stand out as the top candidate. Nine times out of ten the standard professional references gleaned from calling the previous managers you listed on your application won't give hiring managers what they're really looking for, and they know it. So you need to tell them up front that you have what they're looking for. Real references who can give actual information about you as an employee, worker, team member. What you want are "personal professional references" that you give to a hiring manager yourself.

It's very easy for a hiring manager to end up with three top candidates, with access to very little useful information on any of them. If you're the only one of the three who provided an additional list of personal and professional references, you will easily become the safest recommendation in the group and will jump to the top of the list.

This reference list consists of at least three names of former bosses, colleagues, or clients who you know will say absolutely stellar things about you. Don't put anyone on that list who's not a sure bet, and make sure you stick with people you've worked with in some capacity.

Here's the four-part formula to effective reference crafting:

> **Reference Crafting Part 1:** Contact each one and ask if he or she would be willing to be a reference for you. (Don't ever put someone on your list who doesn't know

ahead of time he or she is going to be called and hasn't been coached on what to say.)

Reference Crafting Part 2: Give them a few pointers on the types of positions you're going for, things you'd like them to emphasize, and specifically things you'd like them to avoid talking about (such as problems they may know about concerning your current or previous employer or any other negative or bad-luck issue—you always want your references to stick to the positive).

Reference Crafting Part 3: Openly offer to reciprocate if they ever need a job or other reference.

Reference Crafting Part 4: Ask for these as "personal job references." As agents of the company many will not be willing or able to give a professional reference because of the policies and regulations, but they can usually give a "personal reference" as someone who has worked with you. In most cases, the same questions will be asked of them by a hiring manager and the same type of job-related information will be given, but the reference is not giving the information as an employee of the company but as a personal acquaintance. It's a technicality that will allow you to get people signed up for references who normally would not be able to participate.

Type up your list with the words "Personal Professional References for [your name]" and list each one, followed by his or her relationship to you and phone number. They should all be people you've worked with in some capacity, but within that definition there is some leeway. They can be clients, bosses, vendors, or even members of a professional organization or association you belong to who have worked with you on association business. Stay away from family, religious affiliations, and hobby-related references. As long as the relationships are strictly professional in nature and you know the potential references will say glowing things about you, they are good candidates for your reference list.

Make sure you have this list ready to go before you begin your job search. Once you have them set, you may then write "REFERENCES AVAILABLE UPON REQUEST" at the bottom of your résumé. This is the insider handshake the hiring manger has been looking for to put you at the top of the pile.

This statement signals something completely different to a hiring manager than it used to. It now says you have something other candidates don't have, references who are willing and ready to give actual information about your performance. This gives a hiring manager more to go on for a safe recommendation, makes you appear confident in what others will say about you, and will result in you ranking higher on his or her list.

People who are afraid of what their previous managers might say about them don't put this kind of bold statement on their résumé. It tells a hiring manager immediately that you are confident in your track record.

Having this list of personal/professional references featuring individuals who are ready to eagerly provide additional information about you can mean the difference between being a candidate and being the *top* candidate. These are the people who can give real information about your wonderful skills and talents, and the best part is, they are your hand-picked references ready to say exactly what you want your potential new employer to hear.

This whole idea may seem a little self-serving. And it is. But why not? Your job is to appear to be the safest bet for the hiring managers' recommendation. They may know they're checking your hand-picked references, but having glowing recommendations on you when all they've got on the others is rank and file will still make you the more solid choice compared to other candidates.

Having your own list of references to give is also good protection. Without a separate list of references to check, a hiring manager will typically try to dig into any information he or she can get from your previous employers and ask trick questions—anything to get them to open up and share some useful information they aren't supposed to share. Even if you know these prior employers will say good things about you, misunderstandings can occur with sneaky inquiries of this type. So make their job easier and prepare the field beforehand by filling your references with all your best allies.

Real references are a critical piece of your submission process. Make sure that they are carefully managed, all of them are saying exactly what you want them to, and the hiring managers know you have them. Assuming your references are handled by listing your previous companies and bosses on an application is a truly missed opportunity.

Clearly a résumé submission is much more than just a piece of paper with your work history on it. Crafting your entire résumé image has become a critical aspect of a successful job search process. To get squarely in the door involves a delicate combination of personal advertising, marketing, Internet awareness, and reference crafting to create a solid platform for your candidacy. In order for you to look like the best bet for recommendation, everything hiring managers look at during the submission process must support and reinforce your marketing image.

Use every available platform to your highest advantage, craft the items that can make or break decisions in your favor, and give your résumé the best chance of getting and staying on top. The name of the game is to look like the safest and most enticing choice, so you can continue to move forward into higher levels of the hiring process. It's up to you to ensure there is nothing standing in your way that could confuse or scare off a potential hire recommendation.

Once you've gotten your entire résumé submission package as strong as possible, you're ready for the next level in the hiring process.

It's time to talk about the all-important interview process, where the stakes are much higher and snares are waiting around every corner. It's time to teach you the basics of interview survival.

STOP PLAYING RÉSUMÉ ROULETTE KEY POINTS TO REMEMBER

SECRET 6: STAY OUT OF THE TRASH. Treat your résumé like an enticing advertisement, not a dry historical document. It's critical that you learn how to stand out from the stacks to entice your consumer, the hiring manager, into picking up that phone and calling you. If your résumé is not as enticing as possible, don't bother sending it out at all.

SECRET 7: TAKE IT OFF. Think you have to put everything in your work history on your résumé even if it's working against you? You don't. Learning what you *must* put on a résumé and should *never* put on a résumé can mean the difference between a frustrating job search and a quick offer for the job of your dreams.

SECRET 8: DON'T GET SCANNED OUT. If you can't get your résumé past the computer scanners, it will never be seen by a human being. Learn the trick to getting the key words you need on your résumé and cover letter so you can stay in the game.

SECRET 9: GET THE RECOMMENDATION. Do what you can to get an insider to hand-carry your résumé to the hiring manager's office. That is still the very best way to get noticed and stand out from the crowd of hopefuls. But if you don't have an insider, you can fake it.

SECRET 10: BEWARE THE BORING COVER LETTER. The way most of us have been taught to craft a cover letter is wrong. It will ensure your letter looks boring and like everyone else's. Make sure your cover letters are punchy, exciting, and enticing enough to inspire the hiring manager to put your résumé on top.

SECRET 11: DO YOU YAHOO? The Internet is now a secret weapon for hiring managers to use against you. They will do an Internet search on you, and if you don't Google well, you'll be out of the running. Make sure you know what's out there with your name on it, and even better, put something up that's targeted to the hiring manager who you now know will be looking.

SECRET 12: CAN I CHECK YOUR REFERENCES? The reference game has changed dramatically over the last few years. Be sure you know how to use it to your advantage. Craft your own set of references to stand out from the crowd and leverage them on your résumé to make sure you're on top.

3

YOUR INTERVIEW IS OVER

YOU WEAR YOUR BEST SUIT, ARRIVE EARLY, AND TRY TO keep your hands from visibly shaking. Your hair is in place; there's no spinach in your teeth; you've got copies of your résumé and a portfolio ready for taking notes. They usher you into "the room" and seat you in an uncomfortable chair as you try to smile at a complete stranger who now holds your entire future in the balance. You try to read his facial expression; you try to read his mind. What's he looking for? What kind of answer will make him say "Wow"? What answer will get you to the next level?

Suddenly he's asking questions you weren't ready for. Anxiety peaks as you realize there's no way for you to know what this gatekeeper is really looking for. Will you get another phone call after this? Or will you find yourself in a sea of unreturned calls with a dry form letter in your mailbox that says: "We're sorry, but this job is going to someone else"?

I think we'd all agree that this familiar process is bad enough. But today many feel the process has gotten much worse. And unfortunately, they're right. What we used to experience in an interview just a few years ago has moved to a whole new level of smoke and mirrors.

Did you know that interviewers will trick you into sharing information that's not in your best interest? That you will not only be asked questions designed to reveal your past work behaviors but also be put in situations during the interview to evoke those behaviors so the interviewer can see them firsthand? Did you know that your body language is examined more closely than what you say? That asking questions will make you look like a risk? Or that the way you answer interview questions will be given greater weight than your qualifications and skills for the position?

Interviews, whether over the phone or in-person, are hands down the most important part of the process, and the trickiest. This is where all a company's secret criteria and predilections, hidden within a carefully crafted veil of questions and tactics, come to the surface.

Gone are the days of the straightforward interview designed to allow you to talk about your skills and qualifications. The interview process of today is one of intense behavioral analysis, psychological profiling, and underhanded tactics that can spell disaster for an unprepared candidate.

I'm going to show you the most common tricks and tactics interviewers will throw at you and what they're looking for when they employ each one. You'll learn the practical survival tactics and insider secrets that will allow you to recognize and effectively handle each one to give you the upper hand in the process.

You may have heard of some of these tactics, but there is little truthful information out there on how to effectively deal with them. Some will seem new and utterly shocking. Failure to recognize and defuse even one of these can jeopardize your hiring process at a critical moment.

Think some of the most underhanded and stringent interview

tactics are only used in the larger corporations? Not so. While it's true that the larger companies tend to have hiring practices that are more developed and involved, with hiring mangers highly trained in how to use the tactics I'm about to describe, smaller companies can be even worse in their use of underhanded strategies and tricks in the hiring process. Why? Because they have more at stake.

Smaller companies tend to run much leaner than the large corporations and can't afford to make any mistakes in hiring. They have more to lose if they find themselves with a bad hire in their midst or have to deal with a difficult or litigious employee. Don't discount these interview survival tips simply because you prefer to work within smaller organizations. These tactics are used in companies with as few as a dozen employees and in corporations employing tens of thousands.

These screening tactics are prevalent for a reason: They work. They help screen out those individuals a company feels for whatever reason are undesirable based on their hidden criteria. But it's important to know that all these screening tactics, as scary as they seem, can work in your favor. If you are the only candidate who can recognize and neutralize them, you will naturally stand out as the top choice among the crowd. And if you know what to look for, the tactics a company chooses to use in its interview processes can tell you a lot about whether or not it's the right place for you.

You may not want to work for a company that uses some of the more underhanded styles described here. But many of the top companies in the United States and around the world are using these very tactics to screen out the competition for the most coveted jobs.

This chapter will show you exactly what you're up against in the interview process, from a perspective you've never seen before. And you'll know exactly how to handle and avoid each one of these traps threatening your interview survival.

INSIDER SECRET 13
Hiring managers are not on your side.

"SUSAN" HAD SUBMITTED HER RÉSUMÉ TO A COMPANY SHE dearly wanted to work for. This was the third time she'd sent her résumé to this company, hoping for a phone call. She was overjoyed to get one, quite out of the blue, on a Saturday. The person on the other end of the phone was so nice it almost felt like Susan was talking to a close friend. It didn't seem like an interview at all. They soon began speaking about each other's families and kids and even the unique challenges of being a single parent. The phone call went on for over an hour, and afterward Susan was on cloud nine. She definitely had the support of this hiring manager and knew the next phone call would be to schedule a face-to-face interview with the very same person she'd just made friends with. She felt like she was in.

But now two weeks had gone by with no call and Susan was beginning to chew her nails. She had left several voice mails for her new friend, but to no avail. What had gone wrong?

After waiting and wondering for almost a month with no return phone calls, Susan heard from a friend at the company that someone else had been hired for the position. No call, no letter, no explanation, no nothing. What could have made such a positive phone call go bad?

Susan fell into one of the biggest traps that catch unsuspecting candidates off-guard.

Those people who sound like they're your best friend, your new advocate throughout this next phase of the hiring process, are not what they seem.

Phone screeners, interviewers, and hiring managers are trained to sound that way. They're trained to be enthusiastic, friendly, and upbeat representatives for the company.

It's certainly exciting to get that initial call from a hiring manager that lets you know you've made it to the next level. It's even more exciting to get that in-person interview. But the most common assumption candidates wrongly make at this point is something most people never consider: A hiring manager is not on your side, ever.

You already know from Secret 1 that hiring managers aren't looking to include you as a candidate for hire but are looking for any reason to exclude you from the remainder of the process. But when you begin talking to these powerful gatekeepers in person, a strange thing can happen. You are speaking with a friendly person who is putting you at ease, chatting with you on a wide variety of topics, and you suddenly find you're letting your guard down. Certainly the connection you've made with this individual isn't just professional; you must be creating some sort of friendship. Certainly this individual is rooting for you to get the job and will help you do so. Wrong.

No matter how friendly hiring managers are, no matter how supportive or empathetic they seem, there is one key thing missing. Loyalty. You will never hold the primary position on their scale of loyalty because of one simple fact: You don't cut this person's paycheck. A hiring manager is only loyal to one entity, the company that employs him or her, and its interests. Your interests, no matter what kind of connection you make with this individual or how pleasant the meeting was, will always be secondary to the company's interests and secret criteria. Always.

What does this mean? From moment one these friendly people on the phone or sitting across the desk from you are looking for reasons to eliminate you that have nothing to do with the qualifications for the position. As empathetic as they may seem, they won't be able to give you the benefit of the doubt and won't look the other way if red flags are raised.

Hiring managers are not there to find the best fit for the position; they are there to protect the company from the wrong fit. There's a big difference.

The truth is: A hiring manager's primary secret agenda is to screen out all candidates who could potentially cause problems or inconvenience for the company. That screening comes first, above all else. The hiring manager has already looked at your résumé and believes you have the appropriate skills to recommend you for moving forward. So the purpose of the interview is not solely to find out if you can do the job; it's also to see what kind of person you are and if you have the potential to cause the company any inconvenience.

What was Susan's big mistake? She got comfortable. During Susan's exciting phone call, she'd become so comfortable with her "new friend" she chose to openly share the details of her chaotic family life. Recently divorced, she was trying to juggle raising three small children, fighting a tough custody battle, and working full-time. Her new friend on the phone had been very understanding and even stated she had been through a difficult divorce herself several years earlier, leaving her as a single working parent as well. They lamented together over the unique challenges this posed. But Susan forgot that she was not talking to a best friend but rather an agent of the company she wished to work for. An agent required to screen out any candidate who showed potential for inconvenience or, in this case, an inability to focus completely on this important position due to a variety of looming personal challenges.

Susan's hiring manager, as nice and supportive as she may have been, could never recommend someone for hire who was going through a series of difficult personal issues. If anything were to happen that jeopardized the position, especially something related to a previously disclosed issue the hiring manager had known could be a problem, that hiring manager could be in danger of losing her job.

Which do you think this hiring manager would be willing to choose: supporting a fellow single working mother through a difficult time or protecting her position so she can continue to feed her own kids? I think you know the answer. This isn't about making a new friend; it's about being a safe recommendation for someone whose job hangs in the balance every time he or she recommends a hire.

"Beth" was thrilled to get an offer from a large company she'd dreamed of working for. The job was perfect for her and she was feeling on top of the world. She had been through three months of interviews with all sorts of people within the organization, and the human-resources manager had walked her through the entire process. The manager had been so nice and so helpful. She had been the one to personally call and extend the offer that would be presented to Beth in writing in a personal meeting that next Monday. "It's just formal paperwork," the human-resources manager said. "We want you to start right away." The offer was great, with everything Beth had wanted and more.

But Beth had been harboring a secret throughout this process that made this fantastic job offer even more important. She was a single mother of a child with disabilities and needed this job to pay for her child's lofty medical bills and other care essentials. This new job would be the answer to Beth's prayers.

Thinking everything was in the bag now that an offer had been discussed, she decided to relax a little and share the reason for her overwhelming enthusiasm with this human-resources manager who had been so nice. After all, wouldn't she want to know that this offer was helping a struggling family more than anyone could imagine? Beth excitedly blurted out her situation and struggles, explaining that this offer was even more timely because her child was going in for a series of risky surgeries and she was unsure of what was going to happen. This job would now help her pay for that as well as provide some much-needed stability.

Monday morning, when Beth arrived at the company to sign her paperwork for the formal offer, she was told that something had come up and the meeting would have to be rescheduled. Thinking nothing of it, Beth left with the understanding that her new human-resources manager friend would be calling her later in the day to reschedule. That call never came.

After two weeks of trying to reach her friend and others Beth had interviewed with at the company, she finally received a dry letter in the mail thanking her for interviewing and telling her that the position had been filled.

Outraged, Beth talked to a lawyer who then contacted the company. They abruptly denied that a verbal offer had ever been made. Denying that Beth had ever been a solid candidate for the position, they also denied any knowledge of Beth's private personal issues with her child. It had all been discussed over the phone, so of course there was no proof, no paper trail. And no more job.

This is one of the more heart-wrenching stories I've experienced in all my years of doing this kind of work, but I share it because it illustrates what's at stake here. A hiring manager, no matter how sympathetic to your personal situations, would never be able to recommend continuing with a hire if he or she knew there could be a potential for higher medical insurance premiums, lost time, and severe inconvenience for the company.

Yes, they do care. Yes, they do want you to have a job and take care of your family. But they are acting as agents of the company, and the company wants serious inconveniences to be someone else's problem, not theirs.

Hiring managers are required to operate in the best interest of the company at every stage in the process, but they are not required to tell you that. As nice as they seem, the minute your interests appear to run contrary to those of the company, the two of you are on opposite sides. And you will never know it.

Companies large and small run too lean these days to be able to absorb a difficult personal situation with an employee. It's not that they don't care about your well-being, but they will always care more about the well-being of the company. Most companies feel they have to have every position filled with someone who can put in 110 percent at all times or the company will lose its edge. That fear will trump concern for your personal issues every time.

How do you avoid all this? Remember whom you are talking to at all times—an agent of the company required to put its best interests first, not yours. Remember that your personal information is yours. You do not need to disclose anything personal or private during the hiring process, or after you've been hired for that matter.

Don't allow yourself to be lulled into a false sense of security by a friendly approach and an "I'm here for you" attitude. Like salespeople, hiring managers are trained to sound that way as emissaries of the company, but they are not your friends and are not *allowed* to be on your side. In fact, many will try to trick you. . . .

INSIDER SECRET 14
Interviewers will trick you.

YOU SPOT A PICTURE OF CHILDREN PROMINENTLY DISPLAYED on an interviewer's desk and make a friendly comment. The interviewer shares a personal story, and you feel compelled to respond in kind. This is a friendly meeting after all, not an interrogation, right? Could it be a trick? Yes.

Interviewers use a variety of tactics to get you to volunteer sensitive information that would be illegal to ask in an interview but that can be highly valuable in this high-stakes selection process.

Where most candidates get into trouble is during the small talk before an interview really begins. It's important to understand that once you walk through the doors or talk to any company representative in any capacity, you are in the interview. It all counts. Anything you choose to say, even in jest or small talk, can and will be used against you. Whether it's talking to the receptionist, security guard, or even someone in the bathroom, you are in the interview.

I know a hiring manager who enlists the receptionist to gather personal information on each candidate who comes in. The receptionist hands out the application and then opens a dialogue for small talk. If the information shared puts the candidate outside the company's hiring criteria, a specific-color Post-it is placed on the application. That Post-it is a secret signal that will turn the candidate's in-depth interview into a ten-minute courtesy meeting. The interview is over before it begins.

Another hiring manager works for a company that is keen on avoiding the inconveniences of employees with small children. She keeps a picture of children on her desk facing potential candidates. She has no children. The tactic is designed to trick a candidate into asking questions about the children and spontaneously talking about their own kids. If no comment is made about the picture, the hiring manager might encourage it by saying that she's sorry she's late but she had to pick up her daughter from soccer practice, followed by "aren't kids just great?"

This kind of open question invites the social response of reciprocation. We've been conditioned to feel that if we don't respond to an open statement like that, we're being rude—certainly not how you want to be perceived in an interview. So we reciprocate in kind and start talking about things that are actually not in our best interest.

How about an interviewer who makes a comment as he sits down for the interview that his back has been giving him problems and he's worried he may need surgery, casually leading the conversation so that you feel compelled to share your own medical issues in sympathy? What if I told you the hiring manager had no back problems?

These underhanded tactics are used because it's illegal to ask about such things, but it's not illegal to subtly encourage candidates to confess information on their own.

Sometimes a tactic isn't even necessary. I've been in countless interviews where candidates suddenly felt the need to confess completely inappropriate information with no prompting whatsoever. In that situation, interviewers are trained to pretend nothing serious just happened. They're trained to ignore it in front of the candidate, even though they know it means the end of this individual's bid for the position.

This begs the next logical question. Why would interviewers try to trick you like this? Why would they feel the need to resort to such tactics?

There are very few opportunities or legal avenues busy hiring managers can use to quickly get to the heart of your personality. They know most candidates will be able to put on their best behavior for an interview, telling hiring managers what they think they want to hear. Hiring managers need to find out who you really are—fast—so they can make the best choice for their company. These entrapments and tactics are used because of that time constraint, in addition to the high stakes of the hiring process. It's not that these hiring managers are trying to be malicious; they are simply trying to get the company's needs met in the midst of a variety of legal constraints they feel keep them from doing so.

In fact, most people who employ these tactics see nothing wrong with them. They view such a tactic as a protective measure for the company, while allowing them to excel at their jobs. After all, it is your choice to volunteer inappropriate information in an interview; they are merely providing the opportunity for you to do so. If you choose not to share, there is nothing they can do. In their minds they are doing nothing illegal; they are simply providing opportunities.

As scary as all this sounds, these underhanded tricks are very simple to avoid: Don't share your personal information—for any reason. If you find yourself being baited by one of these tactics, the best course of action is: Don't bite.

Don't share your personal information just because it appears that the interviewer did. You can sympathize with what an interviewer just told you, but don't reciprocate. If it's on a topic that would normally be illegal to ask about: marital status, children, sexual preference, religion, medical issues, ethnicity, age, then don't share it. Now, I'm not recommending you bring this to the interviewer's attention unless you want to end the interview for good. But I do recommend you maintain awareness of whom you're talking to and what his or her agenda may be.

If you find yourself feeling painted into a corner, the best defense is to turn the interviewer's questions back on him or her, like this:

> INTERVIEWER: Sorry I'm late; I had to pick up my daughter from soccer practice. Aren't kids great? [Long pause waiting for reciprocation.]
>
> CANDIDATE: Yes, they are; how old is *your* daughter? What position does *she* play?

• • •

> INTERVIEWER: Hey, we went to the same school. I was class of '94. [Open-ended statement designed to get you to reciprocate by telling what year you graduated so the interviewer can get your age. *It goes without saying you should never put graduation dates on your résumé unless you wish to invite age discrimination into your job*

search. Graduation dates are only appropriate when there is a degree pending.]

CANDIDATE: Such a great school, isn't it? I had such a good time there. What was *your* major? Mine was business. [Avoiding the reciprocation of which year you graduated.]

• • •

INTERVIEWER: I've been having the worst problems with my knee lately; the doctor says I may have to have surgery. [Open-ended statement designed to have you sympathize by sharing your own medical issues.]

CANDIDATE: Gosh, I'm so sorry to hear that. How did you hurt it?

Asking questions in response will allow you to put the spotlight back on the interviewer without giving anything away that shouldn't be discussed. A response like the preceding ones won't allow interviewers to get anything out of you about your parental status, age, or medical issues, unless they ask a direct question—in these cases illegal ones. And since you didn't reciprocate as most candidates would under that kind of social manipulation, the interviewer is forced to assume there are no issues of concern and move on.

The truth is: An interview is not a confessional. This is not a safe place to discuss your personal issues, preferences, or private information. As you can see by the preceding examples, you will still be able to maintain a friendly connection with the interviewer while protecting yourself from inappropriate screenings and deceptive tactics.

We all have personal, medical, and family issues we have to deal with, but these are our private concerns. No company and no interviewer need to know about them.

Asking questions about your children, age, martial status, and medical issues is illegal for a reason. Don't let anyone trick you into giving away your rights to privacy.

INSIDER SECRET 15
Your body will betray you.

MOST OF US PUT ALL OUR ATTENTION ON WHAT WE'RE GOING to say in an interview, but is that really what's most important?

A recent study featured in *Forbes* and *BusinessWeek* showed that only 7 percent of an interviewer's impression of you is based on what you say. A full 55 percent is based on your body language, and 38 percent is based on your tone of voice.

This means you could be the very best candidate for the job and know all the right things to say, but if you aren't dressed right, give a dead-fish handshake, don't look the interviewer in the eye, or exhibit negative body language, you will be out.

Most people work on polishing their verbal skills for an interview, which is obviously important, but if you don't work on your overall presentation, you may never get the chance to dazzle the interviewer with your verbal skills.

When you first meet an interviewer, creating a positive first impression will solidify your foundation for a successful interview. That means dressing up (even if you are interviewing for a casual company, you want to present a polished appearance), smiling first, looking him or her in the eye, and extending a firm, confident handshake. If you are sitting when the interviewer approaches, always stand up to greet him or her.

Failing to do any of these will erode an interviewer's first impression of you and cause you to have a more difficult interview.

If you appear to lack confidence, look sloppy, seem evasive, or exhibit any negative body language during the encounter, an interviewer will want to know why and will dig for reasons. This means you will get a tougher interview than others.

Why are body language and appearance so important? If you appear to be a polished, confident candidate, exhibiting positive body language and appearance, it will support and reinforce everything you say during interviews. It will put interviewers at ease, cause them to relax, and make them feel that you have nothing to hide. You appear to be exactly what you say you are, a qualified professional candidate. It will make interviewers feel as though they don't need to go searching with trick questions or tactics. That will translate into easier questions and easier interviews.

Here's how it's done:

From moment one, it's important to smile and keep your appearance a confident one. That means sitting up straight, planting your feet firmly on the floor, avoiding nervous gestures (they can make you appear untrustworthy or evasive), and making eye contact. Positive body language will make you appear confident and qualified. Negative body language, even if accidental, will turn the interviewer's impression against you. Once that impression has turned negative, no matter how qualified you are, you will not get the job.

Here's a list of a few things to avoid:

> **Slouching:** This will be seen as a sign of disrespect, lack of interest in the interview, or a lack of preparedness. It makes it appear as though you do not have confidence in your abilities.
>
> **Staring at the floor:** Many of us tend to do this when we're nervous, but this will be interpreted by the interviewer as an indication of lack of interest in the conversation.

Arms folded: Standing or sitting with your arms across your chest will be interpreted as a defensive posture, will make the interviewer think you have something to hide or are uncomfortable, and will tend to shut down the conversation.

Hands in pockets: Standing with your hands in your pockets makes it look like you may have something to hide and suggests unease or a lack of confidence.

Touching your nose: It is widely thought that when someone rubs his or her nose when speaking, he or she is not being truthful. Touching your nose during an interview, even if it itches, will be interpreted by the interviewer as an indication of dishonesty.

Rubbing your neck: This is seen as an indication of boredom or unease.

Movement: Shaking one leg or jiggling a foot will be interpreted by an interviewer as an indication of severe nervousness and discomfort.

Facing: Failure to face the interviewer with your body will be interpreted as suggesting avoidance, that you have something to hide. Pointing your feet toward the door or leaning in that general direction will make it look like you want to flee.

Dress: First-round candidates are often eliminated for the way they dress. Wearing jeans, looking sloppy, or wearing wrinkled or overly casual attire will be viewed as a sign of disrespect by the interviewer. Dress is also treated by interviewers as an insight into what kind of thinker you are. A sloppy dresser will be interpreted as a sloppy, disorganized thinker.

Each of these, even if done accidentally, will put up red flags in the mind of an interviewer. These red flags will trigger tactics and questions designed to dig deeper into your background, getting you to reveal why your body language seems to contradict what you're saying.

Here are a few things you can do to increase your chances of making that great impression and getting an easier interview:

Adopt an open posture: That means arms and legs uncrossed. It suggests a relaxed, honest, open demeanor and conveys confidence.

Make regular eye contact without staring: There are three statistically significant actions that build a good impression: making eye contact, smiling, and nodding your head. If you do nothing else, focusing on these three things will reinforce your positive image.

Steer your body: If you must cross your legs to be more comfortable, make sure you point your knees at the interviewer and keep your body straight. You don't want to lean to one side or the other.

Lean forward: Leaning forward in your chair conveys interest and engagement in the conversation.

Use your hands: Complementing your answers with physical expression conveys confidence in what you're saying. Feel free to talk with your hands; use them for emphasis and to form ideas. It will make you look like you know what you're talking about.

Match the ideal: Dress to the company's ideal image. Every company has an ideal of how they'd like their representatives to dress and behave. If you don't know what the company's ideal is, look at the directors and executives and copy what they wear. If you don't have the opportunity to see what the top people are wearing, always go for the well-groomed, polished, conservative look. You can't go wrong with dressing up. Even if you get there and find that everyone is very casually dressed, all it takes is one comment to get you back on track: "I can see you have casual dress here; that's wonderful, what a great benefit."

All qualifications being equal, a company will choose the candidate with the most polished and positive presentation in an interview.

Creating a polished, conservative, and ideal image, exhibiting positive body language, and avoiding behavior or appearances that make interviewers nervous will support and enhance everything you say in your interview. It will allow that 7 percent, "what you say," to become the main focus, and all your wonderful qualifications will shine through. Plus you'll get an easier interview than everyone else.

INSIDER SECRET 16
There's one trick to all trick questions.

THERE ARE COUNTLESS BOOKS, ARTICLES, AND SEMINARS DEvoted to helping you craft the best responses to all kinds of interview questions. But you don't need to drive yourself crazy over potential trick questions, memorizing them all so that you feel prepared. It's much easier than that.

In fact, memorizing lists of questions and trying to prepare set answers for every scenario will work against you. You run the risk of sounding like a robot, with a boring and flat delivery, and being utterly forgettable in the interview process.

All you need to know is why companies ask these trick questions. Once you know the reasoning behind them, you'll know how to spot one, you'll understand what the interviewer is secretly screening for, and you'll be able to avoid all trick questions with ease.

The secret is: All trick questions, even the really scary psychological questions, are crafted so that you will give a negative answer. The interviewer is trying to trick you into giving away something unflattering about your personality or to get you to talk negatively about a previous employer or boss. Once you are tricked into saying something negative, the interview is over.

The secret to steering clear of this trick is to remain positive in everything you say. Even if you must say something negative for a moment to properly answer a question, be gracious and forgiving, and move on immediately to your successes using positive statements.

If you have a tendency to be the glass-half-empty type, the skill of consistently presenting information in a positive framework may take some practice, but it is an absolute must if you want to score the top jobs.

The truth is: Positive people (candidates who speak and present their information in the most positive way) **are hired more often than any other personality type.** Companies tend to hire positive people because they believe those people are successful and will draw success to the organization. Companies fear that people with negative tendencies will attract negativity and even cause the company to be unlucky.

Now why doesn't anyone tell you this? Because it's a test. Companies don't want candidates doing these things because they know it will temporarily help them be successful. They want candidates to "just be themselves" in the interview process so the company can see what you're all about in an uncensored way. They want the negative nellies to tip their hand and save the company time and effort. Companies want to hire the truly positive people who approach interviews and their work with optimism and confidence.

If you're asked what high school was like for you, what your father did for a living, or what was the worst job you've ever had, no matter what those scenarios were really like for you, it is imperative to stay positive in your answer. It's not about sharing exactly what happened in your personal or work past; it's all about packaging your answers to put you in the best light and help your best qualities shine through.

Here's what I'm talking about:

> **INTERVIEWER:** Why are you leaving your current job?
>
> **CANDIDATE:** Well, my boss and I haven't really seen eye to eye on things. I'm interested in moving the company forward and implementing some things that will take the company out of the Dark Ages, but he's just too set in his ways. Eventually this kind of thing can get frustrating, and I'm looking to find a company that's more forward thinking.

Think this is a good answer? It's not. Your interview is over.

But why? You showed that you are forward thinking and you're not willing to stay in an unprogressive situation. What employer wouldn't want that? Besides, this potential employer is going to realize everything wasn't perfect at your previous company; otherwise you wouldn't be looking to leave.

This all makes logical sense, except for one thing. This is a trick question that succeeded in getting you to speak negatively about your previous employer. You negated your boss and made it look like you only cared about your agenda. Yes, it's an agenda that many potential employers might value, but not at the expense of the relationship with your previous boss, the key gatekeeper in your career. Nor at the potential expense of hiring a negative employee only interested in what he or she wants to do. What does the answer look like when it's done right?

The Fix:

> INTERVIEWER: Why are you leaving your current job?
>
> CANDIDATE: I've really enjoyed working for the company, and I've learned a great deal, but I'm also very intrigued by your company's commitment to forward momentum and dynamic growth. That's something I highly value and enjoy, and I'd be very interested in bringing the skills I've learned to an environment like this.

You're hired! Now this is basically the same answer as the preceding one, but without any of the negativity. This one got the best points across without bashing the previous employer or the boss. There's no need to say that the previous company didn't keep up with your desires for forward momentum; that's implied in the fact that you are out interviewing and wish to make a change. See the difference in the two approaches? One was completely positive; the other shared a negative premise. That's all it takes to avoid being taken down by a trick question.

Here's another one:

> INTERVIEWER: Tell me about the most difficult boss or client you've ever worked with.
>
> CANDIDATE: Well, there was this one boss who was so difficult. She could never make up her mind. You'd do something the way she asked for it, but it was never good enough, and she'd turn around and want something else. It was so frustrating that I eventually transferred onto another team. She got fired soon after that, so I guess the company agreed that she wasn't a very good boss.

Well? What do you think? This may have been a very valid and accurate answer, but once again, your interview is over if you give this type of response.

The person interviewing you for this position is not going to care that you had a boss who was unfair or even inappropriate. If you share a negative experience during an interview, it will make you look like you have a track record of unsuccessful relationships. Remember, anything shared in an interview setting is given magnified importance. Interviewers will look at this kind of answer and think, *This candidate can't get along with his bosses, and isn't willing to find out what his manager needs.*

Even though we've all had bad bosses and even though the interviewer can most likely sympathize with you, the fact that you've chosen to share a negative experience (or got tricked into it) will knock you right out of the running.

Don't allow yourself to get tricked or fooled by an interviewer's questions. Your job is to maintain as positive a message and image as possible, no matter what the question. Even if you are asked to talk about a difficult or unsuccessful past situation, find a way to sidestep any negativity and emphasize the positive aspects of the experience.

The Fix:

> INTERVIEWER: Tell me about the most difficult boss or client you've ever worked with.
>
> CANDIDATE: Well, I've been pretty lucky in this regard, but in the work setting there are always going to be challenges that arise. A few years ago, I had a boss who appeared to have trouble making up her mind. It was causing frustration for the team. I soon realized it was because she was highly distracted and didn't have the time to communicate exactly what she wanted up front. Realizing she was dealing with too much, I made sure I got a

> clear idea of what was needed and expected on the project so we could give her exactly what she wanted the first time, without any additional effort or follow-up on her part. I learned a lot from that experience and still value it today.

This version is all positive, with none of the negative aspects. It's essentially the same story, but told without the negative emotions and personal baggage. It's more objective, putting you and the situation in the best light. Rather than ending your interview early, this positive answer just got you hired.

The truth is: In a high-stakes interview, it's not about sharing every detail of what actually happened; it's about packaging. It's again about marketing yourself effectively.

Interviewing is like blind dating. Rather than going on a first date and sharing all the realities of your life: "I'm a bad cook, a slob, and my last three relationships ended with a restraining order," you may want to emphasize all your good points: "I make great chocolate-chip cookies, I love animals, and I'm a good skier." The good and the not-so-good may all be true, but the first set of disclosures is just a little too scary for a first meeting. A first date and a first interview will not be able to get to know who you are, the real you, during this brief initial meeting. So it's key to package things in their best light. It's true that some of the not-so-good things may eventually come to light later, but that's usually after the person has gotten to know you and can get the full-picture perspective.

Rule of thumb when answering interview questions? Never give an answer or share an experience that doesn't have a happy ending, doesn't end successfully, or doesn't showcase you as a star in some way.

Here's another classic trick question:

> INTERVIEWER: What are your three biggest weaknesses?

> CANDIDATE: Well, I tend to procrastinate, but I get my best work done when I'm under the gun. I don't like getting additional tasks when I'm working on a deadline, but nobody likes that, do they? And I'm not great at organization, my desk always looks like an explosion—but that's just 'cause I'm so busy and such a hard worker.

Think this one will keep you in the game? Possibly, but it's not doing you any favors. This candidate tried to answer in a way that continued to put her in a positive light, but it didn't quite make it.

Sure, this is a better approach than stating weaknesses that aren't really weaknesses, which most people have heard is the best approach to this question. It may have been at one time, but interviewers have gotten too smart for that now and won't let you get away with it. Thus this question has become a lot more difficult to answer properly.

"Well . . . I'm a workaholic, a perfectionist, and I try too hard to please everyone." That kind of answer just isn't going to fly in interviews anymore. A trained interviewer will say, "Hmm, very interesting, but those aren't really weaknesses. Why don't you give me three more?" And if you try to say, "Gee, I don't have any weaknesses," be prepared for a much stronger and more aggressive response from the interviewer.

There's a better way to get past this type of trick question, and that is to share three things you've become aware of as potential or previous issues that you've already fixed and how you did it. Identify, then neutralize.

The Fix:

> INTERVIEWER: What are your three biggest weaknesses?
>
> CANDIDATE: Well everybody has something they'd like to be doing better, and I'm always looking to improve my

> skills. About five years ago, a previous boss told me that I needed some help with my organizational skills, and I appreciated him telling me that. It really helped me. I took a wonderful course, put together a great system that I still use to this day, and I really enjoy it. It has helped me work so much more efficiently and I have a lot less stress because I know that nothing will slip through the cracks even when I'm under tight deadlines. Second, I realize that this industry has a tendency to change the software it uses every few years, and that used to be quite frustrating. But now I plan for it and I try to find out what the shift might be ahead of time so I can work learning about it into my schedule and get it done ahead of the curve. And third, I've noticed that I tend to get really focused in on my work, especially when I have a deadline. But I've found that my work is much richer when I shift over and do other things on my to-do list in between project tasks so I can keep my thought process fresh and can return to the project renewed.

The best way to address this question is to answer with previously identified potential weaknesses you've already fixed. This shows a willingness to accept feedback and critiques and that you are conscientious in improving your skills and talents in the workplace. It also acknowledges that everyone has something they are working on. Just make sure the weaknesses don't put you in a negative light.

I once interviewed someone who answered that question with "I used to smoke a joint at lunch to calm myself down when things got stressful at work, but that really started to hurt my work. So now I only do it on weekends."

I had another one say, "When I work too many hours, my back really starts hurting me, so I guess my biggest weakness is that I can only go for about six hours before I become pretty useless."

Needless to say, neither of these individuals got a recommendation for hire. Be sure to pick somewhat benign weaknesses to feature as things you are working on or have already fixed.

How about this innocuous-sounding trick question?:

> INTERVIEWER: Where do you see yourself in five years?
>
> CANDIDATE: Well, I see myself still working here but hopefully at a higher level, handling more responsibility, expanding my role, and maybe even one day becoming a vice president.

Sounds good, doesn't it? What could possibly be wrong with an answer that shows investment in the company, continued growth, and upward mobility?

This is a trick question because it's again looking for you to speak negatively, but under the guise of a positive question. Most candidates believe that this question is only looking to ensure you want to stay with the company for a long time and that you aren't going to flake out and disappear to potentially greener pastures before the company gets its investment out of you. But that's not all interviewers who ask this question are looking for. They are also looking to see if you'll get bored where you are, if your ambitions lie elsewhere, or if you could even potentially become a threat to their position.

The Fix:

> INTERVIEWER: Where do you see yourself in five years?
>
> CANDIDATE: I'd love to be working for this company. I think this is someplace I would enjoy working for a very long time. This position seems like a great match for

> me. And the company has such a stellar reputation for forward movement and bringing new ideas to the marketplace, I love the idea of continuing to expand my skills and talents to help drive the success of this company.

This trick question is a wonderful opportunity to showcase your enthusiasm for the job and company that shouldn't be passed up. You want to show the interviewer you are interested in this position at *this* time.

Don't let a time-frame question trip you up. The interviewer is not really asking you about the next five years, so this is not the time to say that you hope to be running the company one day. Your private hopes, plans, ambitions, forward movement, and expectations for promotion are things you should keep to yourself in an interview. Not just because you could inadvertently step on your interviewer's ambitions but also because moving up is not your decision; it's the company's. Before they get to know the real you, this kind of talk will too easily be construed as "He'll be unhappy with this position soon because he's already hoping for more responsibility and thinking of moving onward and upward."

Here is another popular question that trips people up:

> INTERVIEWER: Tell me about the job you've had in your career you liked the least.

To properly answer this one, you take a challenging job and turn it into a positive learning experience or success. Carefully avoid any negativity or bashing of former employers, responsibilities, or bosses; instead follow up with "I really learned a lot from that job" or "I still use those skills to this day." This will help solidify your positive message.

An interviewer is always looking for you to answer negatively and start talking trash about a former work experience so that he or she can get a glimpse into your true personality and behavior at work.

What if the interviewer asks about the best job you've ever had? Make sure your answer puts you in a positive light, not just the job. For example, you should steer clear of things like "I got to run the projector at a movie theater for a summer, and all I did was eat candy and watch movies and get paid for it; it was so great!" It is much better to share a story about what a hard worker you are and how much you learned from a great opportunity, even if it wasn't your best job, rather than to share a fun work experience such as getting paid to watch movies and eat candy all day.

One more word of caution: Don't take your cues from the interviewer about what you can and cannot say. Interviewers will go into a negative story of their own to try to get you to do the same: "Boy, I had this terrible boss once; you wouldn't believe what he did. . . ." It's okay for the interviewer to be critical of a former boss or share a bad experience, but not you. Don't give in to the tendency to reciprocate or you will fall into the interviewer's trap. It's never okay to speak in the negative, even if everyone else in the interview room is doing just that.

Staying positive during a job interview and avoiding sharing any information that touches on bad luck or negative experiences you've had in your career will take you straight to the top of the list.

Companies and hiring managers will never openly share this secret because it takes away too many of the tricks that make the interviewer's job easier. But if you know that what interviewers are secretly looking for is stories of positivity and silver linings, avoiding anything negative or critical, then you'll survive with flying colors as the number one candidate.

INSIDER SECRET 17
Storytelling is your best defense.

MANY OF YOU HAVE HEARD OF OR EXPERIENCED FIRSTHAND the new behavioral interviewing techniques. They are nerve-wracking, and they're designed that way on purpose.

Questions are fired at you in a way that actually keeps you from knowing what to say in response. This new trend forces unsuspecting candidates away from the traditional questions we're all used to answering and into behavior scenarios from past experiences: "Describe a moment where you had to publicly disagree with your boss on an important issue and how you chose to handle it."

But there is a way to prepare for this particularly aggressive and off-putting new style so that you always have something positive to say that makes you stand out as a top candidate. This preparation can also help you feel more comfortable and confident in a process designed to make you feel uncomfortable.

When interviewers fire off a question, they are looking for a quick and well-prepared response. That is what's going to make the best impression. If you stammer and stray, it will look like you have something to hide. Rather than winging it on these key questions, you can come in prepared with powerful, prepackaged answers that are so flexible you can apply them to any question.

Behavioral interviewing is a new way of formulating questions designed to make you sweat and put you off-guard, in the hopes that you will share something you shouldn't or normally wouldn't. But because of the nature of behavioral questioning, it opens the door for storytelling as a qualified and effective response to any question. This new shift in interviewing allows a candidate to prepare positive stories in advance to use throughout the process for both protection and advantage. Traditional and behavioral styles are still essentially looking for the same things, for you to go negative or become critical. So preparing properly for the most difficult style—behavioral—will help ensure success with both.

Now this is where most people say to me, "How can I possibly prepare?" "How will I know what they're going to ask?" **The truth is: They all ask the same things in different ways. They are all looking for the same things, no matter what style or tactic the interviewer chooses to use on you.**

You don't have to know what questions they're going to ask ahead of time; all you have to do is develop a positive key message and stick to it.

Politicians are famous for the way they use this tactic, referred to as "staying on message." Politicians develop their message, with the main issue they want to get across. Once that message is set, it doesn't matter what an interviewer asks, because what comes out of the politician's mouth is his or her prepared message. Politicians do this to protect themselves from talking about subjects they know could get them in trouble, to keep from being trapped by a tenacious interviewer, and to ensure that their best points are always highlighted. They do it for exactly the same reason you sweat in an interview: They know they only have one shot to steer this important opportunity in their favor. While politicians take this tactic to an extreme degree, you can absolutely use the same strategy for easily and effectively sailing through tough and underhanded interview questions.

The best way to do this is by preparing 3–5 short stories. (You can prepare as many as you'd like to have on hand when you need them, but you must have at least three to cover your bases.) They should each take no longer than two or three minutes to tell. These stories should be your greatest career (or school, if you're a recent graduate) success stories. Something you did that no one thought was possible, or that time you saved the day, or that new process you implemented that increased productivity by 20 percent. Make sure each one is told from a completely positive silver-lining point of view, avoiding all negativity. (If you skipped over Secret 16, make sure you review it before crafting your stories.)

Gather up all your greatest hits and prepare them into short, positive statements featuring you as the star. Make sure one of the three shows a challenge or struggle you faced with a boss, co-workers, or deadlines but that you ultimately overcame successfully.

Then when an interviewer asks anything that even remotely points to one of your stories, launch one! For example:

> INTERVIEWER: Tell me about a difficult work situation and how you handled it.
>
> CANDIDATE: Well, we had this notoriously difficult client. At one point this client gave my team a project with an extremely tight deadline, but I'd worked with this particular client before and knew how to make him happy. We had a meeting to prepare ahead of time, anticipated his needs, and we were able to provide him with a highly successful product ahead of schedule. Everyone was very pleased and the client called the head of the company personally to say how happy he was with the results.

Having success stories in your back pocket during an interview will always give you something positive and successful to say, make you look like a sharp candidate, and keep you on track. Even if your success story isn't related directly to the question, you can find a way to link it in.

For example: If you wanted to share your story of the preceding happy client, but the interviewer asked about a difficult situation with a boss, you could say something like "Well, I've been quite lucky and I haven't really had any difficult situations with my bosses, but I have had a few with some difficult clients, and as we all know, 'the client is the boss.'" Then you can continue with your story.

The interviewer will certainly accept this kind of segue. Even if you have to create a somewhat awkward link between a question and the positive story you'd like to tell, it's always better to share a success story than allow yourself to get trapped into saying something that puts you in a negative light.

Once you've practiced this storytelling approach, finding the stories that seem to be the most compelling and successful, you will be able to approach every interview with full confidence, knowing ahead of time exactly what you're going to say, no matter what style is used or what types of questions are asked.

Having prepared success stories can also help you answer your questions in a more powerful and memorable way. Most people who are faced with an interview question they aren't ready for fall into the typical rut of answering with a list of items. For example: "Oh yes, I've worked with a variety of software like that; let's see: I've worked with *x, y, z,* and *a* software." Although lists can be effective, it always has greater impact to follow up such a list with a specific example that shows the skills or qualities you've just listed in action. Something like "Oh yes, I've worked with a variety of software like that, such as *x, y, z,* and *a*. In fact, for the last project I worked on, I had to quickly learn the newest *b* software and was able to do it in record time while producing the finished product ahead of schedule. The client was very pleased."

You should use your natural tendency to answer with a list of items as an opportunity to mentally process and choose a success story to tack onto the end of that list.

I recommend that savvy job seekers practice answering key questions with this powerful formula: a sweeping positive statement (setting the right tone while buying you time as you think about what you will say next), followed by a short list, and ending with one of your success stories.

This formula is highly effective and makes you sound like the ideal, positive candidate. It also gives interviewers exactly what they're looking for: a glimpse into what kind of behavior you exhibit on the job. Behavioral interview questions are usually designed to get you to tell a story. But because most people don't have their best stories prepared and ready to share, this can all too often turn into a trap that will cause you to say things you shouldn't. But if you have your stories ready to go, you give interviewers exactly what they're looking for, while putting yourself in the best light possible.

If you are in doubt over a particular question or feel trapped in a particularly difficult interview style, you can always tell one of your prepared success stories and know that you're on the right track. Even if it doesn't come close to answering the question, it's always better to launch a success story than to allow yourself to get trapped by a trick question.

Another effective preparation tactic is to write down your top ten best qualities as an employee, i.e.: organized, energetic, detail oriented, hardworking, team player, quick learner. What do you bring to the table no one else has? What makes you the stellar choice as a candidate? Writing these down can help you remember illustrative success stories and can also serve another purpose. Reading your list of best qualities and reminding yourself of your success stories before each interview will help shift your mind-set from that of a job seeker to that of a great employee any company would be lucky to have.

This strategic review of all your best qualities will bolster your confidence, remind you of what a great catch you are, and keep these qualities top-of-mind so you can easily sprinkle them throughout your interview. You'll know exactly what you're going to say no matter what interview tactics and questions are thrown at you, so you always look like the winner.

INSIDER SECRET 18
There's one "type" that always gets the offer.

THERE IS A POWERFUL SECRET ABOUT THE HIRING PROCESS that interviewers hope candidates never find out: Many hiring managers are taught to watch out for the "halo effect." It causes hiring managers to hire one type of candidate more than any other. What is that type? The candidate who seems most like themselves.

When hiring managers find a candidate they like personally, whom they feel a connection with, suddenly that candidate can do no wrong. It's like a switch goes on in the interviewer's brain that says, *This is it.*

This feeling can override concerns about skills, talent, all sorts of things you'd think would be much more important during an interview process. This "halo effect" phenomenon can be so strong that even though many hiring managers are specifically taught to look out for it, they still most often hire the person they've experienced some sort of personal connection with. Unfortunately, most candidates don't know this phenomenon exists, let alone how to invoke it.

This connection can be created as easily as smiling at the interviewer, making eye contact, seeming at ease, asking him questions about pictures on his desk, or paying him a heartfelt compliment. It can also be done by mirroring, which will create the sensation that you two are somehow very much alike and in sync. Mirroring can be accomplished by keeping pace with the interviewer's tone and style. If you have a very mellow interviewer, switch gears to your mellow side. And if you have someone really quick, firing questions, moving a million miles a minute, you may want to ramp things up to match his or her pace.

Mirroring is something we all do naturally and subconsciously when we're speaking to someone we feel comfortable with. You may notice that when you cross your legs the person you're speaking to suddenly does the same, or that when you make an arm movement the other person follows without realizing it. It's an unconscious response created by a feeling of unity.

This can work both ways, meaning you can use it to create a sense of instant connection and rapport. The interviewer you are mirroring will suddenly begin to feel that you are just like him. He will feel more comfortable and will begin to feel connected.

One of an interviewer's biggest fears is whether or not he or she can trust what you're saying. We all tend to trust those who seem most like us. If you match the interviewer's tone, pace, breathing, and even posturing, the interviewer will tend to feel in sync with you.

Mirroring is something that must be done subtly to be effective, especially when you are attempting to match something as obvious as body postures and mannerisms. You don't have to match everything to be effective; just one or two subtle mirroring movements during the interview can create the desired effect.

You can try practicing this technique with family members or friends. Try matching their breathing pace, tone of voice, and body movements without being obvious. Then, after a while, try switching one of your movements or your pace and see if they follow. If you've done it correctly by creating a subtle and unconscious rapport, they will follow you. If they don't follow, go back to mirroring them and try again. The ability to create this kind of rapport with a stranger during an interview is a powerful skill that can make you seem like the only candidate the hiring manager felt a connection with.

Another insider trick for creating this magical halo effect is to treat the interviewer like a good friend. Mentally imagine that you've known this person for years and he or she is someone you're very fond of. Now, don't get confused here. This person is not to be treated like an actual friend, so there should be no sharing of personal information, no personal boundaries should be invaded, and you should not be letting your guard down. It's just in your imagination. Pretend you're having this interview with a really good friend and this "interview" is just a formality. If you can make that mental shift into the place you normally reserve for close friends and other people you feel comfortable with, you will seem more confident, personable, comfortable, and friendly. It will help you relax and you will naturally seem less stiff and more likable. If you've done this correctly, the interviewer will feel the imagined connection you've created and may even reciprocate in feeling and tone.

Even though you don't want to share any personal or negative information with this individual, you do want him to like you. The more an interviewer personally likes you and the more he believes you are just like him, the more likely you will create that halo effect.

Being prepared with your success stories and positive message so you can steer away from focusing so intently on yourself and focus on the interviewer instead will help you create that all-important connection. You'll be able to easily see opportunities to create and reinforce connections. Even simple phrases like "I know exactly what you mean" can make an interviewer feel connected to you.

The biggest mistake most candidates make in terms of connecting is concentrating solely on themselves in the interview. They end up walking into interviews in their own personal bubble and miss all the cues and opportunities for connection. The interviewer is left feeling like he wasn't even in the room, that some stranger came in and barked information at him with nervous gestures, trying to sell themselves as a candidate as hard as possible. This kind of experience is what most interviewers encounter 90 percent of the time, so even if you are able to escape your nervousness and focus on connecting with the interviewer for a just few minutes, that may be all you need to make an impression. Being able to focus on the interviewer and create that connection is so rare that the one person who can successfully accomplish it, even for a moment, is usually the one who gets hired.

Rather than concentrating on presenting all your information and going for the hard sell during the interview, try practicing your stories ahead of time until you feel comfortable with what you're planning to say. You can then concentrate your primary energies on making a connection with whoever turns out to be your interviewer. If you stay in your own head, concentrating on yourself and your answers, you'll never make that connection and you will have lost the halo.

The truth is: An interviewer is ten times more likely to recommend someone for hire who seems similar to him- or herself, who he or she likes and feels comfortable with. If you become that person, you're in.

INSIDER SECRET 19

Your interview may not be real.

NO ONE TALKS ABOUT TRICK INTERVIEWS, AND NO ONE wants to admit their company uses them. But they are common, and they can spell disaster for an unsuspecting candidate.

I'm going to share six of the most common trick interview tactics and how to combat them. These are the ones you will encounter most, but there are many variations. Trick interviews are in heavy use across all workplace structures, from large corporations to small start-ups. They can shake your confidence to the core, and they are highly effective for an interviewer. They provide a window into a candidate's true nature more quickly than anything else.

These tactics are crafted to purposefully fluster, frustrate, and generally stress you out to see how you respond under pressure.

These actually aren't interviews at all. They aren't designed to get to know you, find out about your skills, or have a pleasant meeting. They are carefully orchestrated to see how you'll behave in a difficult or stressful circumstance. Companies believe this is much more effective than the standard interview and will tell them what they need to know about your true character.

Rather than reacting to the emotional stimuli, you need to know what to look out for and how to respond to each scenario to get to the next level. These tactics can also tell you a great deal about the type of company you would be working for should you choose to accept a position with them.

Trick Interview Tactic 1: The Abrupt End

THIS TACTIC IS ONE OF THE MOST WIDELY USED TRICKS. IT'S the classic abrupt ending to an interview, making you feel like you must have done or said something wrong that caused it. It will be almost impossible to tell whether you have actually offended the person, said something wrong, or are in the midst of a planned tactic. Luckily, the save is the same no matter what's truly going on behind the scenes.

It goes something like this: You feel the interview is going well, even though your interviewer seems a bit stern, with no visible sense of humor. She sits stiffly in her chair, glancing at you in a judgmental fashion over her designer glasses, and only says "hmmm" after each of your perfectly crafted answers. After twenty minutes, when you have just masterfully answered the interviewer's latest question, she suddenly closes her binder, makes a face, folds her arms, and says with a big sigh, "Well, thank you so much for coming in; that will be all. This interview is over."

You nervously jump up from your chair with insecurities racing through your mind. Did you say something wrong? Did you offend her in some way? Should you apologize? Without another word, she sternly shows you to the door.

This tactic can make even the most seasoned professional go back to the car and burst into tears. But it is actually designed to see if you'll crack.

If you find yourself in this situation, review your answers and overall conduct. If anything seems fishy, remove it from any future interviews. If you think back and honestly can't identify anything that might have ended the interview, you are probably a victim of this rather nasty tactic. Even if you find you may have said something wrong, there is only one way to deal with it while preserving your chances to move forward, and that is to pretend nothing happened. Leave the interview with poise and confidence intact, smile, thank her for the interview, ask for her card, and walk out like you're on top of the world. Do not let her see that you are flustered in any way. This is key, because if it was a trick, you've just passed the test with flying colors.

Whatever happens, make sure you go ahead and send a warm thank-you note without mentioning what occurred. Many people make the mistake of thinking they've blown it, so they neglect to send the note, which is a big mistake.

This tactic says a number of things about the company that employs it. It could signify that this company has particularly demanding clients who provide an inordinate amount of stress. Or it can signify that the company has a demanding set of managers who don't easily hand out the kudos or support one would normally expect. This company is looking for people who can support themselves and maintain their confidence in the midst of an unsupportive and stressful environment. You may want to think carefully about working for a company like this if you are someone who likes development, friendly chitchat, support, or even open rewards in your work environment.

Trick Interview Tactic 2: The Constant Interruption

YOU SIT DOWN IN THE OFFICE OF A HIRING MANAGER, ALL ready for your big interview, but as you start to answer questions, you suddenly become aware that something's not quite right. He's clearly too busy for this interview. Maybe he doesn't even care about this interview at all! The phone is ringing, he's taking messages, writing things down, sending e-mails, and typing on his BlackBerry, and to make matters worse, people keep coming in and out asking questions and disrupting the flow.

It's impossible to keep your train of thought and provide the answers you were hoping to wow him with, let alone have him actually hear what you're saying. But every time you pause, he motions for you to continue, even though it's clear he hasn't heard a thing.

You are in the "cruncher." This tactic is designed to see firsthand how a candidate deals with stress and multitasking. This is a company that moves very fast, with lots of different things going on at once, and the best way to tell if you can handle their pace is to put you squarely in the middle of it. So here you are, trying to give a good interview in the midst of total chaos. Here's the formula for making it through:

Concentrate on the questions and give your best answers as though nothing is going on. Don't be fazed by the interruptions or the fact that he's not paying any attention to you whatsoever. Stay on target, stay positive, stay on message, and try to make a connection. Even saying something like "Hey, I have that same BlackBerry; don't you just love it?" will help you make some sort of connection in this chaotic environment.

The object of this game is to make it through with a smile on your face as though nothing strange is happening, like this kind of chaos is your most favorable work environment. Knowing that how you handle chaos and stress is the point of this trick interview tactic, you can even get right to the heart of the matter by saying something like "This company sure has a fast pace; I love that."

Don't worry about how a constant-interruption interview actually went. These tactics are usually the first trial, followed by a real interview if you pass the test. In a true interview, your interviewer will certainly focus on your answers and do a proper screening. You'll know you've passed this test if you get a call for another round of interviews.

There are scenarios where you will encounter a combination of the standard "real" interview with an interruption or two thrown in to see how you handle it. If the interviewer only takes one call during the interview, this may also be a test. In this instance, the secret is to look away and shuffle through your paperwork or jot down a few notes for yourself to provide a sense of privacy. You may even want to gesture to him to see if he'd like you to leave the room while he takes the call. These responses will make you seem both conscientious and in tune with the interviewer's needs.

Once the phone call or interruption has ended, you can help get things back on track by saying something like "In response to your question about customer service . . ." But whatever you do, don't show any anger or resentment if the interruption goes longer than what you feel is courteous. Remember, you are in a behavioral test.

Trick Interview Tactic 3: The On-the-Spot Question

THIS TACTIC FORCES YOU TO ANSWER HIGH-PRESSURE QUESTIONS on the spot as though you've prepared for weeks. For example: Right when you're feeling comfortable that this is just a traditional interview setting with standard questions, the interviewer suddenly thrusts a generic yellow pencil toward you and says, "Sell it to me, right here, right now!" Or you find yourself suddenly faced with the calculation of how many balloons it takes to lift a grown man off the ground.

If you suspect you may be interviewing with one of these companies, it can be extremely helpful to speak to someone on the inside who's been through it. But there's really no set way to prepare for these. The best course of action is to prepare for the unexpected based on your area of expertise. If you are in marketing, advertising, or sales, it might be good to have a prerehearsed sales pitch you could launch at a moment's notice. If you're a computer programmer, engineer, or mathematician, it may be prudent to practice some off-the-wall technical scenarios to keep yourself in practice just in case.

When you are feeling stuck, faced with a daunting scenario to role-play or an impossible question, it's always best to go with what first comes to mind. Don't try to give interviewers what you think they want to hear, because it's not that kind of question. Keep your cool, take the time to think before answering, take a deep breath, and give it your best shot.

In many cases, the on-the-spot tactics are designed to make you sweat and see how you can handle the pressure. Sometimes the correct answer will give you additional points, but often these questions are designed to see if you can get through the pressure with your poise intact. So don't worry as much about the correct answer. Concentrate on handling and answering the question as professionally as possible.

This kind of tactic is yet another reason to get as much interview practice as possible, even if it means going on interviews for jobs you aren't sure you want. There tend to be similarities in tactics and questions within industries. So if you get surprised by one of these stressful on-the-spot scenarios and don't answer correctly, you can recalibrate and practice for your next opportunity. Then, when you get the interview for your dream job, that on-the-spot question won't throw you quite so hard.

Trick Interview Tactic 4: The Food Interview

THIS INTERVIEWER WANTS TO TAKE YOU OUT TO LUNCH OR dinner. That must certainly be a good sign, right? Not so fast; the trick here is that when you're out dining you tend to let your guard down and behave more casually. This is exactly what the interviewer is hoping for. He has put you in a scenario you usually find yourself in with family and friends, so the tendency will be to relax and fall into those familiar patterns. Don't. The interviewer may act casual and friendly to help facilitate this shift and you can certainly be friendly in return, but you need to remember that you are still in a formal interview.

Then there's the ordering. It goes without saying that you can't order what you normally would if you were out with friends. Nothing messy. No BBQ ribs or big salads with ranch dressing. You are not only in an interview; you are in the food interview, which means that on top of having to answer the interview questions, you will need to eat like you're having tea with the queen.

Not only is the food interview designed to get candidates to loosen up and share things that wouldn't normally be shared in a formal office-interview setting; it is also designed to get a good look at your table manners and social graces. Companies look at these things when they know you'll be taking clients to lunch or having to represent the company in a variety of social situations. So if you're used to eating with your elbows on the table, talking with your mouth full, or belching to signify satisfaction at the end of a good meal, you may want to brush up on your dining etiquette.

One of the biggest mistakes candidates can make is to take their cues on how to act from the behavior of the interviewers. This is what they may be counting on. Don't do it.

And what do you do when the interviewer orders alcohol? Many believe if the interviewer orders a drink that means you can, too, and in a stressful interview it can seem like a good idea to relax a little with a drink. It's not. You need to be on your guard. You are still in an interview.

Many times an interviewer will order alcohol to see if you will do the same, to see if you'll relax and let your guard down. It is completely inappropriate to drink during an interview, even if everyone else at the table has ordered something and is encouraging you to do so. If you feel you must order something to fit in with the group, sip it slowly, if at all, and leave at least half still in the glass. Treat it like the test it is.

Another reason to refrain from drinking is that the interviewer is most likely hoping you will loosen up with a drink or two, to see what information you may volunteer. You can drink with the gang and relax with them after hours once you've been hired. Until then you are a candidate under extreme scrutiny, and you have to remember that, even when you are outside of a traditional business setting.

Trick Interview Tactic 5: The Nontraditional Meeting Place

YOU GOT THE CALL YOU'D BEEN WAITING FOR, BUT IT DIDN'T quite progress the way you'd hoped. The person who wants to interview you for that new job is only in town for an hour while she waits for her next flight and wants you to meet her at the airport for "a quick face-to-face."

There are lots of variations on this one: "Meet me in a company lobby in between client meetings," "Come to my kid's Little League game and we can talk on the sidelines." I've even heard "Come ride with me in a cab on my way to a client meeting."

This is either the move of a very busy person who genuinely wants to meet you so she'll do anything to fit you into her schedule, or it's a trick. You'll never know for sure, so the safest bet is to treat it like a trick interview. This one is all about elemental stress to see how you handle yourself: "Let's put this person in a strange setting for an interview with tons of distractions and see if he can stay focused." "Let's see if he can handle a casual interview at a kid's softball game." "Let's see if he can answer questions in a fast-moving cab as I check to make sure I have everything I need to get on the plane."

These interviews aren't much fun, but you should always say yes to them anyway. Unless of course the request is so bizarre that you are worried for your safety, i.e., "Meet me in my hotel room." Those should certainly be rescheduled for another time and a public place. Otherwise, it's important to show that you're up for anything and can give a good interview no matter the setting. The trick is the same every time, and they're all looking for the same thing: Can the candidate handle this situation with poise?

Trick Interview Tactic 6: The Good Interviewer/Bad Interviewer

THIS IS AN EFFECTIVE VARIATION ON THE "GOOD COP, BAD cop." In this interview, done as a team, one takes the role of the good and kind interviewer, while the other takes the role of the aggressive or mean interviewer.

For example: One interviewer abruptly puts you on the spot or asks inappropriate questions, and the "good" interviewer steps in and says something like "Oh, you can't ask that. I'm so sorry; you don't have to answer that if you don't want to," leaving it open for you to be the nice guy and say, "Don't worry about it; I'm okay to answer that for you."

The good interviewer/bad interviewer is designed to make you feel comfortable, as if you have someone looking out for you, so you can let your guard down. These interviewers are secretly hoping you'll let your guard down enough to share things with the "good" interviewer that you wouldn't normally share.

The main idea when facing all these tactics is to keep your cool no matter what you encounter during the interview process. If it's a trick, keeping a cool head will help you move to the next level. Even if it's not a trick, your ability to handle this type of environment effectively will help you go far in the interviewer's estimation of you as a candidate and will give you a glimpse into what it will be like to work for that company.

INSIDER SECRET 20
One size does not fit all.

DID YOU KNOW THERE ARE EIGHT DIFFERENT INTERVIEW styles? Did you know that each one can tell you where you stand in the process and even what kind of company you're interviewing with? Many candidates mistakenly believe that the various interview styles a company uses are just a matter of personal preference, but that is not the case. The interview style a company chooses is a carefully crafted decision based on the organization's hiring philosophy and secret criteria.

Failure to recognize and adapt to each interview style will cause you to appear out of sync with what the company's looking for. And it will cause you to miss prime opportunities to make connections with the interviewer who has chosen this particular style.

Understanding these variations will help you make the most of each opportunity without getting flustered.

Interview Style 1: The Unskilled Interviewer

BELIEVE IT OR NOT, THIS IS A STYLE. ALTHOUGH AN UNINtended one, the absence of a chosen style and the absence of skill as an interviewer is a style in itself. A company that hasn't bothered to train its managers or human-resources representatives on how to conduct a proper interview can tell you a great deal about the company. A company that doesn't know how to hire the best people or craft a powerful team may prove quite frustrating to work for. Aside from that, meeting with an unskilled interviewer can spell disaster for a candidate if he or she doesn't know exactly what to do in this situation.

How do you know if you are faced with an unskilled interviewer? It looks like this: The interviewer stares at your résumé as long periods of silence go by; then he looks up at you and says something generic like "Why don't you tell me a little bit about yourself." These interviews usually don't have any direction or set format. The interviewer doesn't seem to know what to ask or what to say. In many cases, he may do all the talking, instead of asking the questions he should.

It is critical that you learn how to take charge of the unskilled interview and stick to your message to get your success stories and qualifications across. This is still your opportunity to sell yourself and land the job, but you won't be getting any help from the interviewer.

Untrained interviewers rarely know what they're supposed to be looking for, don't know how to screen, and don't know how to ask questions to get the process moving. But they do tend to hire candidates they personally connect with more than any other type of interviewer. So this is an excellent opportunity to build rapport, create a connection, and get this person to like you. You will have a better chance of activating "the halo effect" with this interviewer than with any other type.

In addition to creating a connection with this individual, you may also have to take charge of the interview. You may need to get things going by asking a question that will allow the interviewer to begin but then allow you to take it the rest of the way. This will allow you to lead the interview so that you can actively target all the points the interviewer needs to hear to recommend you.

"I'd love to know a little more about what the position entails" is a good way to start. It gets the unprepared interviewer off the hook by giving him something to say, and while he is talking, you can take notes and gather your key points for response. By the time he's finished telling you all about the position, you should have three key things the interviewer shared that you can capitalize on. This will tell you exactly what to emphasize about your experience and work history that will make you look like the perfect candidate.

In this disorganized scenario, it is critical to stick to your message. An untrained interviewer won't give you many obvious opportunities to share your success stories and best qualities, so work them in wherever you can. Don't worry about awkward segues in the conversation; getting your message across is much more important.

The biggest mistake candidates make in this situation is to let the interviewer lead. The interview will lead to disaster if all you end up doing is chatting about inconsequential matters in between awkward silences. You may not feel completely comfortable taking charge of an interview, leading it in a favorable direction for yourself, but you will have to. Believe me, the untrained interviewer will be eternally grateful and you will make a positive, lasting impression.

Interview Style 2: The Interrogation

NOT ONLY IS THIS INTERVIEW STYLE HEAVILY STRUCTURED, but most candidates feel it to be the most stressful and intimidating of all styles. It goes a little like this:

"Hi, I'm here for a two o'clock meeting with the head of human resources for your open position."

"Of course," the receptionist says. "You will be having that meeting in the conference room." He leads you down the hall to an open door, and in you go, only to be faced with four men and two women at the end of a long conference table, all staring at you. Believe it or not, this is your interview.

The best way to get through the interrogation interview is to understand that this group is looking for two things: how you handle stress and how you conduct yourself in a client meeting or presentation. So treat it like a professional presentation to clients. (If you're a recent graduate with no client presentation experience, think about a large presentation you've done for a school project or how you might present an important issue to the school board for formal consideration.)

Put on your most charming smile, bridge the Grand Canyon gap between you and the group of interrogators, and go shake every hand like you would in a client meeting. Put on your game face and jump on in. There is little chance you will know about this style of interview before it happens, so how you deal with the initial shock of the format will be critically important. The rest can be accomplished by treating it as the formal client presentation it truly is.

There will be only one problem: It will be difficult to create a personal halo effect connection with any of your individual interviewers, so don't even try. Direct eye contact is always a good idea, but trying to create personal connections in your comments or with mirroring will not come across well to a group. It will be much easier in this scenario to create a connection with the company itself and the group as a whole. You can do this by saying things like "This company has such a great reputation; I'd love to be a part of a company that's known for putting quality first."

Depending on how comfortable you are addressing a surprise board-of-directors meeting, this may not be the best interview you've ever had. However, if you can get through it with a smile on your face and not too much sweat, you've done well. This is one of the most difficult interview styles that exists, and you need to give yourself credit for surviving!

However, an interrogation interview does say something about how the company views you as a candidate that should make you feel better about the experience. It says that all these important people think you might be "the one." These people don't just waste their time gathering together for an interrogation all at the same time. Having them all take time out away from their work says something important. The interrogation is typically reserved for positions that deal with clients, broker important deals, and represent the company in high-level meetings. Even if the position you're applying for does not have those things listed as current responsibilities, it will most likely lead in that direction down the road, or the company wouldn't bother with such an extreme format.

Interview Style 3: The Tag Team

THIS INTERVIEW STYLE IS ONE OF THE MOST POPULAR TODAY. In a tag team, there's a preliminary interview, followed by a series of interviews with a variety of people, lasting most, if not all, of the day. Some even go on for multiple days at a time. The tag team interview style is most convenient for the key decision makers at the company but is completely exhausting for the candidate. So make sure you are fully caffeinated and have a snack in your pocket, because these don't always include lunch.

The tag team interview can prove quite stressful, but it's important to realize that the tag team style says much the same thing as the interrogation. It says that you are a key candidate. All these people don't set aside time to talk to you unless you are one of the top two or three candidates. In fact, the tag team interview is often only reserved for the one primary candidate who's been recommended by the hiring manager or human resources.

This is a good thing to know, because it means you can relax a little. That doesn't mean you should let your guard down or start talking about your personal life, but it does mean that you don't have to sit in each interview nervously worrying about every question. You wouldn't be in this tag team interview if the group wasn't already sold on your qualifications and experience. What they're looking for is something else. They're each looking to see if your talents and work approach will fit into their particular areas of concern.

Will you be a good support to the accounting department? Will you be nice or fun to work with? Will you be a threat to my position or be an ally? Will you have better technical skills than the last one? Each person you interview with will have his or her own agenda, and it's your job to find out what that is. Even though it's best to let each interviewer lead in this tag team format, it can be helpful to ask questions like "How do you see this position supporting your agendas and goals?" or "What would you consider to be high success for this position as it relates to your department?" You are trying to find out why this particular individual has asked to be part of the interview process and why this position is important to him or her. If you can figure that out and then *be* his or her answer to it, you're in.

Be prepared for each individual interviewer to have his or her own unique style (which could include any of the tricks or tactics listed in this chapter). Listen for any fears or issues the interviewer is screening for and try to neutralize them in your answers. The interviewers you will meet in a tag team will be most concerned about company fit, so this is a good time to make that halo connection with each person you interview with. If enough of them like you and feel you'd be nice to work with, you have a good chance of being hired.

Your biggest challenge in the tag team interview will be to stay fresh and sharp for each person as you're handed off from one to the next. You may feel like you have nothing left when you get to the last person's office, but you'll have to rally. It's important that this last interview feel as fresh and energetic as your first one. Remember, it's all part of the test.

It's also important as you meet with each person that you treat him or her like the only person you're interviewing with and as though he or she is the most important person on the list. Most people have a tendency to save their energy for the vice president meeting and then not worry so much about the human-resources assistant. You can't. You never know who really has the last word in this hiring decision, and many times it's not who you think.

In the interest of treating everyone like they're the most important person you're meeting with that day, you'll want to completely focus in on what he or she is saying and what that person's unique agenda is. Don't worry if your time with one person is going too long. Don't look at your watch and say, "You know, I'd love to keep talking with you, but I was supposed to meet with the vice president twenty minutes ago." This could be dangerous and could ruffle some feathers. Besides, going overtime can be a good thing. It means this person is really engaged and is enjoying the discussion. Let someone else come in and move you along if the schedule is really that tight. You can always come back, and even if you don't, the company will go on the opinions of those you did have time to meet with. And I guarantee, if you've gone overtime, you're doing well.

In fact, progressing through the levels of a tag team interview usually means you're doing a great job. If you weren't, the word would have been sent out and the people at the end of the line would suddenly become too busy to meet you.

Interview Style 4: The HR Interview

AN INTERVIEW WITH HUMAN RESOURCES (PERSONNEL, TALent department, etc.) typically takes place during the initial screening before you're interviewed by the person who would be your direct boss or manager, but not always. Some companies like to mix it up.

It's important to understand that no matter when in the process HR steps in, an interview with anyone from human resources holds a unique agenda separate from any other interview. The secret edict of a human-resources representative in hiring is to keep out any potential inconveniences, litigiousness, or problems. Secondarily, the HR interview is screening for good company fit along with their secret list of criteria and qualities that the top candidate must meet.

Human-resources people will usually be the most highly trained interviewers, with all the best tactics and trick questions. That means you should be most on-guard when meeting these people and be aware that anything you choose to say will become part of the decision-making process. It's also important that the people in human resources personally like you, because they will have the final say in whether or not you get hired. It's an interesting balancing act.

Once you've moved through the second level of interviews, you will find that you often meet with someone from human resources again, usually toward the end of the process. But this HR interview is very different from the previous one. In this interview, the human-resources person seems more relaxed, gives you details about the company benefits, perks, sick time, vacation time, company parties, shows you around the office, and talks openly about compensation. Many candidates mistakenly believe this means they've got the job. Although it can be a good sign, it is usually designed to open discussions regarding salary and benefits before an offer is presented, thus lessening your ability to negotiate effectively at the appropriate time. This is a good time to take notes, but don't let this interview style trick you into thinking you are negotiating an offer or actually beginning salary or benefit negotiations. You're not. Negotiations should always be held until you have the formal offer letter in hand. (More about the secrets to negotiating for top dollar in the next chapter.)

Even though you can learn a lot from this kind of "interview," while secretly gathering the information given to determine whether or not this would be a good fit, you must refrain from opening negotiations too soon. All you should say in response to this type of interview is "Everything looks fine" and "I'm happy to entertain any offer."

The human-resources person may even ask you point-blank questions like "Do you think you'd be happy with these benefits, these work hours, this much travel, or this level of compensation?" The answer is always "I'm excited by this opportunity, and that [salary, benefits, travel schedule] definitely sounds like something I'd consider." Don't be fooled by the grand tour and "This is where you'll sit, and these are the people you'll be working with." This interview is *not* an offer.

Interview Style 5: The Boss

IN SOME CASES, THE PERSON WHO WOULD BE YOUR BOSS will be the one and only hiring manager for the position. So you need to be aware that he or she may not have received any formal training on how to do an interview. You may be walking into a highly trained trick-question or trick-interview, or an untrained-interviewer scenario. But no matter what style you walk into, be aware that a boss who has to do all his or her own hiring is probably stressed out and overworked. Most bosses don't have time to do the work they have, let alone play hiring manager for every open position. So the more helpful and understanding you can be, the better.

The key to a boss interview versus interviews with human resources or others at the company is finding out what's most important to this individual. You can bet it's entirely different from what's most important to human resources. Human resources conducts the prevention and protection screening. The boss will be looking for something else entirely. He or she is looking for a good fit on the team and a qualified candidate, but there's something else. The powerful and secret boss desire is: *Will this person make me look good, support me, and remain loyal?*

A boss is looking for a true supporter, a foundational partner. Someone he or she can count on. Bosses live their lives squeezed from all sides, dealing with unruly and resentful employees, the competition of other managers, and demanding executives constantly wanting the impossible.

If you want to go straight to the top of this boss's list, ask a question like "What would be your ideal for this position?" or "How do you see this position supporting you and your goals?" Be sure to take notes, because once you've been hired, this is the information you'll need to look like a star. Feel free to butter up with statements like "I'd love to work with you" or "I think I could learn a lot from someone like you." Bosses don't get too much of this in the day-to-day. There's usually a lot more eye rolling behind their back and irreverent e-mail exchanges complaining about something they did at the last meeting. Paying compliments in a boss interview can go a long way, but only if they are sincere. A boss can smell a canned suck-up from a mile away. So whatever you say, make sure it's genuine. If you really think you'd enjoy working with this person, make sure you say so!

The key to a boss interview is support and loyalty. This should be the focus of your answers and the stories you choose to tell. Share stories of how you supported your previous boss on a project, how you took on tasks you knew your boss dreaded doing, or how you worked all night on the presentation that helped your boss win the clients he'd been after for over a year. These are the kinds of stories that will make a boss interviewer absolutely drool over the idea of having you on his or her team.

Interview Style 6: The Higher-Up

OCCASIONALLY YOU WILL FIND YOURSELF LED IN TO MEET with a very high-level person at the company, and you find yourself thinking, *Why am I meeting with the CEO for this position?*

The position may not seem to warrant this kind of high-level attention, but rest assured there is always a reason. In smaller companies higher-ups sometimes like to do a meet-and-greet with every single hire. Sometimes there's been talk of a candidate with great potential for bigger and better things down the road and the big bosses are curious. Other times the higher-up interview is based on a concern over a particular hire for a critical position. Whatever the reason, these meetings are all intended to put this higher-up's concerns to rest.

Be respectful and let this higher-up lead the interview in any direction she likes; say something nice about the company and how much you'd like to work there; and be professional. This is not the time to be overly friendly or buddy-buddy. This is the time to present your most professional ideal image of a company representative, because at the end of the day that's what this head honcho is looking for.

It goes without saying that higher-ups do not have a lot of time, so the fact that she would put you on her calendar at all is a big deal. Don't expect a standard twenty- or thirty-minute interview. You may only get two to five minutes, standing. But in the world of a higher-up, that's a lot of time to devote to one person. So don't be offended if she doesn't ask you to sit down or if the interview ends abruptly. That's the way these things go. Be sure to send a follow-up thank-you note even if it was just a brief two-minute meeting.

Interview Style 7: The Technical Screen

TODAY YOU ARE LIKELY TO BE FACED WITH A TECHNICAL screening before the rest of the interview or hiring process even begins. Companies are doing this more and more because they don't want to waste their time interviewing candidates who don't have the skills required for the position. There are two types of technical screenings you need to be prepared for: One is an established format with basic skill requirement questions designed to confirm that you have the skills and experience you say you have. These are so prevalent today that if you choose to put something on your résumé you haven't actually done, chances are you will find yourself embarrassingly cornered. There's nothing more mortifying than sitting through a technical screening with questions you can't answer because you misrepresented your background. However, if you have the skills and technical abilities you say you do, this one should be no problem.

The other type of technical interview is the one you'll need to watch out for: the runaway technical screener. Companies tend to ask their smartest, most knowledgeable people to do these interviews, with little or no training. So it is entirely possible that you will run up against someone on an ego trip who is more interested in showcasing his or her smarts than in crafting answerable questions. With a runaway technical interviewer, the screenings tend to be at an extremely high level, filled with questions only the interviewer knows and only the interviewer can answer. Your only chance to shift this interview to a more reasonable level is to openly compliment the interviewer on his or her knowledge of the subject matter. Try paying a genuine compliment that shows you realize how intelligent this individual is and how knowledgeable he or she obviously is in this field. It's usually good to follow up a compliment like that with "my familiarity is really with *x*."

This can appease the ego of a runaway technical screener and allow him or her to take it down a few notches. The follow-up comment also gives this technical screener somewhere to go next in the questioning. If you've given a sincere compliment, he or she may decide to cut you a break and focus on your area of familiarity.

If that doesn't work, I'm afraid you're on your own. Your only chance is to smile through it and do the best you can. Asking clarifying questions in this situation can show the screener you are interested in learning, and that can certainly help.

Your best bet is to hope that the company soon realizes that no one can pass this particular brand of technical interview and that there need to be adjustments made. Whatever you do, don't complain about the screening or comment on how impossible it was. You never know, it could actually just be a test to see if you get frustrated. The company may have done this to you on purpose to see what reaction you'd have. So no matter how defeating and unfair the experience, it's best to say something generically positive like "I love to learn new things and I'm looking forward to taking my knowledge to the next level."

Interview Style 8: The Weather Channel

NOTHING IS MORE FRUSTRATING TO AN UNSUSPECTING CANDIDATE than going into an important interview with a key player only to talk about the weather, a sports team, or his last vacation, instead of your qualifications and why you are the best person for this job. But this can actually be a good thing. Unless you clearly have an untrained interviewer on your hands, this may mean you're close to an offer. So go ahead and discuss the weather with a big smile on your face.

When you're passed to someone in the final interview stages

who only wants to chitchat, it usually means this interviewer is already sold on your skills and qualifications. He believes you to be the right person for the job. What this weather-channel interviewer is looking for goes beyond skills and experience. This person is screening for personality, congeniality, partnership. He is looking to see if working with you every day for the next few years will be enjoyable.

He chooses to talk about the weather, a favorite sports team, or his vacation to get to know you and find out if you're likable. Go along with it. As long as you remember you are still in an interview and steer clear of personal information, this should be an easy conversation. This is your chance to be friendly and likable and to make a personal connection. This is your chance to go right for the halo.

If this usually easy interview turns into one where you feel cornered into sharing personal information that may be inappropriate, just remember to turn the conversation back on the interviewer by asking questions about what he has already chosen to disclose: "Oh, your son plays softball; what a great game. How old is he?" "Oh, you've got tennis elbow; I'm so sorry to hear that. Do you play any other sports that you could switch to for a while?"

It's okay for you to share personal anecdotes that put you in a positive light. Try talking about sports you play that match his interests, what school you went to, any work acquaintances you have in common, or any travel destinations you've both been to. Just censor any information that shouldn't be part of the interview process, such as when you graduated, whether you took your kids on any of those vacations, how you also hurt your back playing tennis and never fully recovered—things like that.

The key to this interview is that the more likable you seem, the better your chances of getting through to the offer letter.

These eight interview styles are a few of the most common. There are many variations, but learning how to best approach each of these will allow you to easily adapt. You'll see many different tactics and styles as you interview more and more. Each interview style can tell you a great deal about the company and the people you'd be working closely with.

I highly recommend interviewing in as many different settings as often as possible to gain experience and build your interview skill set.

INSIDER SECRET 21
The thank-you note is too late.

YOU TOOK THIS INTERVIEW FOR THE PRACTICE. *IT'S ALWAYS good to practice,* you say to yourself. You didn't think this job was for you, but it'll help you sharpen your skills for when a key interview emerges for a job you *do* want. Lo and behold, a strange thing happens during this interview process—you discover in the course of meeting with people and hearing more details that this may just turn out to be your dream job after all!

During the process you go from being completely unsure to champing at the bit for an offer. You're surprised and excited but suddenly flash back to the interviews you went through solely for practice. Oh no, what if you didn't convey the proper enthusiasm? Maybe you should have answered some of those questions with a little more care? You decide to put your enthusiasm into your thank-you letter, letting the hiring manager know that you're truly interested in the position and are excited to work for the company. This scenario happens more often than you might imagine. And the truth is, it's already too late.

Many candidates go into an interview unsure if they want the job. They believe they will decide after the interview is over and they've learned more. Big mistake. An interviewer will sense that hesitation and take it as a sign that you aren't truly interested.

One of the things an interviewer is secretly screening for is enthusiasm for the job and a passion for the company or the work being done. In many cases this can be more important than your skill level or experience.

Why? Because companies know this kind of attitude cannot be taught, but skills can. Companies also know that genuine enthusiasm can motivate an entire team or department. It is highly prized by hiring managers. So those who go into an interview with arms crossed waiting for the company to impress them, or those who have been taught to be "professional" and not show their enthusiasm for the job, could be greatly hurting their chances for consideration.

This is usually where I get questions like "Won't you seem desperate if you show them how much you want to work there?" The answer is no. Companies and hiring managers are secretly screening for enthusiasm for both the company and the position. They want to know they are hiring someone passionate about working there. Now, I'm not talking about becoming a stalker or telling a hiring manager that you collect newspaper clippings on the CEO and have them pasted all around your living room, but a respectful and sensible level of enthusiasm will improve your chances.

"What if I show enthusiasm for something, get the offer, and don't really want the job?" That particular question means you're getting ahead of yourself. My suggestion is to go for the offer, then see if you really want to work for the company. You won't hurt your career by having multiple offers. A company that's been turned down by a passionate candidate will most likely never forget it—in a good way. In fact, it can make it easier to be hired by that same company should you choose to go back to them down the line. So why is showing passion and enthusiasm during the interview process such a powerful tool?

Imagine you're a hiring manager interviewing many people every week for a variety of positions. Everyone comes in droning on about their experience and why they're the perfect fit for the position—blah, blah. Then just imagine you get someone into your office who takes the time to make a halo connection with you while showing genuine enthusiasm for the company, the position, and the opportunity.

This is the kind of person who will stand out among the crowd. These are the candidates who are remembered and who make an interviewer genuinely feel good. You should approach each interview as though that company is your number-one choice, ensuring that your enthusiasm sets you apart from the pack. Pretend it is the job you want more than all others. The interview is the only chance you get to sell this potential employer on you. If you wait until after the interview to convey your interest in a thank-you note or follow-up phone call, it will simply be too late.

Even though you should always send a follow-up thank-you note or e-mail, it will never have the impact that an interview has. **The truth is: A hiring manager's mind is completely made up after the first twenty minutes of an interview, and very often nothing will be able to change it.** That decision tends to be final and unwavering. So showing enthusiasm after the fact will do you no good whatsoever.

Go on every single interview that you are offered. There is no way to tell what kind of opportunity lies before you until you get into the interview process. Your dream job could be lurking behind the smokescreen of a poorly worded or incorrect job advertisement. So go into every interview as though it's your top choice. That will give you the status as a top candidate and convey the proper enthusiasm should you end up genuinely wanting the job.

This is excellent practice for the interview you know for certain is for your dream job. Those are always much more stressful interviews, and people tend to sabotage their chances by getting too nervous or trying too hard. If you treat every interview like it's for your dream job, then when you get to the real thing you will be perfectly prepared to make the best impression and be the top candidate.

INSIDER SECRET 22
Calling to "follow up" will cost you the job.

ONCE THE INTERVIEW PROCESS IS OVER AND THE THANK-YOU notes have been sent, the dreaded waiting game begins, punctuated by long bouts of nerve-wracking silence.

What does that long silence really mean? Does it mean they don't want you? Does it mean they do? Is there something you should call to say that would sway things in your favor? "To call or not to call?"—that is the age-old question.

You think, *What if they lost my contact information? What if they're looking to see that I'm really interested and really want the job? What if I didn't answer that one question the best I could have? Shouldn't I call them?* No. Don't call to follow up—ever.

Any call you make after the interviews are over will make you appear needy and desperate, and you will lower your standing in the company's estimation with each follow-up call.

You need to wait for them to come to you, even though it's tough. The hard truth is that if they want you, they will call you. If they don't want you, no amount of follow-up will change their minds. The decision is made in the interview process, not afterward. You will not be able to sway things in your favor or help the process, but you will ruin your chances.

Following up after an interview can absolutely cost you the

position, even if the hiring manager had decided you were "the one" during the interview itself.

"Jonathan" had just finished interviewing candidates for a key position he'd been looking to fill for months. It was an important position for the company, and he was feeling really good about his recommendation. He had a stellar first choice and a solid second choice whom he was moving up for further consideration. He had begun working on doing background checks, Internet searching, and reference checking on both while the final considerations were made. But then something strange happened.

After the first week, Jonathan began getting calls from his primary candidate. It started with a follow-up phone call with a clarification on an answer to a question asked during the interview. It seemed very important to the candidate to convey additional information, and he appeared unhappy with his original answers. Jonathan assured him that everything was okay and his original answers had been quite satisfactory.

Two days later Jonathan got another call from this candidate asking about status. Jonathan felt it was important to tell the individual that he was in fact one of the top candidates and that things were moving forward. Jonathan didn't expect to hear from this individual again until it was time to extend the formal offer. But Jonathan was surprised to see that this candidate had called another two times. Intercepted by Jonathan's assistant, he had been calling about status, when an offer might be extended, and if references were being checked.

It became clear that this individual was not the confident candidate Jonathan had originally thought him to be. What if, once hired, he pestered others within the company like this when stressful times arose? A shift occurred in Jonathan's mind and this top candidate fell to second position, if that. Jonathan's once self-assured top candidate now seemed insecure, needy, and not a good fit for the company culture. The offer was extended to the second-choice candidate.

The primary candidate never knew what happened or why he was not the one to receive the offer. Had he not called, he would have had that job offer he seemed so desperate for.

Think this is an isolated incident? It's not. Hiring managers have seen it time and again. An interview is not a standard business meeting requiring a courtesy follow-up phone call. It is more like an audition, and those who refrain from calling will be viewed as more confident and desirable.

It's important to remember that you cannot sway things in your favor after the interview is over and that you will ruin your chances by appearing too needy or pestering an already-busy hiring manger.

You should always send some sort of thank-you note, either handwritten or e-mailed, thanking the interviewers for their time and reiterating your enthusiasm for the position. You can send one to each individual you met with. I recommend always getting a business card for this purpose from each interviewer before you leave his or her office. But that brief thank-you note is all you get to do. That's it. That note is the last time you should contact the company except in response to *their* phone calls or e-mails. From this point on, you only respond; you do not initiate. They get to follow up with you as much as they like, but you do not get the same courtesy.

Contrary to popular opinion, nothing influences the decisions of interviewers or hiring managers after the interviews are over. There is no way to change what is already in motion. It's too late for anything you wish you had said in the interview, enthusiasm you wish you'd conveyed, stories you could have told, or additional practice you should have had. Your interview will have to speak for itself and stand on its own merits. There is no way to sway things in your favor with a follow-up after the fact. Make sure you are prepared before you go in for those interviews. You will not get a second chance.

INSIDER SECRET 23
Asking questions makes you look like a risk.

"JANE" WAS TRULY EXCITED ABOUT HER INTERVIEW WITH A large competitor. This would be a big jump in pay and level. She was ready to do her due diligence to get this job. She had read several books on how to shine during the interview process, and she knew it was important to do some homework on the company so she could ask intelligent questions that showed knowledge of the company. During her research she found lots of fascinating things she thought she could use to show her smarts. She carefully crafted her questions to show how much she'd learned about the company and its unique issues.

But one of the things she discovered during her search caught her off-guard. It seemed that several former employees had been in the press saying negative things about this company. They were saying it was just a "résumé factory" and the employees weren't really happy there, not mistreated, per se, but definitely driven beyond what was reasonable for lower pay than the industry standard. Jane became concerned about this and decided to include this topic as one of her questions so she could get this concern answered and dealt with directly by the interviewer. When the interviewer asked, "Do you have any questions?" Jane knew she was ready.

In fact, the interview seemed to go so well Jane felt sure she'd be getting an offer. Her questions showed how much she knew about the company, and the interviewer had definitely seemed impressed with Jane's level of understanding. However, when Jane asked about the recent negative press and the issues these former employees had voiced, the tone of the interview changed. Jane thought she had asked an educated and valid question and still left the interview feeling confident.

When Jane got an e-mail telling her that the hiring manager had enjoyed meeting with her, but the position had gone to another candidate, she felt compelled to ask why. The hiring manager responded (quite candidly—and this is rare for a hiring manager to do) that he felt she really wasn't that interested in the company, and he pointed to the question about the negative press.

Job seekers are often told that it's important to have questions prepared and to be knowledgeable about the company they're interviewing for. But that doesn't mean you can, or should, ask about everything. You have to strategically pick your questions, and you must avoid any negativity in an interview—especially something the company doesn't want to draw attention to. All kinds of things may come up in your research, but not all of it should be brought to the table in a delicate interview situation.

Everyone seems to believe they must come prepared with questions to ask, but **the truth is: An interview is not an appropriate forum to get your questions answered.**

Asking questions at this time can throw you right out of the running if you aren't careful. It's just too easy to ask questions that inadvertently make you look like a risk or that make you seem like you don't understand the company well enough. In fact, I recommend candidates hold all questions until a formal offer is made. That is the only time you can ask questions without risking your chances as a candidate or inadvertently putting yourself in a negative light. Once you've got a formal offer, you've passed the initial company screening and standard sales pitch. You now have the best chance of getting some real answers without having your questions factor into the company's fears during the initial screening process.

If you must ask questions during an interview, I'll tell you the four best questions to ask, which pose no risk to you and will increase your chances of being seen as a top candidate:

> **QUESTION 1: Can you tell me a little bit more about the position?** The answer to this question is a great

opener and will tell you exactly what to focus on in the interview so you can tailor your answers to highlight things you know they're looking for. It will allow you to focus on selling your attributes instead of wasting time and energy focusing on things they're not interested in.

QUESTION 2: What would be your ideal match [**or candidate**] **for this position?** The answer to this question will allow you to focus in on anything you have to offer that's tailor-made to the hiring manager's ideal for the job. This also opens a perfect avenue for you to share one of your success stories and illustrate why you're such a good fit based on their ideal criteria.

QUESTION 3: What kind of progress and success would you want to see from someone in this position within the first 3–6 months? Not only does this question give you invaluable information on what to focus on once you've been hired; it also helps the hiring manager to envision you in the position. As the hiring manager details his vision of greatest success for a person in this position, he will begin to imagine you operating in that position at that ideal level, simply because you were the one to ask the question. Then, as he's describing it, imagining you already in the position operating successfully, you can follow up with examples in your work experience and skills that mirror this kind of success. This is one of the most powerful questions you can ask during an interview.

If you know that this position involves replacing someone who has left the company or has moved on to another department, there is one other question you can ask. These can be strange shoes to fill depending on the circumstances of departure. You don't want to ask anything about the nature of the departure, but you can absolutely ask strategic questions that will differentiate you from that individual, such as:

> **QUESTION 4: What did the previous person do that you felt was especially successful? What are some things you wish he or she had approached differently?** While the interviewer is answering this question, something magical will happen. She will be mentally separating you from the previous individual. As she describes what should have been done differently, she will separate you from any previous failures the position may have experienced. And as she describes what was done well, she will imagine you in that position operating successfully. It is a great psychological trick you can use to stand out from the other candidates.
>
> All candidates are dealing with the shadow of the person they would be replacing. Once you ask this question, if you have anything in your background you can share to complement the interviewer's list of keys to success, go ahead and share them at this time to really bring your successful image into focus.
>
> A hiring manager will be afraid of hiring another person into a failed position who has the same issues or does not have an ability to be successful. By addressing this fear head-on in your question you will alleviate those qualms and put your name at the top of the list.

All other questions, no matter how pressing in your mind, should be held for a more secure time within the hiring process—like after the offer letter has been extended.

Don't try to ask questions that show how much you know about the company. Those rarely go over well. There is very little chance you can find out everything you need to know to really make a good impression. And if you ask a question that's off-base or makes you seem like some sort of risk, you will do more harm than good.

Let the interviewer tell you all about the company, the position, and the competition. Do your research and be ready to answer questions about your knowledge of the company, should these questions arise, but try not to ask your own questions until you're standing on more solid ground.

Even general questions about something as simple as benefits can get you into trouble very quickly. A benign question about work hours, compensation, health care, or time off, within the pressure cooker of an interview, will give the impression that you aren't as dedicated as you should be or that these are your biggest concerns about the job. None of those questions, even the little ones, should be attempted until a formal offer is on the table. And I don't mean a verbal over-the-phone offer; I mean an in-your-hand, sign-on-the-dotted-line kind of offer. If you're dealing with a company that says they "don't do written offers," request they at least send an e-mail outlining the points of the offer so you can review it (and so there are no misunderstandings down the line).

A formal offer will typically include all the details that will answer your questions. If you still have one or two that need to be answered, you now have a secure foundation from which to approach them. The company wants you, sees you as one of them, and will now be able to answer your questions without feeling threatened by them.

You can clarify benefits, negotiate for higher salary, and/or ask about negative press or other concerns at this time. You can also ask to speak to the person who had the position before or some of the team members you'd be working with to get a feel of what a typical day will be like. If you ask any of these questions before you get a formal offer, you will severely jeopardize your opportunity. Hiring managers don't take well to those types of questions or requests until you get all the way to the end, until you are already "one of them."

Some companies will try to get you to discuss salary, benefits, and work hours early on in the process. Salary is a notorious topic for these early discussions. Don't let a hiring manager try to trick you into talking about salary, benefits, or other negotiable issues too early in the game. They do this to try to get you to tip your hand to what's truly important to you, to find any red flags, and to lessen your ability to negotiate these issues effectively later on.

The best response to an interviewer's attempt at early discussions of these matters is to just say, "Everything sounds great and I look forward to learning more." (More about negotiating salary and benefits effectively in the next chapter.)

The best response to an interviewer's direct request for questions is to either use one of the four questions I gave you earlier (1: Can you tell me a little bit more about the position? 2: What would be your ideal match [or candidate] for this position? 3: What kind of progress and success would you want to see from someone in this position within the first 3–6 months? 4: What did the previous person do that you felt was especially successful?) or give the same statement that "Everything sounds great . . ."

Don't worry about saying "Everything sounds great" and that you don't have any questions, then having lots of them once an offer is in hand. That is expected.

INSIDER SECRET 24
Screening the company will screen you out.

HOW DO YOU KNOW IF THE COMPANY YOU'RE INTERVIEWING with is the right one for you? What should you look for? What kinds of questions should you ask?

It's completely understandable that you'd want to avoid potential problems like you've had at past jobs, but trying to find out if this is the right company for you during the screening process will end your chances on the spot.

"Carl" had a bad experience with his last company. He'd gotten into a position that had no end to the workload and little support, which resulted in his working sixteen hours a day, seven days a week. He'd been able to keep up with this work schedule for a while but eventually burned out, and what had seemed like a promising opportunity ended badly. He hadn't been able to see what he was getting into during the initial interview, and that worried him. He certainly wanted to avoid getting into that same kind of scenario with his next job, especially now that he had a new baby.

In every interview Carl decided to share his story and ask about the support network and hours for the position. It seemed like a good approach, but he was beginning to wonder if this was the best plan. He'd had several interviews that had all ended after only a few minutes (not a good sign) and had received no offers, even though he had all the necessary qualifications for the positions. What was happening?

The story about his bad experience, along with his seemingly logical questions about work hours, was being interpreted by interviewers in an unintended way. Interviewers were viewing Carl as a candidate who didn't want to put in the required normal hours and only cared about being home with his new baby. No matter how Carl worded it, his questions were raising a red flag that made him look like he wasn't a hard worker.

Now of course this wasn't the case or his intention, but it's what happens when a candidate tries to openly screen a company against his or her personal criteria or past experiences to see if it's a good fit.

No company likes to think you are screening them while they're screening you, even though everyone does it. I'll show you the foolproof way to identify your own personal style and the company culture that will make you happiest and how to secretly screen for those things during the interview process so no one knows what you're doing.

Figuring out whether you're accepting an offer with the right company is something that falls squarely on your shoulders. But any concerns and issues that you feel would keep you from accepting an offer are things that must be kept to yourself until just the right moment.

Once Carl stopped sharing his story and learned how to screen for the things that were important to him without having to verbalize his concerns, he got an offer right away for the well-supported nonburnout job he'd been looking for.

Most interviewers will tell you what kind of culture the company has if you know how to read between the lines. Careful observation will answer most of your questions.

The first thing to do is determine the company culture that will be best for you and will support your natural work style. Not all companies are created equal. They all have different styles and cultures and value different things. For example, a fast-moving entrepreneurial company will tend to value creative problem solving, quick decision making, radical changes, and brainstorming. If this matches your natural style and personality, then this is a company that will automatically value your efforts and approach to your work. On the other hand, if you are a methodical process worker who values details and systems, you may want to look for a company culture that values those things. You can certainly work for a company that has a culture opposite to your natural style, but it will be an uphill battle for your career. It is much easier to get ahead if your natural tendencies complement what the company values and rewards.

Company cultures will give themselves away in their history, employees, interview style, and even decor. Watch for the clues and you'll quickly discover what kind of company you're interviewing with. What a company chooses to show you during the interview process will be very similar to what it will be like to work there. Keep your eyes open to how happy the employees look, how overwhelming the paperwork stacks on the desks look, how the facilities look. Does it seem as though these people have what they need to get their jobs done, or are they piled on top of one another and sharing equipment? These are the kinds of things you want to look for.

Identify concerns you'd like to avoid such as intense work hours, bad morale, or financial problems. Whatever those concerns may be, do not let on that you are screening for them. Simply watch for them. Even the biggest, most tightly organized companies will give something away if you know what to look for.

Don't ignore questions like "Do you have problems with tight or shifting deadlines?" That is a dead giveaway that they consistently work long hours on short notice.

Pay attention to statements like "We don't believe that money is the best motivational factor for employees." That kind of statement means the company doesn't have the money it would like for compensation or bonuses.

Don't disregard questions like "Do you have anything that might get in the way of last-minute business trips or conferences?" That kind of question shows that this is probably not a family-friendly company.

Don't believe that a question like "What motivates you to do your best in difficult situations?" is just a question. It most likely means that the department or company has a morale problem and employees aren't happy.

Don't let anything slide through as you do your silent analysis of the information and clues you've been given. Process all of it to make your decision.

Interviewers are very much aware of the weaknesses of the company and the position. This knowledge tends to bleed through into their communication and questions. If you listen carefully, they will give away all you need to know with their choice of questions and veiled statements.

Most, if not all, of your questions will be answered through this method. No interviewer or company representative will tell you the straight-out truth about the position during the interview process, not even if you come right out and ask. If, after the interviews, you still feel the need to ask a question on an issue that's critically important to you, you'll have another chance to get your answer.

The rule is, you should only ask the questions that if not answered to your satisfaction will jeopardize your ability to accept the offer. And those questions, like all others, should be held until the very end.

Concerns about how the position is structured or issues over money or job title, work hours, or benefits, all of these should be held until an offer is in place.

Once you get the offer, you are on the most solid ground possible to get your questions answered without looking like a risk or threat. If there is something critically important that you simply must have answered in order to properly consider the job, then by all means ask it and make sure you get a satisfactory answer before you accept the offer.

So many people stress over issues too early in the game, issues that distract them from the critical job at hand—surviving the interview. Don't stress over your questions and issues until you actually have to make the decision of whether to take the job or not. Take it one step at a time, and don't get too far ahead of yourself. Once you get that offer in hand, then you can consider and discuss the things that you need in order to accept the job.

Now that you've learned the secrets to successfully navigating the interview process, it's time to go deeper. It's time to delve into the taboo topics and hidden dangers lurking within various aspects of the hiring process. These are the things many of us don't think about until it's too late. I'll show you how to recognize, avoid, and neutralize each one in the next chapter.

YOUR INTERVIEW IS OVER KEY POINTS TO REMEMBER

SECRET 13: WHO'S ON YOUR SIDE? Friendly hiring managers or interviewers may seem like they're on your side, but they aren't. Interviewers and human-resources people are agents of the company and must be treated as such at all times. Failure to understand this and protect yourself accordingly can lead to interview disaster.

SECRET 14: AREN'T KIDS GREAT? Beware of the secret tactics interviewers are trained to employ to get you to disclose personal things that would be illegal to ask in an interview.

SECRET 15: WHAT'S YOUR BODY LANGUAGE SAYING? Answering this question is the key to creating a solid first impression with an interviewer. Your body language and appearance will determine the course of your interview, the types of questions you'll be asked, and if not managed properly will cost you the job.

SECRET 16: WORRIED ABOUT TRICK QUESTIONS? You don't have to be. Interviewers are all looking for one thing: negativity. As long as you practice avoiding giving negative answers, you will be able to answer every question that comes your way with ease.

SECRET 17: THE KEY TO BEHAVIORAL INTERVIEWS (or any interview for that matter) is to come armed with your own stories. When you find yourself painted into an interview corner, unsure of what to say, launching one of your carefully crafted success stories will always get you on the right track and make you look like a star.

SECRET 18: GET THE HALO. Interviewers are subject to a phenomenon known as "the halo effect." You can easily work it to your advantage by creating a rapport with the interviewer and by creating an air of trust and connection. In this interview game, the one who makes the connection is the one who wins.

SECRET 19: IS THIS AN INTERVIEW OR A TRICK? It's both. There are six common trick interview tactics you need to watch for. They may look like standard interviews on the surface, but they are carefully designed behavioral tests to see what you might do in a given situation. Those who can recognize and use each one to their advantage will not only get the job but will learn a great deal about their new employer in the process.

SECRET 20: WHICH STYLE IS THIS? There are eight different interview styles that each require a certain response to win. Don't make the mistake of treating every interview the same or you will seem out of sync with the interviewer as well as miss key opportunities to get your name on top.

SECRET 21: EVERY JOB IS NUMBER ONE. Even if you're only taking an interview for the practice, treat every job like it's your dream job—because you never know when it could be. You only get one shot to give interviewers the one thing they're secretly screening for; don't let it pass you by.

SECRET 22: TO CALL OR NOT TO CALL? Understanding how the system works from the inside will help you understand why knowing the correct answer to this question is so important to your success. Calling at the wrong time will end your chances, weaken your position, and even cost you a pending offer.

SECRET 23: DO YOU HAVE ANY QUESTIONS? Most likely you've been taught to come to an interview prepared with questions, but that is dangerous. Do your homework in case you are asked questions about the company, but don't ask your own.

SECRET 24: DON'T SCREEN THE COMPANY. Or, at least don't let them know you're doing it. Learn how to read between the lines to screen for what you want without doing it openly, or you will knock yourself out of the running.

4

DANGER! TRAPS AHEAD!

DID YOU KNOW THAT BEING A PARENT COULD MEAN you'll be offered less money? Or that bad credit can keep you from being hired? Did you know that if you don't negotiate when you get an offer, you'll lower your chances of being successful on the job? Or that your public records will be part of your hiring process?

There are many myths out there about hiring and interviewing. Sometimes these myths are perpetuated to make hiring managers' jobs easier by giving you information that's not in your best interest. Sometimes they are taboo or politically incorrect topics that aren't openly discussed, so candidates don't know how to handle them properly.

Unsuspecting candidates are taken out of the running by the traps I'm about to share. Just one can stop a promising opportunity in its tracks. I think we'd all agree that interviewing is hard enough without misinformation, secrets, and hidden traps waiting to trip us up, but they are out there in full force.

The hiring process of today is skewed in favor of the companies, so learning about these hidden traps will help turn the tide for you.

I'm about to take you right into the land of taboo topics and best-kept secrets no hiring manager would ever want you to know.

INSIDER SECRET 25
Your public records are working against you.

WHILE IT'S ILLEGAL FOR COMPANIES TO DISCRIMINATE against candidates because of credit scores, bankruptcies, lawsuits, or other private information, they secretly do it every day.

In fact, the number of companies scanning public records to find out more about potential candidates is growing, with 75 percent reporting routinely conducting some form of background screening on candidates. Some companies even have private investigators on retainer to do background checks on every potential hire. A company will never tell you that you've been excluded because of something found in a background check. Many candidates have lost a job offer over personal things they didn't even know were in the public domain.

Even if a company doesn't do a formal background check on you, there are lots of things that can be found online with just your name and Social Security number (standard issue on any job application).

There are several proactive things all job seekers can do to help their chances. Before starting any job search, you should always do the following:

> **Run your credit report:** Run your credit report once a year and make sure it's in top form. Clean up anything you can; make sure old entries are off and everything is correct. If you find something inaccurate or something that you'd like to have changed, you can contact the

company that reported the delinquency or other issue and work things out with them directly. Many companies are willing to remove a negative report if you pay in full or start a payment plan. Some items can be changed and some can't, but it's worth a phone call to find out. A few blemishes on a credit report are fairly standard, but your credit score (also known as your FICO score) should stay above 660 to be considered for the top jobs. (See the resource section at the back of this book for information on free credit-checking services.)

Do a background check: Have a local private investigator or professional reference-checking service do a simple background check on you to see what pops up so you are prepared and know what a potential employer might find. (See the resources section at the back of this book for companies that can help with this.)

Due diligence: If you have something on your public record or criminal record or in your credit history that you might be able to change or even have removed, do so. Write letters, appeal to whomever you need to appeal to, and do what you can to remove items that could impact your ability to get the jobs you desire. Any negative items on your public record or credit ratings will keep you from being hired.

"Maury" had been looking for a job for over six months. He'd gotten very close to being hired several times but kept running into this shocking new trend in the hiring process. Each company was doing a "standard background and credit check" before extending the offer. Once this check had been completed, each of his potential new jobs had evaporated. The only thing he could think of was his recent bankruptcy filing, but he thought it was illegal to exclude someone from consideration because of something like that.

Maury had no idea when he'd made the difficult decision to file for bankruptcy that it would impact his job search, but that was exactly what was happening.

If you have something in your background/criminal/credit history that will impact your ability to be hired and you can't get it removed, there's an insider secret that will help you.

You will usually be required to sign a release form to allow a potential employer to do a formal background check. Refusing to sign it is not really an option, because if you don't you will no longer be up for consideration. Even if you know there's something in there you'd rather not have a potential employer see, it's worth going ahead and signing the form. Why? Because some hiring managers don't actually check. They've found that often they'll present the consent form to look into public history and panicked candidates will voluntarily blurt out the information. Many hiring managers have learned they can ask candidates to sign the form, never do the actual check, and still find out all they need to know—and more.

So whatever you do, refrain from spontaneously confessing whatever may be lurking in your public records during an interview or during a request to sign a consent form. Any explanation you give won't help your chances. Either they will run the report and remove you from consideration or they won't and you'll still be in the running. The secret is you should always call this potential bluff.

The best course of action is to smile and sign the release form. It's also helpful to know that most of the in-depth background checking is being done by the larger companies and corporations, so trying for jobs at smaller companies will be to your advantage.

In Maury's case he was able to switch his focus to smaller companies, which are less likely to check, and quickly found a great new job.

INSIDER SECRET 26
The initial phone call is a trap.

"MIKE" HAD BEEN SENDING OUT RÉSUMÉS FOR MONTHS, waiting for the phone to ring. He finally got the phone call he'd been hoping for just as he and his wife were trying to get their kids to bed. Bedtime had never been a popular event in their household, and this night was no exception. There was screaming and crying in the background as Mike frantically tried to switch gears and conduct a pleasant interview. He wondered why the hiring manager would call at such a strange time.

That's a good question. Why do hiring managers tend to call at the most inopportune times: dinnertime or early in the morning on a Saturday? They say it's the only time they have, but could that be true? Not at all.

These initial phone calls are actually designed to catch you off-guard at the worst possible time in the hopes that you will get flustered and let your guard down. Hiring managers try to call you at home at times when they think they can get a glimpse into your home life and what it's really like. They have very little to go on when doing a full evaluation of a potential candidate, so they'll use every tactic at their disposal.

The truth is: You don't have to talk to this person if it's not a good time for you. If you have something going on, are trying to drive in heavy traffic, or have screaming kids to deal with, tell the interviewer that you'd love to talk with her and you will call her right back. Don't say why. Then get off the freeway or go to a quiet part of the house and mentally prepare for the conversation. Then call her back within ten minutes. Don't go into any details or excuses about why you couldn't speak to the interviewer right away. Just jump right into the interview.

Occasionally you will get an interviewer who will say, "I'm afraid this is the only time I have, so we need to do the phone interview now." That is rarely the truth. So if it's really not a great time for you and you know you won't be at your best for this important screening, thank her for the call and say something like "I'm available tomorrow at your convenience between nine A.M. and noon. You can call me at this number, or may I call you at a particular time?" Turning the tables on her will help ensure your protection, and you may be surprised how flexible this previously inflexible interviewer can become.

However, if the interviewer stands her ground and says no to any other time or option, your best bet is to go ahead and give the interview. Just pretend there's nothing else going on, which may be difficult, and do your best. In the end, it's better to have a less-than-ideal phone screening than to not have one at all.

Usually, interviewers are willing to schedule a time that's more convenient for you, if you ask. Sometimes you just have to deal with bad timing, but be aware that even if there is no treacherous intent, if the interviewer hears anything in the background that might sway her decision, she will use it.

INSIDER SECRET 27
Quitting your job is the kiss of death.

YOU'VE ALREADY DECIDED TO LEAVE YOUR JOB AND GO ON TO greener pastures, so why not do it early and devote all your time to job searching? That's not a good idea, and I'll tell you why.

"Joel" was sick and tired of his job and desperately wanted to find something new. After speaking with his wife, he decided he wasn't going to wait any longer; he was going to get out there and find his dream job, so he quit.

Now devoting his time solely to finding a new job, he worked up his résumé, scoured the Internet, and made what felt like hundreds of submissions. Then he waited for the phone to ring. He felt lucky that he had some money tucked away that would allow him to do this. He figured that this concentrated job search would certainly yield what he was looking for.

One of Joel's friends from his former company had also been looking to make a change but didn't have the nest egg Joel had that would have allowed him to quit and look full-time. He had been doing his job search evenings and weekends and had just landed a great job with a good company for more pay. He was thrilled and couldn't wait to share the news with Joel.

Joel was surprised that his friend had found something so quickly after just looking a few hours a week, but he was also very encouraged by this news. If his friend had been able to do this in such a short amount of time, certainly Joel would be able to do much better. Joel had more years of experience than his friend, better qualifications, and since all he did was job-search all day long, he would certainly come out on top. But it didn't quite work out that way.

Joel got very few interviews and they all seemed overly focused on why he had chosen to quit his previous position before finding another one. Joel eventually found a good job with a good company, but it was six months later and for a lower salary than he'd been earning previously. What happened here?

Did you know that the unemployed sometimes wait twice as long for a hire offer as employed people do, and when they do get an offer, it tends to be for substantially less money?

The truth is: Hiring managers are secretly most interested in candidates other companies also want. That means people who are currently employed while also looking elsewhere. Psychologically, it makes a candidate seem more desirable if a hiring manager has to "steal" him or her away from another company.

But why do those who are employed while looking also tend to get the higher offers? A new employer knows they have to sweeten their offer to get someone away from an already-established job. When a potential employer tries to hire away someone who is already employed, they know they must offer a 10 or even 20 percent increase to sway the person to make a move. Not so for an unemployed person who a hiring manager imagines will simply be happy to be employed again.

When looking for a job, you are ten times more desirable, not to mention more confident, when you have a job. So if you are able to stay where you are while you look, you will greatly increase your chances of finding a better position.

One word of caution: Companies highly dislike it when candidates use their current company's resources to job-search. Sending potential employers your information on the company letterhead, using the company e-mail to correspond, and having potential employers call you at work will all send the wrong message. This little habit can make you look disloyal to your current employer, and that definitely won't make the best impression. It's okay to return a call from a potential employer while at work if no one is around to overhear you, but job searching should be done away from your current work as much as possible. While it's good to be employed while searching, you don't want to look like you're milking your current company's resources to do it.

Job searching while still employed also requires a bit of care. While it can be quite convenient to do your job searching online at work, it also puts you in danger of being ousted earlier than you planned. Employees are being terminated for job searching on company time, and you don't want that kind of blemish on your record.

Companies don't want employees who no longer wish to work there and certainly don't want to be paying for your job search, so they can terminate you for misuse of company equipment.

But how could they possibly find out? **The truth is: If you are us-**

ing company resources like their computer, phone, and/or laptop, the company has the right to "view" them at their discretion. What that means is, anything you do while on company premises or while using company equipment doesn't belong to you. It actually belongs to the company, and there's a good chance some company representative is looking at it. How prevalent is this practice?

"Anna" was working late one night on her computer when suddenly her mouse wouldn't respond. Reaching for the phone in frustration, she could only hope that someone from IT was still at work somewhere in this huge building so she could get her project finished and go home. But what happened next on her computer screen caused her to drop the phone before anyone could pick up. Suddenly on her desktop, folders began to open and close at a rapid pace; her e-mail opened, scrolled, then closed again. Her files suddenly listed on the screen and scrolled before her eyes. Selected folders were opened and copied. As the light show finished, she realized someone was on the other end of the phone. As she held it up to her ear, she told the IT person that something very strange was going on with her computer. After a long pause, a nervous voice on the other end of the phone said, "Oh, um, sorry about that. We do that once a month on every computer, but we never would have done it if we'd known you were here. Go ahead and try again; your computer should be back under your control now." As she started to hang up the phone, still in shock, he said, "And please don't tell anyone about this. I screwed up by not making sure everyone was gone first; this is all highly confidential."

According to a recent survey of the American Management Association, 82 percent of companies surveyed admitted to spying on their employees, tracking where they go on the Internet, reading and scanning e-mails, even listening in on or recording phone conversations. Many companies can also scan your hard drive for key words. So if you are conducting your job search at work, there's a good chance your company will find out and your job will be in jeopardy.

A company is required by law to tell its employees it is conducting surveillance or scanning, but that information is usually hidden in the employee manual with one sentence that briefly states something about how all company equipment can be viewed or used at the company's discretion for its purposes at any time. It's always much safer to conduct your search from home.

Now, there's one more very important reason to keep your job while looking for another one: It can provide critical protection if you have something you'd rather not have your potential employer find out about. For example, if you're leaving your job because you've been having problems with your boss or suspect you're in the stages of being managed out or even in danger of being terminated, you'll definitely want to jump to another company before you lose your job.

If you interview while still employed at the company where you've had some difficulties, there won't be any way for a potential new employer to find out about any of those difficulties. Once you've quit or left the company, a potential employer can call your previous company and ask all about you, but it's a well-established common courtesy, and an unwritten rule,, that a potential employer cannot and will not call the company you're currently working for. The reason being, they don't want to hurt your current job by letting your employer know you're interviewing. So it's perfectly fine for you to respectfully ask a potential employer not to contact your current one because they don't yet know you're looking. This means your potential employer can't find out about any problems you've had and you can present your previous employment experience in the best light possible.

It's important to be able to read the signs that let you know if your job is ending, if you're being managed out or about to be terminated, so you can jump to another job quickly with no one finding out about your bad luck. (In *Corporate Confidential: 50 Secrets Your Company Doesn't Want You to Know,* the entire first chapter is devoted to learning how to read the secret signs of a job in jeopardy and the steps that must be taken immediately to protect your career.)

Professionals who encourage candidates to quit their jobs before looking for another one are spreading the self-serving propaganda of the corporations and are doing a great disservice to job seekers. Potential employers want as much access to information about you as possible. This is most easily achieved when candidates are fully separated from their previous jobs. In addition, it keeps employees from secretly looking for another job while still employed. Thus the message they spread is one in their best interest—not yours. While remaining employed during your search is not necessarily in the best interest of your present employer, it is in your best interest and will provide you the best protection.

INSIDER SECRET 28
Failure to negotiate will cost you more than money.

IF YOU ARE ONE OF THOSE PEOPLE WHO ARE AFRAID TO NEgotiate when faced with a job offer, you are actively jeopardizing the success of your new job.

People who say, "It's a good enough offer; I don't really care about the money; I just want the job," or, "I don't want to get into a tough negotiation and make my new employer angry or make them think that money is all I care about; I'm just going to accept the offer," don't realize that if you fail to negotiate, your new employer will lose respect for you. In fact, they will begin to question if they made the right decision in hiring you.

Many mistakenly believe that by not negotiating they've preserved their position, when in fact they've done just the opposite. They have just eroded the foundation of a wonderful new opportunity.

The truth is: No hiring managers expect you to blindly accept the first offer they throw out. Why? Because hiring managers know they're required to offer candidates the lowest dollar amount first, just to see if the candidate will bite. Contrary to what you may have been told, hiring managers' financial incentives aren't based on hiring people. That's the basic function of their job. Many of their incentives are based on keeping compensation numbers as low as possible for new hires. This happens equally in both large and small companies regardless of how much money the company actually has. Because all future raises and bonuses will be based off this initial compensation number, as well as the possibility of having to pay a percentage of that compensation to a recruiter, it has become standard practice in all-size companies to get new hires to take the lowest offer possible. So the hiring manager will be hoping you take that initial lowball offer. But if you do, she will also secretly wonder why. Candidates who believe in themselves and what they have to offer never accept the lowball let's-see-if-they-take-it offer.

You may be happy just to have a job, but you don't want your new employer to know that. Failing to negotiate is one of the biggest and most common mistakes new hires make. Not only does it ensure you are starting at the lowest end of the pay scale; it also shakes confidence within the company in your abilities before you even walk in the door.

Just imagine for a moment that you are the hiring manager for the position. You present your lowball test offer and the candidate enthusiastically accepts right away. As the hiring manager who has seen countless negotiations, you now begin to ask inevitable questions like: *Maybe this person wasn't such a great catch after all? Doesn't he know what he's worth? Isn't he willing to at least ask for top dollar? Doesn't he think he's worth top dollar? If this guy has such a low opinion of himself, maybe I shouldn't have such a high one.*

This scenario happens quite often, and it can completely take the shine off a new hire. Not to mention you'll soon find out you're making less than others and did not get the benefit perks that some were able to negotiate. By not negotiating you run the risk of soon resenting your wonderful new job and feeling unappreciated when you realize others are making more for doing the same work.

Wherever you start financially with a company becomes the foundation for all your future raises and in some cases a foundation for your bonus structure. It all goes up from wherever you start. That is why hiring managers have such big incentives to try to get new candidates to start as low as possible. But that incentive goes only so far. A hiring manager would much rather get the number one candidate they've chosen than keep costs low. Their priorities are clear: Get the best candidate who will be the most successful in the position, then see how low you can get him or her in for. At the end of the day, their desire to get their top candidate will always trump their desire to keep costs low, so if you ask for more money or better benefits, you'll usually get it.

No matter what the hiring manager tells you, most don't accept the first offer. Not everyone hired comes on board at the lowest mark. Most are hired at the middle range, and if they are really good negotiators, they get top dollar. Even if their experience doesn't warrant top pay, good negotiators who understand how to work the system will get it.

Accepting a new offer with a new company is a golden opportunity to increase your compensation. The company needs you, has chosen you, and wants you. The hiring manager has invested in you, has imagined you in the position, and will do almost anything to make it happen. People are pressuring this hiring manager to get you signed on with a start date on the books. This is the one time you can ask for the money and benefits you desire and have the greatest chance of getting them. Don't ever let such a prime opportunity pass you by. It's three times harder to get a raise once you've started working than it is to increase your salary as you enter a new position.

Negotiating will show the company that you know what you're worth and aren't afraid to ask for it. It will help you enter your new position on solid ground, setting you up for success, with key decision makers squarely behind you.

Failure to negotiate will make people worried that you aren't what they thought. They will tend to stand off to the side with arms folded, waiting to see if they've made a huge mistake or even looking for you to fail. Companies are filled with fickle people who aren't willing to support someone they don't believe is a sure thing. If you don't appear to believe in yourself and what you're worth, why should they?

Now that you know negotiating is *not* an optional activity when accepting a new job if you want to be successful, the fears over negotiation tend to kick in: *What if negotiating ruins my chances to get this job? I don't want to make them angry or make it seem like money is all I care about.*

Fear over salary negotiation is very common, and that fear is warranted. It's absolutely true that talking about money or going into negotiations at the wrong time or in the wrong way is dangerous. You can hurt or even end your chances with a company by talking about money or asking for what you want too early in the process.

But if you know the insider secret to negotiating correctly, you will end up with a top-level offer in hand, knowing you have the best benefits and the pay you're worth.

Even if you are happy with the original offer you received, negotiating for additional items or simply negotiating for the sake of building respect ensures that you will enter with the company behind you, respecting you and supporting your efforts. Even if you don't get any of the items you requested during your negotiation, you have still accomplished your ultimate goal. The company knows you believe in yourself as much as they believe in you. That is how you enter on top.

The power of negotiation, along with the tendency to throw you the lowball offer first, are both well-kept secrets that no hiring manager wants you to get your hands on. They don't want you to employ this powerful tactic as a formula to increase respect and support, and they don't want to have to pay top dollar to every candidate. In fact, most hiring managers are trained to try to intimidate you out of negotiating and will in fact try to keep you from effectively negotiating at the right time.

It's not just about negotiating, although that in itself will be valuable. It's about effectively negotiating to increase your chances to get what you want. The hiring managers will be working against you and they are highly trained in tactics that will make you sweat, but the process is easier than you think, and you can be more successful than you've been told. I'll show you the secret to negotiating perfectly and powerfully every time, without jeopardizing your opportunity. Your ability to get what you want can be as simple as this three-part formula:

> **Negotiation Part 1:** Don't allow the hiring manager to trick you into talking about money or benefits too early. And don't volunteer what you're looking for.
>
> **Negotiation Part 2:** Wait for the security of the formal offer letter to begin your negotiations, asking for additional money or benefits. Until that point, everything is "negotiable" and something you would be "happy to consider."
>
> **Negotiation Part 3:** Present your top three most important items for negotiation first, one at a time, completing each one separately until you get what you want or a mutual agreement has been reached.

Hiring managers will try to trick you into talking about money and benefits too early in the process so that you tip your hand, boot yourself out of the running, or ruin your chances for a strong negotiation down the road. Why do they do this? Two reasons: The first is to keep from falling in love with a candidate who is out of their price range. They know that once they've decided you're the one, they will do almost anything to get you into the position, even potentially blow their compensation budget for the quarter. Second, they try to get you to discuss these things early to keep you from effectively negotiating once you've been chosen. Because they are tasked with keeping compensation numbers low, they don't want you to have the upper hand down the road.

They know that if they can get you to say early on in the process that you are happy with *x* money, it will make it difficult for you to ask for more than that when the time is right. So, during the initial interview, a hiring manager will ask things like "What are you looking for as far as salary?" Well, that's a little like asking children what they'd like Santa to bring them for Christmas. It automatically makes you want to blurt out your highest number, your ideal salary. But this is not the time to discuss numbers. If you allow this innocuous-sounding question to trigger you into talking about compensation at this early stage, you've just given the hiring manager the upper hand. If you share a number that's too high, you may have ruined your chances to move forward, and if you throw out a number that's too low, the hiring manager may suddenly feel you aren't the qualified candidate he or she imagined you to be.

There are two great ways to answer that question while still preserving your chances of moving forward in the process. One is to answer the question with a question: "What is your range for the position?" Once you hear what it is, you say, "That sounds like something I'd definitely consider."

The second tactic is to state what you're currently making (or were recently making) followed by a statement such as "Money's not the most important thing to me; what's really important is finding a company that's a good match. I'm open." That is exactly what they want to hear, and it works.

Requiring candidates to state their "salary requirements" in their cover letter is a variation on the same theme, forcing you to tip your hand too early in the game. Again, the safest route is to state what you're currently making, followed by the same statement from the previous paragraph. The same goes for applications that force you to state your "desired salary" for the position. Simply put "currently making [*x* amount]/negotiable" in the box.

The idea is to keep everything "negotiable" while remaining open to any offer the hiring manager may throw out. What you're doing is keeping the process going rather than shutting it down prematurely. Don't worry if the range they give you for the position is less than what you're looking for. If the hiring manager decides you're the one, there is a good chance this range will suddenly shift higher. If not, then it's still your decision to accept the offer. There may be other things you can negotiate that will put the offer back in the running for you.

If you use tactic number two, sharing what you've currently been making, it's important to understand that you can adjust your compensation numbers for each opportunity. For example, if you're looking at a job that has a top pay range that's much higher than what you've been making, feel free when stating your current compensation to mention your bonus, commissions, benefits, stock options, and any other perks that add up to a higher overall compensation. And if you've been making a larger salary and are looking to accept a job that's a little lower in pay, you can leave out any additional perks like bonuses while stressing that money is not the most important thing to you in this situation.

During the entire process, whenever anyone representing the

company talks about money, don't bite. It's a ploy. Just stick with "everything's negotiable" and "what's most important to me is the position and the company." Don't let them corner you into negotiating salary before the time is right.

When you get the formal written offer letter in your hands, then the time is right to talk salary—not when they've made a verbal offer and not when they've let you casually know you're their top candidate. Even if the hiring manager calls you to tell you they're sending an offer and asks if *x* amount of money would be satisfactory, you still shouldn't bite. This is another opportunity to sidestep: "I'll need to see the full offer, but I'll definitely consider it" is all you need to say.

When you get a formal offer in writing, you know two things: First, they want you!—and that is the most solid foundation for negotiation you'll ever get. Second, they are counting on you saying yes. They are now invested in you, they have imagined you starting at the company, and they've put all their eggs in your basket. Instead of excluding you and screening you out, they are now imagining you as "one of them." They are finally on your side, working toward the acceptance of that offer. This is the time your negotiations begin. If you haven't allowed anyone to get you to go into depth about your compensation or benefits up until this point, you have the best chance of getting the highest of both.

The funny thing is, people tend to be most fearful of negotiations when an offer is on the table. "Won't negotiating ruin my chances for the job?" "If I ask for a certain amount of money will the company pull the offer?" Not if you do it right. You don't need to be fearful at this point; you are on solid ground. Negotiations must be done properly, with respect, and showing enthusiasm for the position and the opportunity, but there is very little chance you will jeopardize your opportunity at this point.

The truth is: Negotiating will never hurt your chances unless you do it in a disrespectful manner or become completely inflexible on a particular item. The worst the company can do is say no to your requests, and then it's up to you to determine whether you will still take the job.

Another common question at this juncture is "Won't the company be angry that I've been saying everything sounds fine and I'll consider every offer all the way through the interview process to only now, at the final hour, make a request for more?" No. Hiring managers are expecting this. This is how people who know how to negotiate operate. Hiring managers know this is the strongest time to do it. Even though a hiring manager may hem and haw over your requests, believe me when I tell you they were expecting this. It is all part of the standard negotiation process.

Even though a hiring manager will try to pressure you to move as quickly as possible, a negotiation process is a dance that allows you to take up to two or even three weeks going back and forth with your requests. The key is to take your time, stay respectful, remember you have the upper hand no matter how stressful things get, and follow this secret formula:

> **Negotiation Formula 1:** Determine the top three things you'll be asking for (it's okay to have only one), with your sub-items to use as leverage down the road.
>
> **Negotiation Formula 2:** Go back to the negotiation table no more than twice to negotiate each individual item before moving on to your next item.
>
> **Negotiation Formula 3:** Don't worry about intimidating negotiation tactics. The hiring manager will try to stress you into giving in early, but you hold all the cards.

Here's how this secret formula works:

When the offer is presented in writing, there will always be things you are pleased with and things you wish were different. No offer is perfect right out of the box. It's important to realize, no matter how formal this offer looks, it is just a starting point for negotiations. Make a list of the things you're happy with and a list of the top three things you'd like to see changed. Now wait twenty-four hours. This is for you to gather your negotiating moxie and for the hiring manager to sweat a little. Now the magic begins.

It's important to always start with respect and enthusiasm. Here's what you say to start the negotiation process on the right note: "Thank you so much for the offer; it is obvious you put a lot of work into it, and I'm so excited about the opportunity to work for this company. I really appreciate the [insert here the top three things you thought were perfect, exactly what you wanted, and right on]. But I was really hoping for [insert your number one thing that is most important to you that you'd like to see changed]. Is there anything we could do here [on this item]?"

> *For example: "I'm so excited about this offer; I'm really looking forward to working with Innotech. I really appreciate the 401(k) plan, family benefits coverage, and stock options specified. But I was really hoping for $65,000. Is there anything we can do here?"*

Now, the type of question you use here is very important. It's critical to use a question format that implies you are on the same team, working toward the same goal, a question that will keep the negotiations open and positive.

The kinds of negotiation questions that will work against you and should be avoided are things like "Is this the best you can do?" It's too easy to sound rude when asking a question like this one, and it tends to close down the negotiation process. Even statements like "I really need to get *x* number of dollars if I'm going to take this job" can have a tendency to close down negotiations and might even ruffle feathers rather than keep the process open and favorable. You want to use the question that will maintain the best relationship with the negotiator while moving things in your direction. I like "Is there anything else we can do here?" It keeps everything open and upbeat while suggesting a partnership between you and the negotiator. "We" conveys that the two of you are in this together to find an equitable solution.

Once you've opened negotiations with this positive tone, just let it sit. At this point, the more you talk the weaker your position will become. Be prepared for the negotiator to potentially complain about the request, tell you it's impossible, or tell you nobody ever gets this. That is a common tactic and is one you should be prepared for.

Once the negotiation process has begun, the negotiator will try to make you sweat. But you don't have to. You are actually the one holding all the cards even though it seems to be the other way around. The company wants you, has made a mental investment in seeing you start, has begun to relax at the idea that they've found the right candidate for this position, and feels relieved that they don't have to search anymore. You have the ability at this point to say no and walk away. The company knows that, and they don't want that to happen.

One common mistake made at this point is that candidates tend to ask for everything they want in the negotiation up front. It's best to ask for one thing at a time. Once the negotiation on your most important item has gone as far as it can, then it's most effective to go to your second and third items for negotiation. This will allow you to utilize those second and third items for leverage as you move through your requests. If you put all three on the table at once, you may find you are forced to sacrifice one for another as you go through the give-and-take of negotiations. You want each item negotiated separately so they can't be used against each other by a savvy negotiator.

For most people, their number one item is salary. Here's how to go for the highest salary range without upsetting the negotiation process or your potential new employer:

First, make sure you know the market rate for your position. There are many sources that can help you do this. (See the resources section at the back of this book.) You don't want to ask for a salary you'd like to have but is way outside the established market rate for your new position or out of line for the geographical area you're interviewing in.

Make sure you can back up your monetary request with the established market rate for the position and your skill/experience level. Then when you say "I was really hoping for *x* amount of money for this position; is there anything we could do here?" you are putting in your top dollar request based on the same market-rate information the negotiator will use to determine if the increase is warranted.

It is customary to offer a new hire more than he or she was previously making (especially if you are currently employed when you get that new offer), and you have more leverage during offer negotiations than any other time. So even if you find you are already at the top of the market rate for your position, you can still ask for between a 5 and 10 percent increase over what you were making. Again, as long as you do this respectfully, showing enthusiasm for the position, the worst that can happen is they will say no.

It's not over yet. The negotiator will most likely try to make you sweat by making you wait a few days or so before getting back to you. This is where most people break. As the silence takes over, even the strongest candidates begin to wonder if they've done a horrible thing and lost their chances. Don't sweat it, and don't call.

The negotiator will call you to let you know if there is a revised offer. If you were successful, he or she will say something like "I went to my bosses and really lobbied for you. They said they would be able to offer you ten percent more; how does that sound?"

It's important to understand this response is not the end of the negotiation. You get another round. If you didn't get what you were looking for, you can do it again. You can respond with "I so appreciate you going to bat for me, and I'm thrilled about the additional ten percent, but I was really hoping for *x*; *is there anything else we can do here?*"

You may begin to feel like a broken record by this second round, but there's a reason for the repetition. Using the same question throughout the process is a powerful tactic that gently and respectfully conveys that you are not yet both in agreement. It keeps the negotiations friendly yet effective.

Asking the question again will lay the negotiations right back in their court. There's no need to elaborate or try to soften the request. The less you say at this point the better. Especially if your negotiator is using tactics like "This is never done," or "Do you really want this position?" or "If you're asking for that much, maybe this position isn't the right fit for you." These tactics are designed to get you to stop your negotiations out of fear. For every frightening remark a negotiator makes, you should simply reply with your enthusiasm for the job, reassure him or her that you feel this is a great fit for you, and gently restate your question: "Is there anything else we can do here on the salary?" Remember, as long as you do this very respectfully, showing consistent enthusiasm for the position and the company, along with a genuine desire to work there, there is little chance you could lose the offer.

You will know when you've gone beyond negotiation intimidation tactics and actually hit their bottom line because the negotiator will tell you. He or she will say something like "Gee, I wish I could do more, I really do, but this is absolutely our bottom line; we can't go any further; this is it." You'll hear a difference in the negotiator's tone and a change in wording that will signal this is as far as he or she can go. However, the negotiation is still not over. It's now time to go back to the other items in your top three that are important to you.

At this point in the negotiation, it's important to keep your primary requests limited to your top three. If you have more than three, then you need to reprioritize. You can have a "B" list of requests that are not at your highest level, but those should be negotiated after you've gotten your top three or thrown into the negotiations when one of your three is not something your new employer is willing or able to negotiate on.

If you weren't able to get all the salary you were asking for, now is the time to ask for the remainder in a signing bonus, extra vacation time, or additional stock options. Many times hiring negotiators can be more flexible on these things than they can be on compensation guidelines. Even though they may not be able to be flexible on salary, they may be very flexible on vacation time, additional benefits, or a signing bonus to make up the difference.

The way to ask for it is (again starting with respect and appreciation) "I so appreciate you going to bat for me on the salary and I understand you aren't able to go any further, but *maybe there's something else we could do here*. Would it be possible to make up the difference in a signing bonus?" The negotiator might say, "Well, we don't do signing bonuses." Your turn: "Well, okay, what about an additional week of vacation time?" Or you may say, "Is there flexibility on the job title; maybe we could make the title *A* instead of *B*?"

You'll notice I didn't say "Are you flexible?" but "Is there flexibility?" You'll also notice the use of "we." This kind of wording is very important in creating camaraderie and a sense of partnership that keeps the negotiations out of the realm of you against the negotiator. This kind of wording will inspire the negotiator to work on your behalf rather than against you. People who have tried this secret negotiation tactic have been amazed at how flexible a hiring manager can become on these issues and how much they're able to get.

Many candidates going into these negotiations find that having a loftier title or an extra week of vacation ends up being worth much more than an increase in salary in the long run. Often candidates find that they end up with every single thing they've asked for!

Even if you find there is no flexibility in the offer for the items that are important to you, you get to decide if it's worth it to you to go ahead and accept the offer as is. If you'd still like to move forward, simply thank the negotiator for his or her time, consideration, and help, and accept the offer.

Even if the negotiation ends with you receiving none of the items you requested, you have not failed! Remember, you aren't just doing this for the money or the extra vacation time. The very process of negotiating will have taken you a long way toward raising the company's level of respect for you. In the company's mind, you are courageous, you know what you're worth, and you're making sure that this is the best placement for both you and the company.

Always negotiate. Even if the original offer includes exactly what you were looking for; even if what you want seems too petty to fight for, the act of negotiating is an important component to your future success.

Now, let's say you were going through an interview process with a company that simply didn't have the compensation or title you were looking for, hoping that during the negotiations you would be able to get them to move to a more desirable platform, but to no avail. You can always turn down the offer. Again, you won't ruin your chances during a negotiation unless you become inflexible in a certain area. If there is something highly important to you and your career that you simply can't budge on, feel free to stand your ground in these negotiations. Negotiators will either budge or they won't, and you can look elsewhere. You are in a much stronger position to ask for these things once you have an offer in hand than you are during the interview process itself. Many times a company will be able to move its compensation levels or change the title for the position if it finds the candidate it really wants. I've seen it done many times. If nothing else, you will get some very good practice in interviewing and offer negotiation.

Please remember that just because a company makes an offer doesn't mean you have to accept it. You won't be burning any bridges if you turn down an offer in a respectful way.

I've heard people say they don't even want to interview with a certain company or move forward with the look-and-see process because there is something in the advertisement that makes it seem like the job won't meet their needs. You may know you can't start working there for several weeks or that the salary they've posted is $10K below what you're looking for, but that's no reason to avoid the opportunity. Not only is it good practice, but if a company wants you they will move as much of heaven and earth as they're allowed to get you in there. Sometimes that means they will hire you but let you start months later or move the compensation to the level that matches your needs—any number of things.

Don't underestimate the power of a company that believes a particular candidate is critical to its success. If a company wants you, you'd be surprised what you can ask for and get. The trick is to wait until you're sure they want you to discuss any of it. Candidates who negotiate tend to be much more successful in their new placements, and many believe it's because of the added respect factor these candidates enter with that helps support their efforts going forward. If you show that you believe in yourself and what you're worth, the company will, too.

INSIDER SECRET 29
There is a hidden employment contract.

ARE YOU LOOKING FOR AN EMPLOYMENT CONTRACT TO PROtect you and your new job? I have news for you. Unless you are a high-level executive, you don't want a formal employment contract. A company can too easily use it against you.

There is a way to protect yourself without a contract and still ensure the company will live up to its promises. There is a "secret" employment contract that all companies are willing to create when you're first hired.

I'm asked on a regular basis about creating an employment contract with a new employer, but that's not a realistic request. With growing fears over lawsuits or getting stuck in a bad relationship with an employee, many companies flatly refuse any requests for a formal contract. Only in high-level executive placement is the formal employment contract still alive and well. Unless you are at that level, you shouldn't count on it; nor should you want one. Companies tend to resent these contracts, and I've seen them used against employees as often as I've seen them provide protection. How can a contract be used against you?

"Bill" had a three-year contract with his organization. If the company wanted him out for whatever reason, they would have to buy out the full value of the contract, which meant paying his salary for each year remaining in the agreement. These contracts are known as "golden handcuffs" to the insiders, and there's a very good reason for that nickname. It doesn't just protect you; it also protects the company by preventing you from leaving if you need to.

In Bill's case, because of the nature of his contract, when the company opened another office in another part of the country, he was forced to move his family and spearhead the fledgling enterprise. He found himself moved into a new area he didn't want to live in, working eighty-hour weeks. His contract hadn't quite worked out the way he'd hoped.

When "Jenny" got her contract, she was thrilled. It was her first one, and she felt a sense of job security like never before. But now, two years later, she wished she didn't have it. The company was asking her to do something she didn't want to do, and she couldn't say no. They gave her an assignment that no one else in the company had been willing to take, knowing she couldn't quit with one more year left on her contract. The company had chosen to use Jenny's contract against her to get an unwanted assignment off their desks, and there was nothing she could do about it. If she refused the assignment, the company said she would be demoted.

Her contract didn't specify that she would keep her same title, only that she would never go lower than her current pay rate (because of course she had been hoping for a promotion during this time). Unfortunately, this meant that the company could demote her to a lower, less desirable position as long as they continued to pay her current salary. A demotion on her résumé would definitely hurt her career. So she had to take the assignment and make the best of it. Once her contract was over, she had no idea what her performance record would show or what her career would look like going forward. At this point, all she wanted was to be able to quit on her own terms, but she had signed that ability away.

A contract is not always as great as it sounds. There are times when a contract is advisable, such as when your level demands it or you know the company is about to be purchased or a large reorganization is coming down the line. However, a contract must be carefully crafted with the help of a professional employee advocate to make sure the company is limited in its ability to turn around and use the contract against you.

However, there is a way for you to create a contract with a new employer without them even realizing that you're doing it. It all lies in the offer letter. Did you know that a formal written offer letter is considered a legally binding contract?

If you wish to hold your new employer to something that's important to you, make sure it gets into that formal offer letter and gets signed and placed into your new personnel file.

Make sure all negotiated items are added into the offer letter. All you have to say is "Thank you so much for agreeing to that extra week of vacation time. Just so we're clear and there's no confusion down the road, would you mind including that in the revised offer letter you'll be sending me?"

If the negotiator can't put what you're looking for in writing in the offer itself, try asking for it in writing in an e-mail or memo. That's not quite as good, but it will certainly provide more protection than a verbal agreement over the phone. Don't ever let negotiators feel that you are distrustful of them, the company, or the process—even if you are.

Getting these items in writing for extra clarification will go far in protecting you should a conflict or miscommunication arise down the road. You don't know if this human-resources person or manager you're negotiating with will be employed by the company in six months when you are ready to activate that aspect of your agreement. Getting things in writing is something you should do at every turn. Just make sure you do it in the same manner you went into negotiations—respectfully and with enthusiasm for the company and the position.

Don't worry about standard things in an offer letter that look scary but should be expected, like "at-will employment" statements. Those statements say that a company can end your employment at any time for any reason and that you have the right to do the same. Lots of candidates freak out over this kind of statement, but it's one that we are all going to have to learn to live with. It's a standard item dictated by state law that the company won't be able to remove. Trying to negotiate away standard language can greatly weaken your standing on other negotiation items.

Don't let hiring managers convince you that they will always honor the verbal agreement you have with them. If it's not in the offer letter, you are not protected. Changes to compensation, vacation time, benefits, and anything else you've been able to negotiate should all be included in a new offer letter before you sign it. Don't be fooled by "Oh, this is just a standard letter and I can't change it, but I've taken notes about what we've agreed upon and I'll put them in your file." That won't protect you. You can still choose to work for that company if you wish, but don't count on any of those agreed-upon negotiations to come through.

I counseled an employee whose company had decided to cut costs. The company cut all employee vacation time from three weeks down to two, and cut everyone's salaries by 15 percent for the year. However, this individual was spared. Why? Because he had a carefully worded specification for "3 weeks vacation each year," with a specified salary amount each year, in his signed and filed offer letter. Don't underestimate the power of an implied contract. Things a company would never be willing to put in a "formal employment contract" are specified in offer letters all the time. It's all about using what you've got to your best advantage.

INSIDER SECRET 30
Mothers are being hired for less.

DO YOU TELL INTERVIEWERS OR HIRING MANAGERS THAT YOU are a parent or that you have a family? If so, you are losing potential jobs and possibly making $11,000 less per year than others.

While it's never advisable to share personal information during the hiring or interview process, many candidates still believe they can and should talk about their parental status, kids, and family. Most people believe it is safe, yet it's one of the most dangerous disclosures a candidate can make during the hiring process.

In a recent study done at Cornell University, researchers found that during the interview process mothers were perceived as less committed to work than women without children. The study found that not only were mothers less likely to be hired due to this perception, but also, when they were hired, they were offered substantially lower salaries. There was a gap of around $11,000 in starting salary between those who stated they had children and those who did not, and the more children a candidate said she had, the greater the gap in pay.

The problem here is an age-old, highly taboo double standard. The fact is that most hiring managers, even if they are women, tend to view mothers as distracted and less engaged in their careers than their single counterparts. Mothers are seen as more likely to have to stay home with a sick child, leave early for school events, and be unavailable for last-minute important business trips.

Fathers are seen in the completely opposite light. A candidate who shares that he's a father is seen as more responsible in character and even more committed to the job than his single counterparts.

That's why when a man puts a picture of his children on his desk he's seen as a solid guy who is responsible and can be counted on. But when a woman puts a picture of her children on her desk she's seen as someone the company may not be able to count on, someone who has chosen to put the company second, or someone who would rather be home with those children. This hidden bias is the reason that these types of classic double standards still exist in our workplaces.

The sage advice is to keep your parental status private when interviewing. A hiring manager doesn't need to know this information during an interview, and you have no obligation to tell. They are hiring you for your skills and experience only. To protect yourself from hidden discrimination in the workplace it's best to keep all personal information private. Keep your photos of your family at home, and keep the focus on your skills rather than on your personal life.

If an interviewer does slip up and ask you about your parental status or you just happen to get a clueless one who doesn't know the laws, don't bristle and say, "That's illegal and I won't answer it." You basically just did answer it, and you also killed the interview. Just smile and sidestep it. Here's how:

MR. CLUELESS INTERVIEWER: Do you have any children?

CANDIDATE: I'm really just all about the work right now. I love my job and I'm really devoted to my career.

This answer lets the interviewer know that you would like him to stay focused on work-related questions, while also reinforcing your commitment to the job. You never said whether you had children or not and you've just effectively dodged the question without ruffling any feathers. Now, to be very clear here, I'm not saying you should lie or ever misrepresent yourself. But I definitely feel that when faced with a sticky and unfair situation involving discrimination candidates can and should use anything in their arsenal to make it the nonissue it should be.

Those questions are illegal to ask for a reason, but the answer is sometimes very important to a company. If it's important to you that you work for a company that values families and supports parents, there are online job search resources out there that will help you find family-friendly companies. (See the resources section at the back of this book.) Or you can choose to be up front about your parental status in an interview and let the chips fall where they may. Ultimately, it's up to you, but if you talk about your children in an interview believing that will not impact your ability to be hired or make top salary, you are taking a big risk.

INSIDER SECRET 31
Don't ever admit you've been fired.

"TERRY" WAS A GOOD WORKER WHO HAD BEEN THROUGH A terribly unfair termination, politically motivated by a dishonest boss. Terry knew he'd done nothing wrong but was now lamenting over what this misfortune might do to his career. He had been on several interviews over the past eight months, and they all had abruptly ended within the first ten minutes.

It didn't take long to diagnose the problem, since each interview had ended at exactly the same spot: "So tell me, why did you leave your former employer?"

Each time Terry heard this question, he felt compelled to explain what had happened. He thought of it as damage control.

The truth is: Interviewers won't care that a firing was unjustified or unfair or has a good explanation. They cannot recommend you if they know you've been fired from a previous position. Their job is on the line with each recommendation. A firing is one of those red flags that require a hiring manager to shut down the discussions.

There are a variety of articles and messages out there telling people they should disclose damaging things in an interview, like having been fired, in order to have more control over the information. I've recently read several articles telling job seekers that companies will find out about your past, so you'd better just tell them what really happened right off the bat in your own words. Don't believe it. It's not true.

This is a campaign created by hiring managers and is not in your best interest. Why would they want you to volunteer information like this in an interview? Because they know they may not be able to get it unless they can trick you into volunteering it.

What no company or hiring manager wants you to know is also one of the best-kept and most closely guarded secrets within the job search process.

Over the last several years, there have been laws put in place that many companies feel make it difficult or even illegal for them to openly share certain types of information about their past employees. Generally speaking, the laws allow a company to verify the basics of employment but do not allow an employer to voice personal opinions or add additional information. When it comes to the disclosure of a termination or firing, that is a much stickier subject.

If your state laws allow it and it's company policy to disclose exactly how each employee left, then a company representative is safe to say "He quit to take another job" or even "She was terminated for stealing." If it's true and it is in line with company policy and state laws, then it can be stated. (For a Web site that provides a brief list of reference immunity laws and reference regulations by state, please see the resources section at the back of this book.)

However, this is considered dangerous ground for most companies today. If any company representative steps over the line while giving one of these detailed references and says something he or she shouldn't, the company can be sued for slander or defamation of character. This is not something most companies are willing to risk. So even if a company is allowed to give this type of information, most do not.

When the phone rings in the human-resources office or on your previous boss's desk and the person identifies him- or herself as a potential employer seeking a reference, the human-resources person or boss has no idea who he or she is really talking to. It could be the previous employee's lawyer or a reference-checking service looking for information that could help support a lawsuit for defamation of character. There's a lot of that going on these days, and for a company it's not worth taking a chance.

In most cases, a company representative won't risk damaging complications by saying that you were terminated or fired, that you were a horrible employee, or that there were any issues involved with your employment at all. They sometimes won't even say whether you are eligible for rehire. (Asking if the previous employee was "eligible for rehire" used to be an effective little insider trick to try to find out whether an employee left on good terms without having to ask if the person was terminated, but the laws caught up with this trick and most savvy human-resources people now refuse to answer it.)

All this will largely depend on the company's policy on giving references. Because most companies, even those protected by state immunity laws, are leery of the reference-checking system, most still choose to only give the standard information consisting of dates of employment and titles held on every candidate. That's it. That's all most hiring managers will be able to get out of your last employer.

Now I think you can see why companies don't want you to have this information. If your previous companies do not give separation information, this will protect you if you have a termination or disciplinary action on your record that would keep you from getting hired by another company. That means if you don't volunteer the information, they usually can't get it. And you shouldn't disclose it.

Understanding how the verification of employment truly works is critical to understanding when you should and should not volunteer sensitive information like a previous firing or any other blemish on your work record.

There may be some insider channels for casual chat that would allow hiring managers to get their hands on some gossip about a termination behind the scenes, but that's rare. If you don't want to be eliminated from the job search process, your best defense is to pick whatever positive reason you'd like to share for leaving your previous employer and forge ahead in the interview process as the fabulous employee you know you are. Even if interviewers try to trick you with something like "I hear things didn't end so well with your last company," don't bite. Assume they're fishing. They most likely are. You can say something like "Well, that's news to me; I had a good experience at that company."

Remembering that they may have no true channel for finding out about a termination will help you stand your ground with confidence.

What do you do if you suspect there is someone out there saying bad things about you and costing you opportunities? This is rare, but it can happen even though it's illegal. If you have a suspicion, check it out. You can hire a reference-checking service to run a check on your references and previous employers so you go into the job search knowing exactly what will be said about you. (See the resources section at the back of the book for reference-checking services.) If you do find a previous boss saying things he or she shouldn't, you should contact a career advisor, employee advocate, or reference service to help you get your former boss to stop. If it continues or if what was said was egregious enough to be considered slander, then you may want to call a lawyer.

It's always best to know what will be said about you before you begin your job search, so that you don't learn the hard way.

You can easily find out what your previous company's reference policy is by contacting the human-resources department. Each company will have a set policy on what they're able to say about employees.

When you contact human resources, ask them the following questions:

- What's the company's policy on giving references?
- I want to verify that my information matches yours. What do you have on record as my titles held and dates of employment?
- Do the records show that I'm eligible for rehire?
- What do your records show as the reason for separation?

If you find anything inaccurate, now is the time to get it fixed. If all is correct, this will give you a clear picture of what information will be given when a prospective employer calls.

There is also another little insider trick you can add to your interviews that will help protect your past employment records. The trick is to always present your former experience in as positive a light as possible, so that hiring managers won't see any red flags that would cause them to investigate your previous employment. Most hiring managers are simply too busy to sleuth you out unless they have a clear need to do so.

In Terry's case, he quickly discovered that his company was not sharing separation information or any reference information at all. They were sending all reference inquiries to a third-party company (as many companies are now doing) that was only providing very basic employment verification information. So, on his very next interview, when asked why he'd left his previous employer, Terry smiled and said that he'd been thinking about trying something different for some time and that the current industry he was now interviewing for was exactly where he wanted to be. He got the job.

Most likely, as a matter of strict policy the companies you've worked for won't give separation information. However, what if the one company that does happens to be the one you've been terminated from?

Understand that if a potential employer learns that you've had a termination, the interview process will most likely be over. So you want to do everything you can to keep the termination out of your job search information. If you know for sure that the termination will come up when a potential employer checks, here are a few things to consider:

> **Take it off:** If you were only at the company for a short time, you may want to leave that employer off your résumé, coming up with some positive reason for the gap in employment.
>
> **Seed your references:** Put someone on your reference list from the company that terminated you who will give you a glowing personal recommendation and reference.

This should help balance out the information the hiring manager receives.

Get a "termination" changed: As you leave a company that's trying to terminate you, you may be able to get that designation changed. Most departing employees don't realize that there is some leeway here. Many times you can have a termination designation changed to a mutual agreement separation, a resignation, or even a layoff, which makes all the difference.

Why would a company be willing to change your designation from termination to a resignation or layoff before you leave? Because it protects them. A "terminated" employee is always more of a risk for a wrongful termination lawsuit. A company knows if they give a little at the end and make the departing employee's exit somewhat easier, the chances the employee will turn around and sue are far less.

An employee with a designation of layoff, for example, can now collect unemployment insurance. Employees with a resignation designation won't get unemployment, but they will be able to say that they quit on their own terms and the personnel files will reflect that. Companies have discovered that the more angry the employee and the more abused he or she feels, the greater the chance of a lawsuit. A company may be willing to change your designation simply to protect themselves, and with a little luck it will protect your future opportunities as well.

If the company asks you to sign a "waiver" or "separation agreement" as you leave, you can negotiate your terms of separation as part of that agreement before signing it. A waiver agreement asks you to waive your rights to bringing any type of lawsuit against the company in exchange for a monetary settlement. If a company gives you one of these, they really need you to sign it for their peace of mind. That's your ace in the hole. Don't just blindly sign your rights away; ask for things you'd like in exchange first. The worst they can do is say no, but you may be surprised at what can be changed to give both you and the company some added peace of mind.

If you are leaving a company that gives reasons for separation as part of their reference policy or you work in a state that has reference immunity laws in place, then getting a designation other than "terminated" may be more valuable than any money, severance, or unemployment benefits being offered.

Jump to another job: If you see the writing on the wall at your current company and it looks like a termination is imminent, take action immediately. The best way to avoid the entanglement of a termination on your record is to jump to another company as soon as possible.

The powerful effect the word "termination" can have on your future job opportunities necessitates avoiding it at all costs. Therefore, the best course of action is to begin looking for another opportunity immediately and try to jump to another job before you're asked to leave.

Jumping to another job while still at your previous one will protect you because a hiring manager will not be able to check the references at the company that still employs you. That means you can say anything positive you'd like for the reason you want to leave. The very fact that you are currently employed will make you more appealing as a candidate than an unemployed applicant. This all gives you an edge in the process while protecting your career

> from a bad-luck experience with one company. (For information on how to read the secret signs of a job in jeopardy, see the resources section at the back of this book.)

Many of us have had to go through the painful and humiliating experience of being fired. But it doesn't have to mark the end of your career path. You don't have to move to another state, and you don't have to change your name. All you need is the insider information so you can work this system to your advantage.

Don't let company politics, unfair firings, and uncaring rules and judgments within the hiring process keep your career from moving forward. You are in charge of how your history and information are presented. I'm not saying you should ever lie, but I am saying you can choose to present your information, history, and even little bouts of bad luck in the most positive light possible. You'll find that the more positively you present your previous experiences, the less hiring managers will check into your past.

Nine times out of ten you won't have to disclose during an interview that you've had a termination in your past. A hiring manager won't be able to find out, and you will be able to continue your career successfully.

INSIDER SECRET 32
Age discrimination is shutting you out.

AGE IS ONE OF THE MOST ACTIVE DISCRIMINATIONS IN HIRING today. If you don't know how to neutralize the bias against age, you will lose countless opportunities.

Many of you have seen age discrimination firsthand, as the practice is greatly increasing throughout corporate America. Many of you hope you never will. But it's out there, and at some point in your career you are guaranteed to come face-to-face with it in the hiring process. Unfortunately, it hits both sides of the age equation. Companies have become wary of hiring both older workers and younger workers.

Oddly enough, it's not the actual age of the candidate that will trigger the discrimination issues; it's how old the candidate acts and appears.

What's at Stake for Older Workers?

THINK "OLDER WORKERS" REFERS ONLY TO PEOPLE WHO ARE working into their sixties or seventies (something that's increasingly common)? Think again. Federal law determines "older workers" to be those over forty years of age. Even though all forty-plus workers constitute a protected class in the workplace under federal law, they continue to be the ones targeted for discrimination in the hiring process most often.

The truth is that "older workers" are highly prized for their experience, expertise, responsibility, industry connections, and stability. These tend to be the reasons older workers are hired. It's the fear that companies secretly associate with age that triggers discrimination. But these triggers are simple to avoid. Here are a few of the most common secret triggers and how to avoid them:

Health. The number one fear when hiring an older worker is poor health. This kind of elimination is completely illegal, but companies still do it every day: *Will this person leave us in the lurch due to an illness or injury, go out on medical leave so that we have to hold his or her position for twelve weeks, or make our insurance premiums go up?* Luckily, this is an easy concern to neutralize. As much as you can, you should give the appearance of great health during the interview, and don't talk about any illnesses or health issues either current or in the past.

You want to be able to give the appearance of good health, and that appearance is all a hiring manager will need. Any medical or physical challenges are your personal business. You are under no obligation to volunteer this information to a hiring manager. If the particular position you're applying for has specific physical requirements, then the physical issues that are directly related to the position are all you need to share.

Watch for an interviewer's tricks in this area: The interviewer groans as he sits down and mentions something about his aching knee or back. Then he mentions some recent surgery he's had or is going to have. It's human nature to jump in and say, "Oh, me, too." Or, "That's nothing; I had such-and-such surgery last year and I've never been quite the same." This is the kind of thing we say in conversations with family and friends on a regular basis, but that may be just what an interviewer is counting on. This is a common tactic to get an interviewee to reciprocate and share information that would have been completely illegal to ask about directly.

So, if you get the interviewer who comes right out and asks you the illegal question about your health, you can shut down this inappropriate line of questioning without losing your rapport with the interviewer. The idea is to politely answer this illegal and invasive question as though a complete stranger just asked you, "How are you today?"

> INTERVIEWER: How's your health?
>
> CANDIDATE: [smiling] Fine, thank you.
>
> INTERVIEWER: Anything we need to know about?
>
> CANDIDATE: No.

The company's edge. Another major concern for a hiring manager when interviewing older candidates is their ability to help the company maintain a competitive edge in the marketplace. The fear here is that older workers are not as flexible or may have even become a little stagnant in their thinking and won't be able to add to the cutting-edge momentum that companies thrive on.

This can be neutralized by staying away from saying things that show dated thinking like "Who can keep up with all these changes in our industry?" or "All this new technology gets so overwhelming—thank goodness my son-in-law is in IT; I just call him for help." These casual comments make it appear as though you may be falling behind, which is not the impression you want to give.

Dress the part. One of the easiest ways to negate age discrimination is appearance. A youthful appearance can assuage any fears a hiring manager might have. Why? In an interview a hiring manager is forced to put an overemphasis on surface things because there's not much information to go on. So, whatever you choose to present in an interview will have magnified importance. The way you dress and choose to appear will make all the difference. Also, dress is commonly used to determine what kind of thinker you are. A hiring manager sees sloppy clothing and thinks sloppy thinker or dated clothing and thinks dated thinker.

That means no gray hair, not even if it is nicely styled. Only executives get to have gray hair. Make sure that you're wearing up-to-date clothing and you present a youthful overall appearance. If you've been dressing the same way for the last decade, try going to a style makeover professional who can give you an honest opinion and help you pick out a look that will wow any interviewer. (See the resources section at the back of this book for image therapists and consultants.)

A hiring manager will hesitate to hire an older worker who makes statements that seem "out of touch," is wearing styles from ten years ago, or has an outdated hairstyle. Even if he or she is the most qualified candidate for the position, this type of appearance will send the wrong message and keep the candidate from getting to the top of the list for recommendation.

Every hiring manager will make an offer to an older worker

with great experience, a youthful approach and appearance, an up-to-date hairstyle and clothing, and high energy and enthusiasm for the position. This presentation negates all the lurking fears about hiring an older candidate, allowing the hiring manager to focus on all your best qualities, rather than being distracted by the age factor.

What's at Stake for Younger Workers?

EVERYONE TALKS ABOUT DISCRIMINATION AGAINST OLDER workers, but in many cases younger workers have it much worse. Imagine having the age issue to combat, secret discriminations to overcome, without the years of experience and career clout standing behind you. That's what younger workers are up against. Without years of experience, networking connections, and career successes to point to, younger workers often find themselves severely victimized by age discrimination.

Again, it's not how young you actually are that makes the difference. It's how young you appear and whether or not you are able to successfully avoid the factors that scare hiring managers into activating the discrimination card.

Younger workers are highly desired for their enthusiasm, energy, ability to work hard for longer hours, flexibility, and fresh thinking. Not to mention, a company can hire a younger candidate for a lot less money than a candidate who's been in the workforce for a while. These are all things that work in a younger candidate's favor when looking for a job.

What tends to scare companies into discriminating against younger workers is this group's tendency to be less responsible and more disrespectful and even act inappropriately at times. These are the things younger candidates have to neutralize during the interview process so the hiring manager can concentrate on their skills and attributes.

The best ways to do this are through dress, appearance, and swinging the pendulum of opinion as far away from an interviewer's fears as possible.

Interview coaching. If you are just starting out in the career world, I would highly recommend practicing your interviewing skills on a parent or other trusted adult who has been in the working world for a while. This will help you present yourself as a professional and serious candidate. If at all possible, hire a professional interview coach, even if only for one hour. A coach will help you feel more confident as you face the gauntlet of trick questions and psychological profiling that can make even the most experienced interviewee squirm nervously in his or her chair. The ability to interview confidently and effectively is a skill that will serve you well throughout your career and one that will help you stand head and shoulders above others in your age range.

Dress conservatively. Interviewers focus on what you choose to wear to determine what kind of thinker you are and what kind of employee you'll be. It will also determine how tough an interview you get.

Hiring managers focus on dress because they truly don't have much to go on. So your appearance takes on magnified importance. If you think you can wear sweatpants and flip-flops to an interview without consequences, think again. No interviewer or human-resources professional will tell you what to wear or even that you've dressed inappropriately. This could too easily be construed as a violation of your rights and an opening for a lawsuit. They also don't want to come right out and tell you what to wear to the interview because it's valuable to the hiring manager to see what a candidate naturally chooses. An outfit that is in line with the company image shows that the candidate values the opportunity and would be a good fit for the organization.

When in doubt, it's always best to dress the way older workers do, because they are usually the ones who make the hiring decisions. It's the Baby Boomer generation that created the casual work environment we all now enjoy, but in their minds "casual" meant something entirely different from what it means to you. To those of us in that era, it meant freedom from panty hose, heels, and wool suits. It meant not having to wear a tie, a three-piece suit, and wing tips.

The people of this generation, a.k.a the decision makers who now hold your future in the balance, were never prepared for young people with belly rings or tattoos showing, young women with bra lace hanging out of their tops, or young men with three-day scruff showing up to interviews. Even if you are being interviewed by someone your own age, you can bet this person is answering to someone older who would never okay a candidate who didn't present him- or herself properly in the interview process.

Remember, the people you have to impress probably think of neatly pressed khaki pants and crisp polo shirts as "casual" dress for men and a below-the-knee skirt or pressed slacks (not jeans) with a well-tailored blouse as "casual" for women. Even in extremely casual workplaces, anything less is simply inappropriate for an interview. The rule of thumb is: If you are younger than the Baby Boomer generation, your idea of "dressed up" will most likely be their idea of "casual." So the more dressed-up you are for an interview, the better.

Like it or not, appearance is a major issue at workplaces today. It is one of the primary factors that can make or break a career and make or break a job opportunity. (See the resources section at the back of this book for information on image consultants.)

"Dude, what time is it?" Another main concern with younger employees is reliability, and being late for an interview will certainly reinforce that fear. It's imperative to be early or exactly on time. Again, you want to negate any fears or trepidations the interviewer may have by overdoing it in the other direction.

I recommend (for everyone) that you scope out the location of the company a day or two ahead of time so you aren't scrambling to get there while reading directions. Make sure you know where it is so that on the day of your interview you'll know exactly where to go and how long it will take.

Get there a few minutes early and review your interview material. Go over your top ten best qualities and success stories from Secret 17, so all your information is top-of-mind and you're feeling confident. The rule of thumb is, you should be there early but shouldn't go in until ten minutes before the interview. Being too early can sometimes make you look too eager, but in the case of a younger candidate, this can actually work in your favor.

Beware the dead fish. There's nothing more important than a sturdy handshake, and nothing makes a worse impression on interviewers than a candidate who gives the limp dead-fish handshake and won't look them in the eye. If you don't yet know how to give a perfect handshake, practice with someone you know who has a sturdy, confident handshake. Make sure you're able to walk into the interview head held high, look the interviewer in the eye, smile, and present a solid, firm handshake. This can make all the difference in an interview. First impressions really are everything, especially in a high-stakes interview.

Be overly prepared. I believe that when you are trying to negate a prejudice, the best defense is a good offense. Don't be afraid of overdoing it in the opposite direction so that whatever the issue, it quickly becomes a nonissue. In this case, I'm talking about looking overly responsible by being overly prepared. Bring extra copies of your résumé to hand out if asked. Have multiple copies of your professional references list. Have a professional-looking business notebook or portfolio so that you are ready to take notes—and take some. Ask for business cards from every person you meet so you can send thank-you letters with everyone's name spelled correctly. Have extra pens so you don't have to ask for one. Being overly prepared will make you look like the most conscientious candidate.

Being prepared to negate these hidden discriminations will help you move forward more quickly in your job search and your career without being unexpectedly sidelined, and will allow you to realize your dreams more quickly than others who haven't taken the time to learn these important secrets.

INSIDER SECRET 33
"No" may not mean "no."

THEY'VE DECIDED TO HIRE SOMEONE ELSE FOR THE POSITION. But is that a soft no? Or is that a hard-and-fast, never-contact-me-again no?

Think hearing a "no thank you" at the end of your interview process is the end? It's not. If you really want to work for this company, a no is just the beginning.

None of us ever want to hear that we didn't get the job, but it happens, especially considering the number of candidates and hopefuls for each position. When you are faced with this kind of letdown during a seemingly all-important career moment, it's important to know how to deal with it effectively.

"Amy" had a big interview with the company she'd always wanted to work for but was crushed when she heard via e-mail that she was out of the running. She had a choice to make. She could sulk and close the door on this opportunity altogether, or she could parlay the connections she'd made during this process into potential networking opportunities within the organization. She decided to work her new connections to continue to keep the door open within this company.

She sent a follow-up note to the hiring manager thanking her and emphasizing she'd love to be considered for any opportunities that might be a good fit down the road. She continued to send notes to this hiring manager every few months to check in and stay top-of-mind.

Amy had also made a connection with one of the people she'd interviewed with; they had attended the same university. She chose to contact this person after the interview process was over. Amy sent an e-mail saying she'd heard the position had been successfully filled but that she truly enjoyed connecting with someone from her university and would love to get together for lunch someday.

Amy did end up taking this person to lunch a few months later. Amy was careful not to mention the position or what may have gone wrong during the interview process, knowing it would make the person uncomfortable. They were able to make a successful connection and stayed in contact. Amy now had two contacts within the company she wanted to work for.

It was a year later that her lunch-date contact, knowing Amy was still interested in working for the company, saw an opening that matched her qualifications and forwarded the information to her before the job had been posted. Amy approached the same hiring manager she'd been keeping in touch with and asked her contact to put in a good word. After only one interview Amy was hired and was finally in her dream job.

Many times the first round of interviewing for the job of your dreams is just that, a first round. You don't need to take a no as the final answer. It can be just the beginning of your chance to make a connection with this company, and if you treat it as such, there's a chance you can create the opening you desire.

Now, there's definitely a right way and a wrong way to do this. Most people do it the wrong way. After hearing "no," they call the hiring manager and badger him or her about what went wrong in the process. They ask, "What could I have done differently?" or, "What would you recommend I learn to ensure a better outcome next time?" It's important to take the initial rejection with poise. Wish the company representatives well, thank them for the opportunity, and drop the issue. All those lingering questions you may have will make them very nervous, so keep your questions to yourself.

What you *can* do is keep the lines of communication open. This may be difficult at first, and it may take you a few tries before they realize you aren't going to corner them and ask why you weren't hired. But if you remain positive, confident, and enthusiastic about the company, you have a good chance of being considered for the next opening. You can also work the connections you've made during the interview process, so that when another opening arises you now have a great chance of being an actual internal recommendation for hire. It happens all the time.

There's also another good reason to keep yourself in the loop and continue to communicate with the people involved in the hire. It's related to a common and well-kept secret not too many in the hiring field like to talk about. **The truth is: Many new hires don't work out within the first ninety days and companies are then forced to find an emergency replacement.** Candidates who understand this and stay in touch are often the ones who get the job. As a hiring manager scrambles for a replacement, he or she will usually go to whoever is top-of-mind. If you've been keeping in touch and sending positive messages about working for the company, you have a good chance of being their go-to replacement. Why? Because as long as you have the credentials and skills necessary for the position, you are the easiest choice.

The trap most candidates fall into is to take that initial "no" personally, get upset by the news, and cut off all ties with the company. Don't let your pride keep you from a wonderful opportunity. You've met some very influential people within this organization during the interview process and can use those contacts as part of your networking opportunities.

In fact, there is a large Fortune 100 company that makes it a policy to turn down every single candidate who applies for a job in one particular department. Jobs in this department are so sought after in the industry that the company only wants to hire those who want to work there so badly that they come back after the "no" and keep trying. This company even turns down people who are highly qualified, just to see who is tenacious enough to keep coming back. Essentially, this company will only hire you if you've interviewed once before and been turned down.

The worst thing you can do in this scenario is get upset and ask questions that show a lack of confidence. The best thing you can do is be strong, keep communications open, and keep yourself as close to the "inside" as possible until the next opportunity arises. Hiring managers love to know they have qualified candidates in their back pocket who are enthusiastic about working for the company. This makes their job easier.

If you feel there's a gap in your qualifications that kept you from getting the offer, by all means fix it in the interim. In addition, with each new accomplishment or qualification you garner in the meantime, feel free to submit an updated résumé or send an e-mail to the hiring manager to let him or her know that you now have *x* new certification or skill.

If you believe you may have been turned down for a job due to a mistake you made during the interview process, you will want to work on getting your interview skills in top-notch form. But there's no need to disappear because you once heard the word "no." That little word may not be the end of things. It could actually be the beginning.

INSIDER SECRET 34
Interviewers don't hear what you say.

DO YOU THINK INTERVIEWERS ARE LISTENING TO WHAT you're saying? It sure looks like they are. But the truth is they aren't.

They are listening through a filter that influences everything they hear. This powerful filter can put an unwanted and even shocking spin on everything you say.

As you carefully answer their questions and try to appear confident, they are not listening to your actual words. Interviewers only hear what you say through their own filter of fears, concerns, and secret criteria.

You can't approach this meeting imagining the interviewer knows what a conscientious person you are, that you're a hard worker, a quick learner, and well-meaning. You have to say it. You have to illustrate it in your stories and showcase the qualities you want to get across in your answers, so that you can get through the interviewer's filter.

You must craft your answers to assuage the interviewers' fears and manage their potential interpretations. If you concentrate solely on sharing information, you may find yourself eliminated for something you didn't mean to convey. Interviewers are not listening to the information you share; they are crafting their own interpretation behind every answer you give.

Here's how it happens:

What You Said: "I'm a real people person!"

What the Interviewer Heard: *Oh no, another Chatty Cathy in the office. She'll be gossiping in the mail room instead of getting her work done.*

The Fix:

When you make a statement like this one, be aware of the possible interpretations. It's best to make comments like this in conjunction with your enjoyment of working on a team, bouncing ideas off others, or meeting and creating relationships with clients. When you make statements like the preceding one, put them in a work setting. For example: "I love working with dynamic people in a team environment." Don't just launch the idea that you're a people person and hope the interviewer will interpret it the way you intended.

What You Said: "I'm really looking forward to working here. My last company was so rigid, but this one seems really fun."

What the Interviewer Heard: *This guy might be a slacker who can't follow detailed directions or be held to high standards. He just wants to have "fun" and do things his way.*

The Fix:

Try putting comments like this into a work situation and stay away from making any negative comments about prior work environments or experiences. Instead, say, "I'm really looking forward to working here. It seems like you've created a wonderful company culture and an enjoyable work environment."

What You Said: "I'm looking forward to showing you all that I can do. I'm sure I will soon be taking on additional responsibilities, and one day I hope to be a vice president."

What the Interviewer Heard: *This person isn't going to be happy in this position very long; she's looking for something that this position can't currently give her.*

The Fix:

Avoid statements that show your ambitions. This is not the place for that. The company will decide if you're a good candidate for additional responsibility or future advancement. Talking like this will make it seem as though your ambitions lie beyond the position you're interviewing for and that you won't be happy in it. This means it won't be a successful placement for the interviewer. Try this: "I'm looking forward to working here and applying my skills and talents to this position. It's exactly what I've been looking for and I know you'll all be very pleased with the results."

What You Said: "Do you have medical benefits with 100 percent prescription coverage and that allow you to pick any doctor?"

What the Interviewer Heard: *Uh-oh, this candidate is asking detailed questions about the medical benefits. She may have some serious health issue. We can't just come out and ask if there's a problem, so we'd better not chance it.*

The Fix:

Let the human-resources person or interviewer voluntarily tell you about the benefits when the time is right. Don't ask. If it's not covered during the interviews, it will certainly be covered when an offer is made. When an offer is presented, casually ask if you can review the benefits book that's typically given to new hires—that way you don't have to ask anything specific and can even call the insurance carrier yourself to get specifics.

What You Said: "What? A personality test, an employment analysis test, and a drug test? What's all that for?"

What the Interviewer Heard: *This person is nervous about our testing. Maybe there's a reason he doesn't want to take a drug test. I'll have to look at this candidate more carefully—there may be a problem here.*

The Fix:

No matter what crazy tests a company asks you to take or tells you are part of the process, just smile and say, "Sure." Sometimes the company won't even administer the tests; they'll just mention them to see if you start to sweat. Unfortunately, tests like these are here to stay, and you'll have to take them with a smile if you want the job. (For resources on handling these stressful employment and personality tests, see the "Suggested Reading" section at the back of this book.)

What You Said: "What is the salary for this position? I really need to be making $52,000."

What the Interviewer Heard: *All this one cares about is money.*

The Fix:

If you've read Secret 28, you already know not to bring up money—even if it *is* the most important aspect of the job for you. Always wait until you get to the formal offer letter.

What You Said: "I hope you're not expecting me to hit the ground running and that you're going to provide some training on that proprietary software you mentioned so I can get up to speed on it."

What the Interviewer Heard: *This guy is insecure about the job. He's not sure if he can handle it.*

The Fix:

Try not to voice concerns you may have about the position during the interview process, even if it's something foreign to your abilities. It's always best to assume the company will provide whatever you need to get the job done. In most companies you will have a ninety-day buffer zone to get up to speed on everything. If you find you need training or help on something, that ninety-day period is the time to ask for it. During this time, the company will be most open to giving you what you need to become successful in your position—use it. If they aren't willing, for whatever reason, you will still have that ninety-day period to make it happen, during which most companies won't expect the highest production from you.

What You Said: "Will you be checking references?"

What the Interviewer Heard: *She must be nervous about her references. Maybe she's trying to hide something or hoping we don't find out about a certain issue in her past.*

The Fix:

Never ask about your references and certainly not what any of them may have said. Let the interviewer bring it up. It's always good to submit your list of professional references, but there's no need to comment or ask questions about them at any time during the process. If you do, it will make you look insecure or as if you're concerned about what may be said.

What You Said: "I must tell you I was terminated from my previous job, but I'm sure as soon as you hear the story you'll understand. . . ."

What the Interviewer Heard: *Other companies don't think she's a safe bet for continued employment. She must have done something wrong. I certainly don't want this hire recommendation to end the same way—in a messy termination. Better not risk it.*

The Fix:

This was another little pop quiz. If you read Secret 31, then you know hiring managers' fears will keep them from ever recommending a candidate with a prior termination on his or her record. Disclosing something like this will always knock you out of the running, no matter what the actual circumstances. Don't ever mention a previous termination or any other problems you've had in the past. Even if you have a solid explanation as to why it happened, don't volunteer the information. In most cases, the interviewer will not be able to find out, and if you present your prior employment history in the most positive light possible, most interviewers will assume everything went well and not even check.

What You Said: "I'm a real self-starter and like autonomy."

What the Interviewer Heard: *This person is most likely not a team player.*

The Fix:

Be sure you answer questions to the interviewer's fears, not your strengths. In an answer like this, you could easily avoid misinterpretation by following up your comment of enjoying autonomy immediately with one about teamwork. For example: "I enjoy working on a team but am also known as a self-starter and can work independently when necessary."

What You Said: "I'd prefer you not contact that particular company for a reference; I'm currently in the middle of a lawsuit against them for sexual harassment."

What the Interviewer Heard: *Oh no, this one is litigious. Next!*

The Fix:

Don't ever volunteer in an interview that you have ever filed any kind of legal claim against an employer or are in the middle of one. Even if it pertains to your career history, reason for leaving a company, or directly to your job search, don't disclose it. No matter what the circumstances, any kind of confession regarding a legal entanglement with a prior employer will be the end of your interview and the end of the opportunity.

What You Said: "I'm really organized. In fact, everyone comments on it. I'm involved in this very detailed and complex claim against the home owners association, and everyone continues to comment on how amazingly organized I am and how much it's helped the case."

What the Interviewer Heard: *This one is litigious. Next!*

The Fix:

You may think that because it's a personal legal entanglement it's okay to share. Not true. Even personal legal issues will act as red flags to an interviewer. This includes being a participant in a large class-action lawsuit, a medical lawsuit, or even a custody battle. Those issues are personal and should stay private if you want the job.

What You Said: "I heard your company is family friendly. Do you offer on-site day care?"

What the Interviewer Heard: *This person is just looking for a babysitter. She's not really interested in the position or working for this company. Maybe she'd rather be home with her kids than here working for the company.*

The Fix:

Day care and other personal interests, even if they are perks and/or benefits offered by the company, are the kinds of things you should always sleuth out on your own. Questions like this should not be asked during an interview or you could risk misinterpretation and/or giving your personal issues magnified importance. If the company offers benefits like this, they will tell you all about them when an offer is close to being made. Companies are very proud of their benefits, so you don't have to worry about them keeping these things secret during their hiring sales pitch.

What You Said: "What are your company or personal management philosophies? I had a bad experience once with a micromanager."

What the Interviewer Heard: *This one can't get along with management. If hired, this candidate could be a wild card on the team. Better not chance it.*

The Fix:

Sharing that you've had a problem with a prior boss, for whatever reason, will end your opportunity. Just because you had a bad experience once with a prior boss doesn't mean it will happen again. To conduct a successful interview, you have to give all the players at this new company the benefit of the doubt. There will be no way for you to tell what the company's management style truly is, so there is no point in asking. Even if you are able to interview with the person who would be your new boss, all you can do is look for clues that might give away his or her style and philosophy in the things he or she chooses to talk about, emphasize, and ask during the interview itself. But an interview is not a safe place to talk about such things.

What You Said: "What are your work hours?"

What the Interviewer Heard: *Uh-oh, this candidate doesn't want to put in the hours.*

The Fix:

Wait for the interviewer to volunteer this kind of information, or ask when you get the formal offer. Even if you've had a bad experience with being overworked that you'd like to avoid at your next job, asking about it will only weaken your position as a candidate. As in Secret 24, you can't let companies know that you're openly screening them—they don't like that. You have to be more subtle and look for clues that show whether or not this is a good place for you.

What You Said: "I'm a perfect fit for this job and I can start right away."

What the Interviewer Heard: *Right away? This person may be desperate and may not have any other opportunities. If he's not that busy or in demand, maybe he's not the candidate I thought he was.*

The Fix:

You always want to seem busy and desired. So don't offer that you don't have anything going on and can start right away. Let the company tell you they need you right away and then you can respond with, "I'll see what I can do to move things around and start earlier for you."

What You Said: "I was so happy to get your call; the job market has been really tough. It's been hard for me to find something."

What the Interviewer Heard: *This is obviously not a desirable candidate; no matter what the economy, sought-after employees are always hired quickly. Better move on to the next candidate.*

The Fix:

Don't ever let on that you've had a hard time finding a job. If you've been out of work for a period of time and the interviewer asks you about it, give as positive a response as possible and make it seem like this was your choice: "I took some time to travel," "wanted to get some additional certifications," "always wanted to train for the big marathon," "wanted to take my time to look for just the right placement." Don't share overly personal information or anything that might put you in the danger category, such as medical issues or familial upheavals. A positive response can make this gap in employment a nonissue. There is no such thing as a bad job economy for a sought-after candidate.

Believe it or not, this is what interviewers really think in these situations. But I'm not presenting this to make you second-guess everything you say during an interview or turn you into a nervous wreck. I'm merely presenting it so that you go into your interviews with heightened awareness. Being aware of interviewers' tendency to hear with their fears instead of their ears will help you craft better answers and help you avoid any potential misunderstandings or misinterpretations.

INSIDER SECRET 35
Recruiters must be managed.

THERE IS A DEBATE GOING ON AMONG JOB SEEKERS TODAY AS to whether recruiters are a help or a hindrance in the job search process. Well, they're a little bit of both.

Recruiters can be very helpful in your job search. They tend to have jobs that aren't available or advertised anywhere else. Many are the exclusive hiring portals for the most sought-after companies. They can act as your advocate in the process, help you with your résumé, tell you exactly what to say and do to give you the best shot at being hired, and they are free—to you. They get paid by the company once you've been hired (usually paid on a percentage of the starting salary). This means they also tend to be great negotiators to get you top dollar.

If a company wants you, recruiters can move heaven and earth to make it happen to your satisfaction with all the best benefits and highest salary, without you having to do any of the dirty work.

All of these things would dictate that you should always use recruiters as a key function of your job search process.

However, recruiters must be carefully managed. You will need to treat recruiters just as you would regular hiring managers, giving them the same information and presenting the same image you would in a standard interview. Don't believe you can present yourself one way to the recruiter and another way to the company hiring manager and get the job. This recruiter is acting as your advocate but is also looking for the same things that a hiring manager is screening for: protection, a safe bet for hire, the most qualified candidate, and the right image.

Many people have had their confidence shaken by the advertising tactics recruiters use. Don't let that worry you. That's how they make their business work. Recruiters will place ads of their own for top job listings they know are out there. Those may be for job openings with clients they represent, or not. Those ads are designed to bring you in the door and get you to sign up with their recruiting firm. It is their way of recruiting you, so they can place you. If they don't have lots of qualified candidates to present to their clients, they don't make any money. So they place ads that entice you to call them and send in your résumé for representation.

Why won't they tell you what company they're sending your résumé to? Because they don't want you sending it in yourself, cutting them out of the loop. If they are the ones who found you and represent you to the company, they will be the ones who get paid.

Recruiters are kind of like real estate agents. The name of the game, unless the recruiter you're working with has an exclusive contract with a company, is that the first person who gets the placement wins. Companies usually work with several recruiters at once. That means your recruiter will only get paid if he places one of his represented candidates in that position. If another recruiter places someone else first, your recruiter is out quite a bit of money and he has to start all over again with another job opening.

Recruiters can be wonderful advocates for you, but this rush to placement in order for them to get paid can also create issues you need to be aware of. Often recruiters will pressure a candidate to take a job they know is not a good fit because they want the money. This is the major factor that can work against you, but understanding how this system works will allow you to evaluate every opportunity on its own merits and understand where the overwhelming pressure from your recruiter to take one of his or her jobs is coming from.

You need to make the choice that's best for you, even if it goes against what the recruiter wants you to do. It is ultimately your decision. Don't let a recruiter tell you there may be legal consequences, or that you are doing something unethical by turning down one of his jobs. Working with a recruiter does not obligate you to take one of his client openings. If a recruiter gets nasty or acts unprofessionally toward you over a decision like this, I suggest you move on and not work with this individual or recruiting firm in the future.

Even though the recruiter relationship can get a bit sticky at times, it is always a good idea to work with a few recruiters in your search. They operate at no cost to you, they can greatly increase your effectiveness, and most are highly conscientious, ethical, hardworking individuals who will support your job search efforts.

It's true that there are some unscrupulous recruiters out there, but it's rare. If during the process you begin to sense that something strange is going on, it's best to quickly move on and not work with that particular recruiter again.

However, there is one thing you must always remember. Once you have sent your résumé to a recruiter for a particular position, once you've agreed to have him represent you to a company, he is your representative for that job. You cannot approach that company on your own after that. You can only pursue that particular job opening through the recruiter who represented you and sent in your résumé. This is serious. A recruiter will rightfully respond very strongly to such an act, and you run the risk of potentially being blacklisted by the entire recruiting industry in your area.

Now, if all the recruiter did was call you about a potential job, but you never followed up with him, never sent him your résumé, and never allowed him to represent you for the position at that company, then you have no formal relationship and are free to submit your résumé to the opportunity on your own. This is why most recruiters won't tell you what the position or company is until you agree to have them represent you.

What if you get an unscrupulous corporate hiring manager who wants you to resubmit your résumé without your recruiter because the company doesn't want to pay the commission fee? Don't do it. This is not ethical, and this is not a company you want to work for.

INSIDER SECRET 36
Your inner voice is not as silent as you think.

WE ALL TEND TO BELIEVE THAT WHAT GOES ON IN OUR HEADS and what we tell ourselves in silence stays inside.

The secret is: Interviewers can hear it. What you're telling yourself with your inner voice comes through in every stage of your job search process.

When you have negative or insecure self-talk constantly running through your head, it will tend to govern the tone of your cover letters, e-mails, phone screenings, and interviews. You may have the right skills and say all the right things, but the hiring manager will sense that something key is missing.

What's missing is that the candidate hasn't yet been able to align his or her inner voice with his or her outer voice.

Hiring managers can hear "your inner game" loud and clear, and an interviewer and hiring manager can spot when your inner game is not in tune with what you're saying, because the way you present yourself will feel "off."

Interviewers will say things like "This cover letter lacks confidence," or "I don't know what it was, but it felt like the candidate didn't believe what she was telling me," or "He didn't seem to match what he was saying," or "It seemed like she was just telling me what I wanted to hear."

Athletes practice their inner game on a regular basis. They visualize making baskets, knocking out their opponent, running touchdowns, over and over again in their heads. They don't allow negative images or negative self-talk to creep in because they know what would happen if they did. Negative things would happen in their game.

Athletes don't visualize and imagine for fun; they do it for a very specific reason—it greatly increases their chance of success. If you listen to the athletes who do their self-talk out loud, you know they don't tell themselves they hope their game goes well and they don't mess up. They tell themselves they're "the best in the world, the top, the greatest, the champ!" They do this to get their inner game in line with their outer game. That synergy can create magic, especially when the pressure's on.

When you go into a job search, you may be saying all the right things with your outer voice. But if your inner voice is saying things like *I know I'm not the best candidate, I wish I had more experience, I hope I don't mess this up, I don't understand why I keep losing job after job,* the hiring manager will pick up on it. It will show in your correspondence, tone of voice, facial expression, body language, and even the way you answer questions. In fact, when the pressure's on is when these silent messages tend to shine through the most.

Aligning your inner game can be one of the most powerful things you can do to improve your interview skills. It will show through in everything you say, the way you shake hands, the sparkle in your eye, and all the little things that interviewers pick up on for clues to see if you're really the winner you appear to be.

So how do you make this happen? You start by becoming aware of negative self-talk and consciously breaking those thought habits. The most important step is awareness. Sit down and write out all the thoughts you're having about your job search. It's okay to be honest; no one will see this but you. Write down both the negative and the positive things going through your head on a daily basis.

When you put these thoughts on paper, you will start to notice two very important things: One is that when you're done with your list, you'll see that certain negative messages tend to repeat themselves. They run like a broken record, a habit inside your head. In fact, many negative messages are just the same thing over and over again said in different ways. The second thing you'll notice is that most of these messages, once you see them on paper in the light of day, don't seem to make sense. Negative self-talk is usually based on irrational fears, and when you write them down, their power starts to wane. Sometimes these once powerful messages can even seem laughable. This exercise can help break the mesmeric hold your negative inner dialogue can have over you.

Once you practice this exercise, it will be much easier to be aware of negative thought patterns so you can reverse them.

For example:

> **Negative thought-habit:** I'll never find a job.
>
> **Reversal:** I'm a great catch! There's a company out there looking for someone just like me.

A great way to get your inner game on is to start each day with a barrage of positive statements about your career and job search. It's a great way to build confidence and get ready to go into an interview. Before each interview, sit for a moment and go over your top ten best qualities as an employee, along with your career success stories, so they're top-of-mind. Then say to yourself, *I'm a great catch and a great employee! I'm going to ace this interview and show them I'm the perfect candidate for the job.* Imagine yourself in the interview doing and saying all the right things. Imagine it going the very best it possibly could. Imagine the interviewer making you an offer right there on the spot. Keep going over that positive vision until you feel like it's the dominant one in your head.

Your inner voice and vision will now be able to support you and your efforts as you go into the meeting, and you'll look and sound like the confident candidate you have every right to be!

INSIDER SECRET 37
You can tell when you're "in" or "out."

ONE OF THE BIGGEST STRESS FACTORS IN ANY JOB SEARCH IS trying to tell, through the various phases, how you're doing. Can you tell by how quickly they return your phone call? By the people they ask you to meet? By things they say in the interview? Yes, you can.

There are secret clues, known only by insiders, that will tell you how you're doing at each phase of the job search process. I'll give you the signs to look for, as well as the false positives that can trick you into thinking you're doing better than you really are. I'll even explain why companies sometimes disappear into noncommunication for 2–3 weeks after the interview is completed and why it's not necessarily a bad thing.

Rather than staring at the phone willing it to ring with good news, or racking your brain with questions like *Are they checking references or typing a "no thank you" letter?* these insider secrets will give you some guidelines to go by.

Will my résumé get a response? Hiring managers are too busy to respond to every résumé submission, so don't count on it. If they liked your résumé, you will get a phone call. If not, you will usually get nothing at all.

How quick did they respond? When you send in your résumé and you get a phone call, it absolutely means the company is interested. That is a very good thing, but you shouldn't read too much into it. It's too early in the process for that. Whether they made you wait two minutes or two weeks, if you've gotten a call, they like you enough to continue the process. That's all you're really looking for at this point. Some people feel the speed at which a company calls after getting your résumé will tell you where you stand in the process. It's true that it can tell you how strong your résumé is, but sometimes the person doing the hiring simply had other more pressing matters that kept him or her from going through the résumés right away. And even if yours was the strongest résumé in the pile, the face-to-face interviews are ten times more important. A résumé is designed to get the phone to ring and that interview to be scheduled. If you've achieved that, you're good to go. That's all you need to know.

Did the interviewer sound enthusiastic? On receiving that initial phone call, many try to discern where they stand in the process by how enthusiastic the interviewer sounds on the phone. Again, this might be a little premature. It's certainly a good sign if your interviewer sounds interested and enthusiastic, and it can mean good things. But the very fact that he or she has taken time out of a busy schedule to call you in person means he or she is interested. Whether or not the interviewer still feels that way at the end of the call may be another matter. If the call itself leads to the scheduling of another phone call or a face-to-face interview, then you can get excited. That is the best sign you'll get that the company is interested.

Did they schedule an interview? Companies don't schedule expensive and time-consuming in-person interviews unless they are very interested in you as a top candidate. Most companies only interview in-person their top three hopefuls out of hundreds, sometimes even thousands, of résumés. Whether you are interviewing with a company just down the street or a plane ride away, having key people take time from their work to meet with you is expensive. If several key people have been scheduled for you to meet, then it means the company is very, very interested. Sometimes the initial phone screening will end with talk of a face-to-face interview, sometimes not. Don't let the fact that the initial phone call didn't lead immediately to an interview ruffle your feathers. Often the initial phone screenings are completed with all hopefuls in the résumé pile, then decisions are made separately on whom to call for personal interviews. If an interview is scheduled, you've done very well. But it's not over yet.

Did you progress through the process? When you've done the initial in-person interview, many times you can tell how you're doing if you progress through the various levels and additional meetings. If you are introduced to others within the company or if you find yourself in an interview with another key player or member of the team, it means you've been doing well and the interviewer was inspired to have you meet with others while you were there. Another good sign is if the interview goes longer than expected. If an interview ends after only fifteen or twenty minutes, that's usually not a good sign (unless it's one of the tactics I described in

Secret 19). However, if it continues with additional people being brought in or you get invited to lunch to continue talking, those are great signs.

Did you meet the crew? A spontaneous tour that shows you where you'd be working and introduces you to team members can be a good sign but can also give you a false positive. Candidates have become overly excited because meeting the people they'd be working with is usually something done only once hired. There can also be misinterpretation during these types of tours if the interviewer uses "you." For example: "This is where *you'll* be sitting; this is one of the people *you'll* be working with." This kind of language and these kinds of tours can happen at various stages, but they do not mean that you are the final choice, so try not to get too excited by this kind of thing. The tour can be a very positive sign that you're a top candidate or could merely be the nervous tactic of someone who doesn't know how to conduct an interview. Untrained interviewers spend their time trying to sell candidates on the company rather than screening them properly. Unfortunately, this can give the impression that you're doing better than you really are. So take this one with a grain of salt.

Did they talk about salary or benefits? Everyone gets excited when there's talk of compensation and benefits, but it doesn't mean you're close to an offer. When an interviewer says, "How do you feel about *x* dollars per year?" she's not making you an offer. She's testing the waters to make sure you are within their established salary range. In fact, many interviewers open discussions of compensation early on either to weaken your position to negotiate later should an offer be extended or to find out which candidates would help their financial incentives and which wouldn't. Even though this can be exciting, it's best not to get cornered into a discussion about compensation before an actual offer is submitted and it's best not to read too much into it.

Did they check references? Now, this is not something hiring managers do lightly. This one means you are at least in the top three, if not *the* top candidate. It takes time to check references, and it is only done for the very top candidates. You will have to find out from your references if they were called. You should never ask the company or you will seem too desperate or, even worse, like you may have something you feel nervous about or are trying to hide. But if you find out that references have been called, that's a great sign. In fact, unless your references have been called, no matter what the company representatives say, there is no offer on the way.

Did they disappear? This is by far the scariest part of any interview process. Most candidates believe that when a company stops communicating, it means they are no longer interested. Not necessarily so. If you never hear from them again after you submit your résumé, after the initial screening, or after your in-person interview, it means they have chosen someone else, but sometimes a company will stop communicating with you when they've decided to offer you the job.

Often, when a company finds their top candidate, a strange thing happens. They relax. The stress is over, because they've found "the one." Things slow down from the previous pace. The urgency is gone, and the person in human resources who has been tasked with putting together the final paperwork is distracted by other matters. Too many candidates have misinterpreted this silence and accidentally ruined their chances by sending nasty e-mails, making angry phone calls, or exhibiting a variety of other bad behavior under the mistaken belief that the offer had been pulled. Needless to say, these people did not get the offer that was previously headed their way.

So, should things fall silent, just keep on with your job search and give the company the benefit of the doubt. No matter how good the signs, you should never stop your job search to wait for an offer that may or may not arrive. However, don't assume that silence always means the company is not interested. It's not over until you get that e-mail or letter that says no thanks. And even then it may not be over, as laid out in Secret 33. The secret is that a slowdown can be a standard reaction when the company has found their top candidate. There's nothing to do but wait it out.

Did they send you a formal offer in writing? This is the only real sign that will absolutely tell you for sure. Not a verbal discussion of an offer but the actual piece of paper with a place for you to sign. If you're dealing with a company that only gives verbal offers, make sure you get at least an outline of the offer sent to you via e-mail so you have something to review before accepting (and so you have something in writing for your files). Now you're in.

At this point, the next logical question must be raised: Can you make an offer come faster? Sure you can! If you believe there's a potential offer coming your way or you think you're the top candidate, you can speed up the process, but it involves having another offer on the table. This is why having multiple interested parties and multiple offers can be such an asset for your job search.

It is perfectly acceptable to call the company (I wouldn't recommend initiating a call during the interviewing or hiring process for anything other than this) and say that there is another company that has made an offer and would like an answer within the next few weeks, but that the company you're calling is your first choice.

I'm a believer in making sure the company that is your first choice knows it. I know that makes some feel that they've tipped their hand, but companies love to hear they are your first choice and they're the one you want to work for.

Most companies will put things in swift motion to get you the offer letter if they know you have a decision to make regarding another opportunity—if in fact you are their top candidate. If they don't jump or if they say something like "Well, you have to do what you think is best for you," then chances are they are not as interested in you as you were hoping or their final decisions are still very far off.

I would highly caution you not to do this as a bluff. You should always have another company on the line if you try to use this tactic. I have seen a few candidates try to bluff their way through this with success, but it's a big gamble to take and one that I would not recommend. It can end badly when the company you're looking to get an offer from lags on its deadline and you have to explain why you're still hanging around. No one is going to believe that you've turned down an offer-in-hand for one that's just a potential offer. Then they'll know you were just bluffing, which is never good.

Not only will having another offer and another company interested in you make you look more desirable; it will also help you negotiate for a higher salary by allowing you to leverage the two offers against each other. This is easily and effectively done by using a variation of the negotiation tactics specified in Secret 28. For example: "I greatly appreciate your offer, but I've unexpectedly received an offer from another company. Yours is definitely my first choice, but they've offered me twenty percent more compensation and a larger yearly bonus; *is there anything else we can do here* on compensation?" (Remember, one item at a time. Even though you're hoping for movement on both compensation *and* bonus, it's most effective to wait until you get them to move on compensation, then ask about the bonus.) Job seekers who find themselves in the enviable position of having two offers on the table usually get everything they want. Even if they don't, they still enter with much higher respect than others, and the company will always see them as a sought-after commodity and a great catch. This is a good way to enter!

Whenever job seekers don't go forward with a particular interview because they aren't sure they're interested in the company, they may be missing a key opportunity. You never know what magic may occur, and your job search can only be helped with multiple suitors.

A job search can certainly be a wild ride, but at least you now have a few insider tips to help guide your emotions through the process.

INSIDER SECRET 38
Your dream job is here.

DO YOU HAVE YOUR DREAM JOB? ARE YOU LOOKING FOR IT? You should be. It's out there. And at no other time in history has it been so easy to find.

People are always talking about their "dream job," but how many people do you know who have it? Not too many. So why do so many people talk about it and so few achieve it? **The truth is: Most people don't try for their dream job.** It's not because their dream job doesn't exist; it's because most people don't know how to go about finding it.

Your dream job is not just something you stumble over; it must be carefully crafted.

I have the four "Cs" that will help you land your dream job: Courage, Clarity, Craft, and Consistency.

1. Courage: To find your dream job you have to be unwilling to settle for less. If you allow yourself to stay in a job you don't love and doesn't meet your needs simply because it's there, it's stable, and it's safe, then your chances of finding your dream job will be slim. It takes courage to go for your dream job. And it's not something you find overnight. If you are willing to just go for it, you'll be amazed at what you can find.

2. Clarity: I'm always surprised by how few people can articulate what their dream job really is. What industry is it in? What position would it be? What kind of company culture would it have? This is easily determined by taking the best aspects of the companies you've worked for and positions you've had, and boiling them down to your ideal so you'll recognize it when you see it. If you don't take time to hone your awareness and make a list of things you're looking for, you will miss it when it appears.

Don't get too caught up in the "dream job" title. It doesn't have to be something overly grand or something you've always wanted to do since you were little. It can be something as simple as doing what makes you happy. It may be exactly what you're doing now but with certain lifestyle options that can make all the difference. Would you love to work for a company with casual dress, have your dog in the office with you, have your kids down the hall in day care, work part-time, or work in a part of the country you've always wanted to live? There are online job search sites out there that have done all the work for you to help you hone your job search to the lifestyle choices that will make you happy. (See the resources section at the back of this book.) Don't let the idea of a dream job scare you. Your personal idea of a dream job could be right around the corner with everything you've always wanted.

3. Craft: If you don't have the skills or qualifications for your dream job, you'll need to craft your career path and professional choices to draw your dream job closer to you. If your dream job requires special certifications, experience, or foundational positions in your background, craft your career path so that your résumé shows all those requirements and makes you look like the dream candidate.

4. Consistency: Most people look for their dream job when they find themselves in between jobs. They don't really believe they'll find their dream job, but they look for it anyway at the same time they're looking for a "regular" job. This is a very common mistake. It's very hard to find your dream job when you're under the gun, worried about paying your rent, or worried about how long you've been out of work. When you're under that kind of pressure, it's difficult to take chances and it's not conducive to letting magic happen.

The best way to find your dream job is to get as specific as possible about what you're looking for and then always be looking for it. Keep a constant passive job search going with your criteria in mind. You never know when the magic job will materialize. Your dream job could come when you least expect it. But the chances of you finding it during the few stress-filled months you were out of work and looking for a job to pay the bills are slim.

If you are poised, ready, clear about what you want, and constantly looking, your chances of being one of the few to actually land your dream job are very good indeed. While others are just wishing, you will have it!

DANGER! TRAPS AHEAD!
KEY POINTS TO REMEMBER

SECRET 25: WHAT'S OUT THERE? Find out what your public records have to say about you. Companies are doing regular background checks on their candidates. If you aren't sure about what's out there with your name and information on it, find out!

SECRET 26: "THIS IS NOT A GOOD TIME." When a hiring manager calls you at home, on the road, or at dinnertime, pay attention to your surroundings and the time of the call. It could be a trap.

SECRET 27: DON'T QUIT. Many candidates think it will help their job search to quit the job they have. Don't do it. It will lessen your chances to get the top job and top salary you want.

SECRET 28: ALWAYS NEGOTIATE. You may think that deciding not to negotiate for higher benefits and a better salary makes you look like an agreeable candidate, but you are actually doing harm to your new job. Those who negotiate tend to be much more successful in their new jobs than those who don't. The trick is learning how to negotiate effectively and safely, so you don't jeopardize your new job offer.

SECRET 29: WANT AN EMPLOYMENT CONTRACT? No you don't. Those can too often be used against you. There is another tool, hiding in plain sight, that will provide all the protection you're looking for without any of the drawbacks.

SECRET 30: "I HAVE THREE KIDS; GIVE ME LESS MONEY." Candidates who disclose their parental status in the interview process are being discriminated against. And when hired, they are being hired for less money than others.

SECRET 31: "BEFORE WE GET STARTED, THERE'S SOMETHING YOU SHOULD KNOW. . . ." Many of us feel compelled or have been told that we should share past problems or terminations in an interview—put it right up front to control the information that the interviewer will surely get soon enough. Don't ever do it.

SECRET 32: FIGHT AGE DISCRIMINATION. It's happening in the hiring process to both older and younger workers. But, oddly enough, it's not about your actual age; it's about how old you appear, how you present yourself, and what you choose to say. If you avoid the common statements and behaviors that scare an interviewer, you will get hired no matter what your age.

SECRET 33: IS THAT A "NO"? A "no" may not be the end. Even if you were turned down for the job you wanted, you now have the perfect resources to get the job the next time around. Don't let one no discourage you. It's not the end; it's the beginning.

SECRET 34: INTERVIEWERS DON'T HEAR YOU. It's true that interviewers don't hear what you say in an interview. They don't listen with their ears; they listen with their fears. This can have some shocking and unintended results during an interview if you aren't careful.

SECRET 35: SHOULD I CALL A RECRUITER? The answer is yes. They can be very helpful in the process, but they must also be carefully managed. You need to understand how this process works so you can make the most of the opportunity without getting burned.

SECRET 36: "I'LL NEVER GET A JOB." It may only be in your head, but your negative self-talk is not as silent as you think. It shines through everything from cover letters to your handshake. Get your inner voice in line with your outer voice so interviewers get a cohesive message and they see you as the winner you are.

SECRET 37: AM I "IN" OR "OUT"? There are ways to tell whether you're truly "in" or "out" throughout the entire hiring process. Don't allow yourself to get excited over something that looks good but really means nothing, and don't get upset over a sign that's easily misinterpreted and may not be as bad as you think. Learn how to read the complex signs of the job search process from the inside so you know for sure how you're doing at each stage of the process.

SECRET 38: DREAM JOB, ANYONE? Your dream job is out there, and you can have it. There are four simple steps to finding the job of your dreams. So what are you waiting for?

5

YOU'RE HIRED. NOW WHAT?

IT IS ALWAYS EXCITING TO START THAT NEW JOB. A NEW opportunity, a fresh start, the beginning of potentially great things. But there is another secret as you step into this opportunity that most new hires aren't aware of: Your new job is not secure.

If you want to be successful in your new job, if you want this to be the beginning of great achievements instead of great disappointments, specific steps must be taken immediately to secure your position. And certain things must be avoided at all costs or you will be right back in a job search.

The truth is: When you accept a new job, you are vulnerable for the first 90 to 180 days. What you choose to do in those first 180 days, and how you choose to behave, will determine your overall success with your new company.

A common mistake new hires make is they allow their excitement over a new job to cloud their necessity to protect it.

Accepting a new job is something to celebrate. You have been selected from many candidates for this job. But if you want this to be a winning placement and a solid new step in your career, this is not the time to relax.

Most employees enter into their new jobs focused on fitting in, finding the coffee room, and getting up to speed on the work at hand. This will unfortunately ensure that you look like the standard dime-a-dozen employee whom the company can work to the bone and discard at will. One of those soon-to-be invisible employees who put in the long hours, do everything they are supposed to, but never receive the rewards that were promised.

Those who believe they can relax once they get a new job, thinking that because they're new no one will be expecting great things right away, are doing their career a huge disservice. You have one window in which to set your career with this company, determining either high success or potential failure. If you spend that critical time slacking off, locating the lunchroom, and organizing your paper clips, you will experience the latter.

The truth is: Critical opinions are being formed within the first 90–180 days of your employment that will stick with you for your entire career with this company and beyond.

Within every company there is always an unwritten list of indispensable employees, the ones who are rewarded, are protected, and continue to move forward no matter what. There's another secret list of employees the company wouldn't mind losing. They are the ones who are worked the hardest for the fewest rewards. If the company loses one, they will simply get another—they are dispensable. Which list do you think you typically fall into? Which one do you want to be in?

That will all be determined by the choices you make when you first arrive.

INSIDER SECRET 39
The spotlight is on.

THROUGHOUT YOUR CAREER, THE SPOTLIGHT WILL BE ON you for very short periods of time. It's usually impossible to predict when it will happen because companies don't usually want you to know about it. But when that spotlight does hit, what happens next will become the defining moments of your career.

Here's the secret: When you enter a new company, the spotlight is always on. You can bet on it. You need to make it count.

You won't feel this spotlight, but it's there. When you enter a new company, there's a tendency to feel quite invisible, so it's easy to believe that no one is paying close attention to you.

When you first start, everyone seems to be in a rhythm you can't quite get a hold on yet. They're all working on their own projects, and they all seem to be comfortable in an environment that's foreign to you. All this can make you feel out of sync with the rest of the organization, which will make you feel invisible. In actuality, the exact opposite is happening. Key people are watching you with unseen eyes, to determine what kind of company commodity you truly are.

Why would they be so interested in you among all others working there? Because with each new hire a company secretly hopes it has engaged its newest savior, the person who will infuse the company with success and be the next rising star. Think this is only for the higher-level hires? It's not. This spotlight goes on when any new hire arrives, at any level, because nobody knows where the company's newest success savior may come from.

All eyes will be on you whether you feel them or not. But this critical spotlight is only on for a very short time. It's typically focused on you for between 90 and 180 of your first days. If the company determines you are just one of the typical dispensable employees, the spotlight will shut off early. If you look like you might have potential, the spotlight can stay on for up to the first six months of your new job. At the end of that time, critical judgments are set and will stay that way.

Knowing this, there are four things you should do immediately and consistently to make the best of this fleeting time in the career spotlight.

Overdeliver. Ever had the feeling that you're working harder than anyone else, but nobody's watching? Well, this time they are. This is one time when going the extra mile will most definitely get you somewhere. If you never do it any other time in your career, this is the time to go in early, stay late, work longer hours, go the extra distance on those first few projects. Do not take a vacation. Do not get caught gossiping with your new co-workers in the coffee room. Do not leave early for a doctor's appointment. This is your one opportunity to solidify your image as the ideal employee. This spotlight period is so powerful for new hires that if you've overdelivered and worked harder than others during your first 90–180 days on the job, you can actually ramp back down to a regular work level and the company won't notice. The company will have a set impression of you as the hardest-working, most dedicated employee. The opinions formed during your first few months on the job will stick, even if your work output goes back to a regular or even lower-than-normal output level once the spotlight has dimmed.

Be positive. One of the most powerful things a new hire can do is give voice to positive statements. Companies are hungry for positive employees. They believe positive people will draw success to the organization. Positive behavior and statements are highly prized and will give you a natural air of success. Pessimists, or "realists," who feel they should hold back and see how this new company treats them before saying anything nice about it, are missing a key opportunity. During this critical time, if you exhibit a standoffish approach or give voice to any negative opinions, you will be seen as a potentially negative or even unsuccessful force within the company.

Companies look at your positive statements and approach very carefully. In fact, it's the number one secret determinant they use to tell whether you're going to be key to the company's overall success or not. Companies are afraid of negativity; they know it's contagious and it will cost them success. They love the positive. They know highly positive statements are also contagious and will uplift the company and draw in success.

The more positively you behave and sound, the more you will be seen as a magnet for success within the team and organization. Feel free to openly say how much you like the company, how excited you are to work there, and openly share the things you like about your new boss and co-workers. Keep silent about your concerns. Most of us do exactly the opposite. We tend to stay silent when we're happy with something but get very outspoken when unhappy. You have to reverse this tendency to be successful.

Stay away from any openly negative employees you encounter. You don't want to be seen with them, especially within your first 90–180 days. These people tend to seek out new hires to let them know about all the terrible injustices at the company, and I'm sure they feel they're doing you a great service. But what they don't realize (or maybe they do) is that just being in the presence of an openly negative employee will get you lumped in with them in the minds of key decision makers. And your rise to company stardom can be over just that quickly. Once key decision makers think you may have been poisoned by negativity, the spotlight will shut off. It's that serious. Steer clear of these people and stay as positive as possible. "I actually like it here; I think this is a great place to work" is all you need to say. Don't worry about being "unpopular" with the negative group; this could actually save your job and your upward mobility. Don't worry about being the only person openly sharing a positive voice in a mostly negative environment; it will simply make you stand out even more as the star you are.

Find out what's important. A common mistake new hires make is doing things their own way. You immediately do things the way you think they should be done, doing what you think is most important, instead of finding out what's most important to your boss and to the company. Doing things the way you think they should be done instead of asking how the company or your new boss likes them done will make you immediately seem out of sync with the values and success of the organization. It will put you on the outs before you even get started.

You may know things can be done better than current practices allow. These things do tend to be easier to see as an outsider coming in. But your first few months on the job are not the time to try to change these practices or express your views.

Rather than helping the company, you will be seen as someone who disrespects the established systems, thinks he or she knows better than others who've been working there awhile, and is competitive with others. Only express how you think things could be done more efficiently and how you like to work after you've been with the company for at least six months—when the spotlight is off. That is the proper amount of time necessary to show respect for the current practices and policies before suggesting anything different. Voicing your opinions or going off and doing things the way you think they should be done will do nothing but make you look like a threat, instead of an asset.

Here's the secret: If you take the time during your spotlight period to find out what's most important to the company, your boss, and your co-workers, you will be seen immediately as a valued team member. The company's image of you is what's most important when you first enter.

If you don't want to step on any toes or activate competition against you, you should focus on learning the company's systems and policies with no commentary during your first six months. This is a critical sign of respect that will open the doors to your future with this company. And it must be continued for the full six months in order for you to be trusted by key decision makers and co-workers.

Create a partnership with your boss. Your spotlight time is the best opportunity you'll have to create a solid partnership with your boss, the most powerful gatekeeper in your career. This individual will be the only one who determines the quality of your career path. The type of projects you get, your job security, your compensation, and how the company views you are all tied up in your boss's opinion of you. That opinion will be formed and set during your first few months on the job.

It's critical that you show respect for this key gatekeeper, support him or her in daily work life, and find out what he or she likes and values. Those personal likes and values are what should now be at the top of your priority list.

One of the hardest things for new hires to understand is that doing what's of value to you is not what will get you the rewards you seek. Finding out what is of value to your gatekeeper and doing that is the only thing that will. Doing what your boss values and feels is most important will make you seem like you are in a natural alignment, will make you appear trustworthy, and will cement you as this boss's new MVP. Creating a partnership with this gatekeeper right away and showing him or her that you can be a trusted supporter will open all the gates to what you desire in your career.

You don't have to personally like this individual, but you must absolutely find a way to respect your boss and be an openly supportive force for him or her. No one else has as much power over your livelihood, security, and happiness on the job.

A boss who feels supported by you and who feels you make him or her look good will reciprocate with loyalty, increased job security, promotions, and rewards. A boss who feels threatened by you will immediately and forever take away your key opportunities and erode your job security.

Showing respect first and finding out about the culture you've stepped into can go a long way to making you seem like a good fit and a strong team member. You will make people nervous if you charge ahead on projects the way you've "always done them." Conversely, people will feel they can trust you if you ask questions and take their feelings and comfort level into account first. You weren't hired to show them all how to do things "the right way." You weren't hired to bring the practices of your previous employer to this new opportunity. You were hired to support the systems, processes, and people that are already in place. That's what will make you shine in these first six months.

This approach may seem counterintuitive to many of you. It's certainly not something that is openly talked about within our organizations, but if you concentrate on these four strategies while the spotlight is on, you will be amazed with the results. Even if it involves drastically changing the way you usually work, it is worth it.

Let's face it, you aren't just looking for a new job; you are looking for a new step in your career and a fresh start. How you choose to present yourself within the spotlight will create the foundation for that fresh start. You can either ensure you behave like, and consequently get treated like, everybody else—just another clock-punching employee. Or you can ensure that you exhibit the behaviors that make you look like the newest company star. You can be the one who starts to look more and more like the savior, the one who will make the department and the company more successful, the one who is being flagged for promotions down the line. You can be the one the company feels is the best hire they've made in years.

The foundation you create within these first 180 days will determine the kind of career you can build. Feel free to do the things you'd really like to do once the opinions and judgments are set in your favor. At that point, you're on much safer ground. Until then, don't kid yourself into thinking that you're just another invisible new employee. You're not. You could, after all, be the newest company star.

INSIDER SECRET 40
You must take sides.

YOUR NEW TEAM MEMBERS ARE ACTIVELY TAKING SIDES FROM the moment you enter. They are deciding whether they will be working with you or against you. Which side are you on?

Nothing ends the excitement of a new job like walking into a hostile environment. Rather than being welcomed with smiles and open arms, you find yourself surrounded by crossed arms, sour faces, side-glances, whispers, and nonresponsiveness to your requests.

So many of us show up to new jobs ready to share our knowledge and wow everybody only to find, instead of support, a boss who seems threatened by our talents and a team that sees us as competition instead of an asset. You soon realize that alliances are forming against you, people are excluding you, and there's an indescribable feeling of being an outsider. What do you do? This isn't the high school cafeteria; this is your career. Do you start all over again and prove yourself to all these people? Or do you just forge ahead and do your thing, with the famous "if-they-don't-like-me-that's-tough" attitude?

You'll be happy to know that as common as this scenario can be, entering a new company provides the perfect opportunity to start off on the right foot and get key people on your side.

When you first enter, everyone is looking to see if you are a threat or an ally. Once you have been labeled a potential threat, people will begin working against you and you will not be supported. Their trust is never coming back.

Almost anything can be seen as a threat in this environment, but it's not enough to try to avoid threatening behavior. You have to say you are with them, show that you are an ally, or they will assume the worst: that you are not on their side. You must immediately and openly choose a side right when you enter the company—their side. Or they will assume that you are only on your own side, only out for yourself.

There are only two sides in this game, and the one you choose is critical to your success. One side means being a member of a group who enjoys support, reciprocal favors, and protection. The other is lonely, unsupported, and treacherous. You may think that being on your own side, against everyone else, is the safest course of action in today's workplace. But the opposite is true. If you are alone, without allies to protect and support you, you are ten times more likely to be taken down by company politics, have others steal your work and accomplishments, and be sacrificed for someone else's career aspirations. It is imperative that you build key alliances immediately when you enter a company. Let everyone know you're on their side, or you will be on the outs.

Here's how it's done.

Identifying Inner Saboteurs

FIRST, THERE ARE TWO NATURAL TENDENCIES YOU WILL need to be aware of, and fight against, if you want to keep from short-circuiting the process.

One is the tendency to want to prove to others that you belong where you've landed. You don't need to do this. You were hired. You survived the grueling interview and screening process to become the new hire, and that should be enough for everyone—including you. You don't need to prove anything to these people, and attempting to do so will only weaken your position. The very nature of "proving" will make you seem like a threat to those around you because it tends to emphasize all your qualifications and experience in juxtaposition to theirs, thus automatically activating competition.

A sense of competition is highly threatening to your co-workers' positions and livelihood. If you've accidentally made people feel threatened, they will act against you, sometimes quite strongly, rather than in support of you. This will not create the cohesive team you were hoping to join. It will instead make others distrust you and feel protective of their own territory and even make some feel compelled to sabotage you. Steering clear of competition is critical, especially within the first 90–180 days when everyone is sizing you up to see what kind of potential threat you might be to their position. Truthfully, it's good to avoid the activation of competition throughout your entire career, unless you enjoy the added thrill of having co-workers and bosses plotting against you. It's important to understand that once created, a competitive climate never goes away.

The second natural instinct to watch for and prevent is the tendency to put your personal production over the creation of solid relationships and building alliances. High production is important during your first six months, but it must be secondary to creating the key alliances you need to be protected and successful. Otherwise, all you've worked for will be too easily taken away. I've seen many hardworking employees and even high-level executives taken down because they did not know how to build strong alliances as they entered the company and did not understand the value of inspiring loyalty and support to protect them as they built their career. The foundation of alliances you create can make all the difference between hard work for great rewards and hard work for zero rewards.

Some employees know how important building alliances can be, and they try to manipulate their relationships. This will bring mixed results and create distrust. Others understand that alliances are key but don't know how to naturally create them, so they just come right out and ask for the loyalty and support of others. This also will yield mixed results. However, there is a way to inspire loyalty in others. If you've been able to inspire loyalty, security, and support, you will have it forever. The secret is the "law of reciprocity." This will put you squarely on the right side without having to beg for others to support you.

Activating the Law of Reciprocity

YOU CAN SEE THIS POWERFUL LAW AT WORK WHEN SOMEONE gives you a gift you weren't expecting. When this happens, doesn't it naturally inspire you to reciprocate in some way? What if it's a gift that means a great deal to you and you cannot reciprocate immediately? It will cause you to look for ways to help and support the giver because you feel somehow indebted and obligated to even the score. Most people feel terrible embarrassment over a lavish and unexpected gift that cannot be immediately repaid and will go to great lengths to reciprocate.

Advertisers use this law quite effectively by offering "free" samples, which subconsciously make us feel obligated to purchase the product. Another popular variation on this idea is offering a special discount or "knocking one whole payment off the purchase price," which the consumer interprets as a gift. It makes us somehow feel indebted to the company: "They've done something very generous for me, and I didn't even ask for it. The score between us is uneven, so I must do something in return (like make a purchase)."

This tactic is highly effective in the workplace. When we're given something important to us, without being asked directly for anything in return, most of us will naturally act to even the score. It's a subconscious urge that many of us aren't even aware of.

This instinct is so strong that it will inspire loyalty, respect, and support more quickly than anything else. Because an established team can feel so threatened, disrupted, and distrustful of a new employee, the law of reciprocity is the one thing that will cut through all these issues and turn the situation around—in your favor.

So what gift can you offer? You are the gift! Give others the gift of your support and service first, before you ask for or require anything at all of them.

This is done by casually going to your team members, boss, and other key people and asking how you can be of help to them. In order for it to be a true gift, it should be the first interaction you have with each of these people. Most do just the opposite, going to each person they think they'll need help from and telling him or her who they are and what they need. This will work against you and will create enemies rather than supporters. Instead, present yourself in service and support to others, no matter what your rank.

Ask them how your position could best serve theirs, if there's anything they need from you or your department, if there is any way you can help make their job or position easier. Depending on whom you're speaking to, you could also ask if there are things they might like to see done differently in your position that your predecessor wasn't providing. No matter what it is, make sure you provide it. Timely follow-through is the key to ensuring that your gift is trusted.

As a bonus, you've also just given them a "free sample" of your work and your value to them as an ally. You've shown them how good you are at your job, without making them feel threatened—because it was part of the gift. Now they know you are good at what you do, responsive, caring, an ally, and not a threat. They are also now inspired to provide protection for you and give you support when you need it. Why? Because you offered support and service first. Now, if you were to go to any of them later on and ask for a special favor, what kind of response do you think you'd get? If you've done this correctly, you'll go right to the top of their list.

Offering yourself in service to others as you enter a new job, asking what your co-workers and gatekeepers need instead of assuming you know what's best, will help you focus on what's most important to the company and your career. It will give you immediate insight into the inner workings of the company, what its key challenges are, and how you fit in. These meetings with co-workers will help you get up to speed quickly, as well as ensure that you are supported as you move forward.

Your Boss Is #1

YOUR BOSS WILL HAVE THE MOST POWER OVER YOUR CAREER success and job security. In order to create a partnership with this powerful gatekeeper, you must quickly and openly choose his or her side. This person is the most important ally you can make. Now, of course, there are instances where you may get a boss who is on the way out, has made political mistakes, or has created powerful enemies. If you think your boss is a falling star, you should try to distance yourself as much as possible so you don't get caught in the downfall, but you must still offer yourself in service.

Assuming you have a boss who's on solid ground, this relationship should be the primary focus of your alliance building.

In fact, I recommend starting the very first day with a one-on-one meeting with your new boss to find out what's most important to him or her. Learn what your boss would like to see from you and what you can do to be as supportive as possible. Find out what this boss would view as a huge success for the position and the team that can be accomplished within your first 3–6 months. Then boil down all this information into the top three things you believe are most important to your new boss and those should become your #1 priority.

As you can imagine, when others on your new team see what you're doing (putting your boss's interests first), they will naturally feel threatened, but offering yourself in service to them as well will neutralize those feelings. Instead of being seen as a potential threat or even a brownnoser, you will be seen as someone who offers support to everyone equally and you will be trusted. That's why it's critical that you do this for your team members as well. Your boss's preferences and needs always come first, then services and support for team members. Where do yours fit in? During your spotlight period, your needs are last.

The more quickly you offer yourself in service, the more your efforts will be trusted, and the more secure your position will be.

In fact, for the first three to four weeks of your new job, you should spend around 30 to 40 percent of your time creating alliances and offering services for others and only 60 to 70 percent on your work. Don't worry about becoming overwhelmed with requests for things to do for others. You'll find that most often the people you offer this gift to can't think of anything you can do for them, but they will greatly appreciate the gesture, and a sense of reciprocity will still be created. You will get the most requests and preferences from your boss, and those should always come first. Any other requests from key allies, even if they come later on, should be taken on with secondary yet key importance. Don't worry that other work is not getting done. For the first three weeks on your new job, this *is* your work. There is nothing more important to your career success than choosing sides and building these key alliances. Nothing.

If you inherit a huge workload and think you just don't have time to start your new job building key alliances, think again. Even if you have to work longer hours at first to do both, you will want to do so. You have a very brief window to build these alliances. If done too late, your efforts will be distrusted.

What if important things start to fall through the cracks while you're spending time on key alliances? If you've been building alliances and something critical does fall through the cracks, guess who will come to your rescue?

We all want to make the best impression when we start at a new company and show everyone we can do everything perfectly.

The truth is: When you first start, no matter how hard you work or concentrate on your tasks, some things will fall through the cracks. You won't be able to do everything perfectly right off the bat. What kind of protection do you have when that happens? What do you think would happen if instead of building any key alliances, you concentrated solely on your work? Chances are you'd be seen as someone only out for yourself and your own career, and those around you would let you fall. No matter how hard you'd been working, you'd be on shakier ground than when you started, because you have no allies.

We've all seen those employees, or even executives, who sit back and do nothing and who are seemingly untouchable even when things go wrong. What do they have that you don't? They have allies. They have a loyal base of alliances with people ready to protect them, cover for them, and do favors for them. They don't have to worry when things go wrong or when they make a mistake. They don't even have to worry about political shifting in the workplace because they have so many people in their corner. They have openly chosen sides and openly operated in support of others when they first started at the company, in return for protection and support.

As annoying as this kind of untouchable employee or executive can seem to an outsider, they've worked hard to achieve that level of support. It's created through putting others first, doing favors, offering protection, and providing support for key people along the way.

A support network has become a critical aspect of success in our career paths. We can no longer afford to treat ourselves as an island in the workplace. When trouble comes, we all need the added protection of powerful work allies. These allies provide protection, greater security, more opportunities for growth, and an easier work life. It is within your power to create a supportive network simply by offering a gift.

INSIDER SECRET 41
Your new job is not secure.

DO YOU KNOW WHAT DETERMINES JOB SECURITY THESE DAYS? Most people don't. In fact, many believe it no longer exists. But it does, and you can create it.

Even though it seems like companies are willing to callously discard their employees no matter how hard they work or how dedicated they are, that's not the case. No company will get rid of an employee they feel is critical to their success. In fact, I've seen many companies break the rules to keep a particular employee even when drastic things occurred within the organization. The problem is, company loyalty is not automatic anymore. It's not created by hard work, long hours, or even years of service. It must be inspired. It can be inspired throughout the course of your career, but that will be an uphill battle. It is always easiest to create when you first enter a company.

The truth is: Your job security is determined within your first six months on the job, and that determination will be very hard to change.

How can that be the case? While the spotlight is on, the company will naturally determine how valuable you are to the organization and how critical you are to their overall success. That perceived value translates directly into ongoing job security or lack thereof.

If you are able to show that you are a unifying, supportive, successful, and positive force within those first six months, you will achieve job security while others remain invisible.

While everyone is watching and evaluating you, it is the perfect time to show them you are in line with the values of the organization, willing to go the extra mile, positive about being there, and a successful force within the organization. Those are all the things the company is looking for in their next star. A company will never remove a potential star.

They aren't appraising you solely on your work accomplishments. They are evaluating how well you represent the ideal image the company wants to have. Those who seem in line with that ideal are the ones flagged for "great things in the future." These employees are noted as the ones to watch, while others are mentally dismissed.

If you look like and act like all the others, you will have the same job security they have—none. You will be seen as one of the easily replaced masses the company doesn't need to care about. But if you showcase yourself as the new company star, you will be protected no matter what.

In the creation of job security, you cannot have a more powerful ally than your boss. No matter what your boss says, he is always the one in charge of determining who stays and who goes, who is valued and who is overlooked. The relationship you create with your boss will determine your level of job security. Allowing the company to see how wonderful you are falls squarely within the powers of your gatekeeper. You can't showcase your talents without the support of your boss. There is no getting around this gatekeeper. If you look like the next company star, your boss can choose to convince key people otherwise, or he can allow your image to shine through, as it should.

The image you're going for is not created by showcasing your brains and talents against your boss and co-workers. That tendency, although a natural one, will make you seem overly ambitious and threatening to those around you. Even though it seems like that approach would make your skills and talents more visible, it will actually have the opposite effect as you enter a company.

Trying to showcase your value on your own is always dangerous, but inspiring others to do it for you is golden. Offering your brains and talent in support of your boss and co-workers will cause the entire group to showcase your talents and value *for* you as they say glowing things about you and openly sing your praises for you. This magnifies your value to those who are watching. That's the secret to ensuring you are seen as an asset to the group and organization rather than a risk. The kind of partnership you create with your boss and the quality of the alliances you are able to build are what will provide job protection no matter what comes.

It's not about working hard. It's not about your skill level. It's about your perceived value to the key decision makers. If they feel that you are a potential star, a key to their success, they will move heaven and earth to protect and promote you.

The truth is: You are the one in charge of how the company views and treats you. You are the one who determines if others feel threatened by you or feel inspired to support and partner with you. You are not a victim of the workplace system. The system merely responds to behavioral choices. If you choose to behave like an island only looking out for yourself, the system will respond in kind and treat you that way. If you choose to integrate yourself, treating the company's success as your own and becoming a key support for others within the organization, the system will respond in kind and protect you.

Treating our workplaces as though loyalty no longer exists is a self-fulfilling prophecy. **The truth is: If you show open loyalty first, the company will feel inspired to reciprocate,** much in the same way that offering service and support first to others will bring it right back to you. It's all about reciprocity.

If you are looking to create security for yourself, try making the person in charge of your security, your boss, feel secure and supported. In fact, if you are looking for anything in your career that you feel you've been missing, something that could make all the difference in the level of success you've experienced, try offering and providing it first. I think you'll find it can create the magic you've been looking for.

The judgments a company forms about you are entirely in your hands. Not only can they be carefully crafted to support your goals for success, but they should be your main priority as you start a new job. This will go much further than learning how to work the copier; trust me.

INSIDER SECRET 42
Looking like you don't belong is the key.

IF YOUR GOAL IS TO MOVE UP WITHIN THE ORGANIZATION and be flagged for future promotions, you must stand out from the crowd from the very beginning.

Most of us have aspirations beyond what we've been hired to do. There's certainly nothing wrong with that, but you will be distrusted if you voice those aspirations, either during the interview process or during your spotlight period. You will be perceived as a threat and potential risk to those around you. Besides, you are not the one in charge of making those decisions—the company's key decision makers are. They are not swayed or impressed with speeches about how one day you'd like to have one of their jobs.

What does sway these key decision makers? There is a little-known secret to making those at the top feel inspired to help you move up. Asking for help getting promoted will never work, but inspiring those above to elevate you will always work.

The first step is to emulate those who hold the position you aspire to, not those who hold the one you have. Most believe they should try to fit in with their current group, but that will simply make you invisible to those at the top. Trying to fit in with where you are will do nothing but ensure you stay there.

One of the things most easily seen and recognized by those above you is how you look and outwardly behave. If you look like you fit in at the higher levels, those at the top will start to visualize you there and will soon feel increasingly uncomfortable having you lingering in the lower ranks where you clearly stand out. None of them want someone who looks like "one of their own" sitting at a lower level, so they will unknowingly become your allies in helping you move up.

Don't worry about standing out from the crowd—this is a good thing. You want those in power positions to notice you. In fact, you want them to mistake you for one of them. This is done by openly aligning yourself with the issues they support, the messages they promote, even the way they dress and the hours they keep. Emulating this group is much more powerful than telling these people you wish to join them.

These tactics can most easily be enacted when you first enter the company so that you are trusted without question. If they see you trying to do it later, you will experience a much greater uphill battle to gain their trust.

In addition to dressing like they do and looking like you belong at their higher level, you want to be actively working on any certifications or credentials required at the level you're looking to join, along with any cultural nuances this group values (like a penchant for golf or an appreciation of cigars). Make sure you do these on your own time and they do not impact your work productivity. Also, be sure to let your boss and human-resources department know when you've added a certification or credential that the company values. You certainly don't have to let anyone know about improving your golf game, but when you get good enough, being seen golfing where the key people at your company golf wouldn't be a bad idea. Showing off your new cigar knowledge to the executive group who smoke together by offering them a nice box of cigars doesn't hurt, either.

In addition to crafting your new image to fit in with those at the next level, you will need to pay special attention to your alliance with your boss. If you look like you belong at the higher levels, but your boss doesn't, you could quickly be in trouble. Your boss is the one who will flag you to move up to that next level. Without his support you will never be promoted no matter how much you emulate those at the top. So, offering yourself in service to this individual, making him look good, and working in support of his efforts will ensure that nice things are said about you behind closed doors. It will also ensure that when people at the next level come to move you up to "where you belong," your boss won't be standing in your way.

Don't ever underestimate the power of someone at a higher level feeling uncomfortable seeing "one of their own" languishing at a lower level. Those individuals never languish for long.

INSIDER SECRET 43
Every day is your next interview.

EVERY SINGLE DAY YOU GO TO WORK, YOU ARE INTERVIEWING for your next career opportunity. How you behave day to day will determine the course of your career.

"Diane" was experiencing a typical job search, filled with typical frustrations, but there was one thing that was really starting to bother her—her references. She'd forgotten all about those. In fact, she was having trouble even finding three people to put on her professional references sheet. She was a strong worker, had always put in the hours, and had been a top producer, but she was always a bit of a company loner. She ultimately didn't have a network to fall back on during her job search but figured that she would start looking online and in the classifieds and certainly her credentials would land her on top.

"Mark" was known in his work circles as an all-around good guy. He was a hard worker but would also jump in to help others on his team on a regular basis. When he found his department eliminated, he went right to his network of previous co-workers and bosses. He spent a few days calling everyone he'd worked with previously, asking if they knew of anything he might be suited for and if they'd give him a reference. He had a resounding response and an interview by the end of that week. He had a new job in almost record time, spending only two weeks out of work and joining his new company before his severance check had been cashed.

There's no doubt that networking is one of the most powerful tools in job searching today, and there are many ways to create that network: joining industry groups, through family or common-interest circles. But most of us forget about the most powerful networking opportunity we have—our co-workers.

These are the people who can really speak to our strengths and can vouch for our work talents and industry knowledge. They are the ones who will know about jobs that have come up that are a perfect match for you, and they are the ones who get called for referrals from recruiters and friends at other companies.

People you work with every day, especially your boss, are also the ones whom companies will try to get hold of to find out about your previous work history. These are the people who will be giving you references for future opportunities.

The truth is: Every day we go to work, we are unknowingly interviewing for the rest of our careers. Whether you realize it or not, everything you choose to do at your current job is actively building the references and networks that will support you in finding your next job and the next job after that.

What you choose to say and how you choose to behave will follow you from job to job. It will either cost you opportunities or build bridges to new ones. The support of those you've worked with in the past is incredibly powerful in moving your career forward, recommending you for opportunities, and providing top-notch references that get you hired for the best jobs.

You may feel that what you do day to day doesn't really matter as long as you get your work done. But at the end of the day, the quality of your work can be secondary to the foundational network you've built. It is as important to manage your work reputation as it is to manage what ends up on your résumé.

To get the best jobs, the jobs you desire, you want every boss you've worked for to volunteer glowing recommendations. You want the people you've worked with and helped to become your network army that's always out there ready to support your next move.

What you do in your position matters just as much as if not more than what you work on: how you choose to treat those you work with, how you partner with your boss, if you act in support of others. These all create a reputation that follows you.

Are you concerned that the reputation you've built, or accidentally ignored, may be working against you? You can change it with the very next job you get. New jobs provide the perfect opportunity to start fresh, and they are wonderful places for creating powerful networks and referral pathways. **The truth is: The same behaviors that make you look like the next company star will also create a solid foundation of networks and alliances that will support you throughout your career.**

The easiest way to create a network is to stop thinking of these people as difficult co-workers and demanding bosses and start treating them like important clients. Clients are always treated like the important gatekeepers they are, but we forget that our bosses and co-workers will become just as powerful. Just as entrepreneurs depend on their clients for referrals for additional opportunities and growth, so do the job hunters of today. A personal referral is one of the most powerful influences in interviewing. It can elevate a standard candidate to a top recommendation for hire.

Networking doesn't start once you're out of a job, frantically looking for your next opportunity. It is something you build every day with the people you work with, your vendors, clients, co-workers, and bosses. You will never have more powerful allies than those you've worked closely with and done favors for and the people you've saved when the you-know-what hit the fan. These are the people who become your most powerful job search allies and career support network.

Be mindful of your daily interactions with these powerful people you now find yourself teamed up with. These partnerships will last longer and be more powerful than you imagine.

The truth is: Your number one job is always to protect your job and career path. No one else can do it for you. But it doesn't have to be a daunting task. It is most easily and effectively accomplished within your first few months. And it will have staying power.

Don't let the political pitfalls of the typical workplace operate against you. Take the time to set yourself up for success from the very beginning, so that this new opportunity becomes the gateway to achieving your goals and dreams.

It's not enough to have a powerful strategy to win in the interview process. Make sure you have an equally powerful strategy to create a solid foundation for continued success once you're hired.

YOU'RE HIRED. NOW WHAT? KEY POINTS TO REMEMBER

SECRET 39: WHAT'S THAT BRIGHT LIGHT? You are in the spotlight when you first join a company as a new hire. How you choose to use it will determine whether you are headed for struggle or success.

SECRET 40: WHAT SIDE ARE YOU ON? There are only two choices: your side or theirs. The one you choose will determine whether you are protected and supported or abandoned and sabotaged. Choose carefully.

SECRET 41: THERE'S JOB SECURITY? It may seem like job security is a thing of the past, but it can be created today if you know how. The secret is that it's always easiest to create when you first enter a new company.

SECRET 42: WHAT'S "ONE OF OUR OWN" DOING DOWN THERE? If you want to move up, you can either ask for promotions and go around tooting your own horn, or inspire those at the top to notice you and quickly elevate you to their level. Which do you think is safer and easier?

SECRET 43: EVERY DAY IS YOUR NEXT INTERVIEW. Setting yourself up for future career success is done day by day, with the people working right next to you. They will always be the most powerful job network you have.

CONCLUSION

INSIDER SECRET 44
You have the power.

I'M SURE MOST OF YOU THOUGHT THE HIRING AND INTERviewing process was bad enough before reading this book, and now that you know what's really going on out there it must seem completely overwhelming. Our interview processes seem more and more like brutal Hollywood auditions than the pleasant and professional meetings we thought they were. "Too short, too tall, not confident enough, didn't sell it to me—NEXT!" Don't let this intimidate you.

Behind the scenes of these interviews, there is a lot going on. Clearly not all of it is working in your favor, but here's the good news—you now know what all of it is. You now know that a hiring manager is just as scared as you are, and sometimes even more so. Scared he won't be able to find the right candidate in time to please the department, scared he'll hire the wrong person or cause the company inconvenience, or even lose his job in the process. You also know where all the bombs are buried in the hiring process and how to avoid them. You have the upper hand.

You now understand how to maneuver through the process from the inside to work each interview opportunity to your advantage. You now have the power to choose the jobs and the companies *you* want to work for, not the other way around. The only thing that's been standing in your way is the hiring manager, and it's time we took away a little of his power.

The truth is: Companies don't hold all the power; you do. You are the one who dictates how they treat you, view you, respond to you. You are the one who can direct your job search in any direction you desire. Companies are not as mysterious as they seem; they are responsive entities. They are responding to you. Everything you do and say will elicit a standard and predictable response from the interviewer and the company. Change what you do or say and the response of the company will change accordingly.

Here's even better news: If learning and working all 44 of these secrets into your job search repertoire seems too overwhelming at this moment, you don't need to incorporate all of them to ace the hiring process. These insider secrets will swing the power into your hands in such a way that just incorporating one or two of them into your job search will yield amazing results. Taking just one of the secrets in this book to heart, let alone putting several into practice, can mean the difference between taking whatever job comes along next and enjoying dream job after dream job.

We spend so much time at work, with most of our energy going to our jobs every day, it's important to be able to find and recognize the job for you when you see it. You deserve to work in the best environment for you, to have the job you desire with a company that deserves your efforts and time. If you invest in yourself and your future by managing your résumé, directing your career path, and actively putting into practice the secrets in this book, you will find that you have access to opportunities that others simply won't have.

You can absolutely have a job that makes you happy, puts a smile on your face every morning, fulfills you, and makes you say, "A paycheck? I'd do this for free!" Can you imagine? Yes, it's really out there.

Don't just sit around hoping for the best and hoping for things to change. Make it happen. Use these secrets and every tool you can find to get yourself to a place in your career that makes you feel like you've "arrived," whatever that means for you. For some it may be more money and a corner office; for others it may be more creativity, part-time work, having your kids down the hall in day care, or working in a part of the country you've always wanted to live in. All of these possibilities exist today, and so do the processes and tools to help you find and achieve your dreams.

The interview systems will continue to change. Your career will continue to change, but there is one constant—you. No interviewer will ever be able to assess or uncover the real you in a one-hour meeting. No hiring manager will be able to understand who you are with all your life history, struggles, and victories. It's up to you to present yourself in a way that showcases the best of all you've learned, all you know, and who you know you will one day become. Show them the best of who you truly are. No matter what crazy trick questions or discrimination you may face, know that you are a wonderfully unique commodity. We each have a unique spark inside us. Look within yourself and reconnect with that spark. That's what speaks to people. That's what makes you unique. That's what will shine through even the most challenging interview process.

Finding the right company fit, acing the interview for the job of your dreams, and getting top dollar for the position you've always wanted are the moments we all work toward. Don't just hope that these things will come your way and that you'll be ready if they do.

Get out there and make it happen. Practice all these tools and insider tips now, not just before you're going into the big interview for the job that's perfect for you. Do something to move your career forward every day. Build your certifications, create your network, build your skills, invest in your interviewing and negotiating skills, and turn yourself into the number one candidate every company would love to have.

Don't ever let hidden agendas, underhanded tactics, and inexperienced interviewers keep you from achieving the jobs you desire. All it takes is a little planning and some insider knowledge to get you there.

Now you have all the power in the process. You can do it!

HELPFUL RESOURCES AND INFORMATION

CAREER ADVICE AND RESOURCES

Anti9to5guide.com Showcases the Alternatives to Traditional Jobs

This site offers free articles and career advice for those looking to transition from a traditional corporate job into work that better fits their lifestyle dreams: freelance, part-time, flextime, at-home, outdoor, overseas, nonprofit, etc. It asks us to "explore what life is like outside the cube."

ColorQProfiles.com Career-Matching Services

Find your ideal career and your unique work style. The Color Q profile career-matching system can help you discover your unique style and how to use it to your career advantage.

CynthiaShapiro.com Career and Job Search Advice

Find résumé crafting, interview coaching, negotiation training, cover-letter strategies, career issue resolution, plans for promotion or goal achievement, and career coaching. This site also offers a Career Chat discussion board mediated by the author, free career resources, and articles and interviews on key career issues.

Fortune.com *Fortune* Magazine

The magazine's Web site, part of CNNMoney.com, lists the best companies to work for and offers a variety of helpful and interesting articles for your career.

Free-career-test.com Career Testing and Matching

This site provides a *free* report highlighting your strengths and interests to help you find the career and industry that are best for you. For an additional small fee it will also produce a detailed report with a list of the industries you might enjoy working in, professional organizations related to your field, and sites that will help you learn more about the industry.

VocationVacations.com Try Out Your Dream Job

The only company of its kind, VocationVacations gives people the opportunity to test-drive the job of their dreams—risk-free. If you're curious about a new career or would just like to see what living another career might be like, a VocationVacations adventure provides a uniquely educational experience.

COMPENSATION AND SALARY INFORMATION

Erieri.com The Economic Research Institute

ERI offers career salary and cost-of-living information, and a *free* salary potential calculator and cost-of-living calculator for over 7,200 U.S., Canadian, and international cities.

Salary.com Compensation Information

This site contains all kinds of information relating to compensation. The "SalaryWizard" lists salary statistics for hundreds of positions.

SalaryExpert.com Salary Comparisons and Market Rate

This site provides *free* salary and benefits information for over thirty thousand jobs. Choose a job title and a location from a list of cities in the United States and Canada and find salary and benefits statistics as well as buying power comparisons. This site also compares local data with national norms.

CREDIT REPORT SERVICE

AnnualCreditReport.com Run Your Credit Report

Find out what a potential employer might see if they run your credit report. This site allows you to request a *free* credit report once every twelve months from each of the nationwide consumer credit reporting companies: Equifax, Experian, and TransUnion. They also have a listing of your consumer rights and resources on how to manage the information on your credit report. *(Note: Although it is important to know what's in your credit report prior to job searching and clean up anything you can, you may not want to run your credit reports more than once a year or it may lower your credit score.)*

FIRING AND TERMINATION RECOVERY

CynthiaShapiro.com Recovery from a Firing or Termination

The author Cynthia Shapiro offers special resources for job seekers struggling to find a new position after a termination or firing. A confidential and in-depth analysis of the issues surrounding the termination, reference checking, research, and specialized interview coaching can all help put a job seeker back on track quickly and effectively.

SimplyFired.com Resources and Support for the Recently Fired

This is a wonderful resource for those who have had to go through a recent firing or termination. Sometimes it helps to know that you're not alone. Commiserate with others; read funny stories; get expert help. Share your experience on a site with people who understand—and can help!

GOVERNMENT INFORMATION AND SERVICES

DOL.gov The Department of Labor

The site for the U.S. Department of Labor provides detailed wage and job information, benefits and insurance information, and general legal information for employees.

Info.gov The U.S. Government Information Center

This site can help lead you through the maze of information on employment law and services available through government agencies. Call the 800 number and have them guide you to the most appropriate Web site or agency to get the employment or legal information you need, or click on the "Pueblo" services (generated out of Pueblo, Colorado) to get to the Federal Citizen Information Center. Then click on "Employment" on the left side. *(Note: Some reports are fee based, but they are very low cost.)*

IMAGE CONSULTANTS

GloriaStarr.com Image Coaching and Executive Finishing School

Gloria Starr offers impression management for the workplace, business and dining etiquette, communication skills, and executive finishing school.

ImageTherapists.com Image Therapists International

This sought-after service provides personalized coaching on how to present yourself in dress, appearance, and overall image for greater authenticity, personal power, and career success.

NewYorkImageConsultant.com Image Consulting

These image consultants will help you maximize your visual first impressions in an interview or important meeting to project an overall image of confidence and success.

INDUSTRY AND COMPANY RESEARCH

Acinet.org America's Career InfoNet

This site offers information on occupations, industries, and state labor markets for career research purposes and allows you to build a profile with employment, wages, and skills and find high-growth and high-wage occupations. At this site you can also create industry profiles with employment and wage trend information and find industries projected to grow the fastest or those with the largest current employment.

BLS.gov The Bureau of Labor Statistics

This government site provided the statistical information cited in this book. They keep detailed reports and records on unemployment, job openings, and trends for analysis and research purposes.

CarolWorld.com Company Research

This site provides corporate annual reports for research on specific companies prior to interviews.

Hoovers.com Company and Industry Research Center

Hoover's offers comprehensive company, industry, and market intelligence to help you research the companies you want to work for.

Job-Descriptions.org Find Job Descriptions

This resource provides general job descriptions and details. The site offers over thirteen thousand descriptions, divided into major categories, divisions, and groups.

INTERNET/WEB PRESENCE MANAGEMENT

Google.com *Free* Google E-lerts to Monitor Your Web Presence

When job-searching, you should be actively monitoring your name and presence on the Web. To sign up for this free service, sign up for the "Alert" function and put in your name or the topic you'd like it to search for. You will get an e-mail every time your name pops up on an Internet posting.

LinkedIn.com Create a Professional Web Presence and Online Network for Your Job Search

LinkedIn is an online community that can be used as a powerful job search tool. It allows you to create a personal profile that showcases you as the ideal candidate for the industry and jobs you're targeting in your search. You can network with company executives, find people you worked with previously who may know of job openings, and add a professional Web presence to your overall job search strategy.

JOB SEARCHING

CampusCareerCenter.com Campus Career Center (CCC)

This site offers resources for recent graduates to find their first job. CCC specializes in enabling Fortune 500 companies to recruit the best and brightest students nationwide.

ExecuNet.com Executive Networking

ExecuNet connects senior-level professionals ($100K+) directly with business decision makers, executive recruiters, and peers.

Experience.com Internships and Entry-Level Jobs

Alumni from hundreds of universities and Fortune 500 companies post internships and entry-level jobs on this site specifically targeted to your school. Plus you can connect with alumni and insiders for advice on how to find the best internships and positions to help with your job search and career management.

4ICJ.com International Careers and Jobs

This site, 4 International Careers and Jobs, is a worldwide directory of job sites and career resources for finding overseas jobs. It offers free and fee-based connections to international employment agencies regarding seasonal work, government jobs, internships, full-time jobs, and other services.

Idealist.org Nonprofit Jobs

This site provides a listing of jobs and volunteer opportunities at nonprofit organizations.

SimplyHired.com Target Your Job Search and Find Your Dream Job

This effective job search site does all the work for you. It automatically searches over four million jobs, pulling them from all the big-name job boards, the thousands of lesser-known job boards, company Web sites, even the newspaper classifieds. It will continue your search for you and e-mail you when a job pops up that matches your dream job criteria. As a bonus, it is the only job search site that can search by personal categories like "mom-friendly" "eco-friendly," "age-fifty-plus-friendly," "GLTB (gay, lesbian, transgender, bisexual)–friendly," and even "dog-friendly" workplaces.

LEGAL INFORMATION AND RESOURCES

CynthiaShapiro.com Not Sure If You Have a Legal Case?

Start with a confidential review and analysis directly from the author. Cynthia Shapiro will help you determine where you stand, what your best options are, if you have a strong enough case to move forward with an attorney, and what the ramifications to your career might be. Once you're ready to move forward, Cynthia Shapiro can locate the best lawyer for your case right in your area.

ELinfonet.com Employment Law Information Network

This site provides detailed information and articles on legal issues related to employment.

FindLaw.com Lawyer Finder

Find a lawyer in your state with expertise in your particular area of concern.

LectLaw.com The 'Letric Law Library

This site provides general materials on employment law with explanations and articles on legal topics affecting today's workers.

Legal-Database.com The Online Legal Database

This site provides free legal advice, articles, and the answers to frequently asked labor law questions. It also provides plain-English definitions and explanations of state and federal labor laws.

NELA.org The National Employment Lawyers Association

It is crucial when looking for a lawyer to find one who specializes in employee law (not employer law, and not employer and employee law). NELA advocates for employee rights and workplace fairness while promoting the highest standards of professionalism, ethics, and judicial integrity. NELA is the country's only professional organization that is exclusively composed of lawyers who represent individual employees in cases involving employment discrimination and other employment-related matters. Find a specialist in employee law in your area here.

ORGANIZATIONS AND EMPLOYEE ASSOCIATIONS

dir.yahoo.com/Business and Economy/organizations/professional/

This site offers a directory listing of associations and organizations by industry.

PERSONALITY AND PSYCHOLOGICAL PROFILING

FunEducation.com Free Personality Testing

If you're interested in practicing these tests before you encounter the real thing in an interview, this site may be helpful. *(Note: The site is* free *but has lots of advertisements and offers to weed through; to get your results you will need to click "skip" or "next offer" at the bottom of each page as they pop up. You do not need to sign up for anything to receive your results.)*

Also see the "Suggested Reading" section for a book on preparing for personality profiling and psychological testing in job interviews.

PUBLIC SPEAKING

Toastmasters.org Public Speaking

Toastmasters is a great way to improve your communication skills, lose your fears of public speaking, and develop key tools for success.

REFERENCE CHECKING

ahipubs.net/reports/immunity.pdf Reference Immunity Laws

This unique URL will lead you to a summary of reference immunity laws for each state. Find out if your state has reference immunity laws in place, and get a quick glimpse of the employment reference regulations for your area.

This is an invaluable resource, compiled by the Alexander Hamilton Institute Incorporated.

CynthiaShapiro.com Professional Reference Checking and Employee Advocacy

Find out what your former boss or company is saying about you to prospective employers, and what you can do about it. The author Cynthia Shapiro offers a variety of personalized services and resources for job seekers including in-depth confidential reference checking and practical solutions for eliminating and neutralizing the issues that arise from any negative references.

MyReferences.com Reference- and Background-Checking Service

Allison & Taylor can conduct a professional reference and background check on you before you start your job search, so you'll know exactly what former employers are saying about you.

WOMEN'S RESOURCES

NAFE.com The National Association for Female Executives

NAFE is one of the largest women's professional associations in the country. They provide resources and services through education, networking, and public advocacy to empower members to achieve career success and financial security.

NegotiatingWomen.com Negotiating Women, Inc.

This organization is devoted to the training, consulting, and advancement of women. They offer e-learning courses to help women overcome the natural tendencies that block effective negotiation, and provide guidance to making what you're worth and getting the salary you desire.

NewLadderToSuccess.com Success Support for Women

New Ladder To Success is an online community for professional women dedicated to helping women enhance their knowledge and skills in today's business world. Membership is *free*. You can ask questions, share answers, publish blogs, or post your own career tips and strategies to help others.

WORKPLACE RIGHTS AND INFORMATION

Workrights.org The National Workrights Institute

This nonprofit organization dedicated to fighting for you and your rights in the workplace offers articles, information, and current developments on workplace rights issues. This is a group all working Americans should belong to and support.

SUGGESTED READING

The Anti 9–5 Guide: Practical Career Advice for Women Who Think Outside the Cube, Michelle Goodman (Seal Press, 2007)

If you're thinking of escaping the politics and confinement of the standard corporate environment, this book is a must-read. It presents an entertaining and invaluable collection of expert advice on alternatives to the traditional corporate jobs. It's packed with excellent advice on finding your ultimate dream job, freelancing, flexible work schedules, and nontraditional workplaces.

Career Match: Connecting Who You Are with What You'll Love to Do, Shoya Zichy with Ann Bidou (AMACOM, 2007)

Find the job that truly complements your personality. This book will help you identify the type of work that will inspire and exhilarate you, determine the kind of boss and work environment you need to thrive, confirm the rightness of the path you're on or help you find a better one.

Concrete Confidence: A 30-Day Program for an Unshakable Foundation of Self-Assurance, Sam Horn (St. Martin's Press, 1997)

This is a practical, user-friendly program that is filled with techniques you can begin using immediately. You will learn how to walk into a room full of strangers and turn them into friends, be a self-coach rather than your own worst critic, be able to turn mistakes into lessons instead of failures, and converse with comfort.

Corporate Confidential: 50 Secrets Your Company Doesn't Want You to Know—And What to Do About Them, Cynthia Shapiro (St. Martin's Griffin, 2005)

This international bestseller shares the 50 insider secrets every worker needs to know for job protection and success. Find out how to read the secret signs of a job in jeopardy and what must be done immediately, how to tell if there are imminent changes in your organization or industry coming your way, how to easily get the promotion or raise you're looking for, and how to recognize and resolve workplace issues, deal with a difficult boss, and work the system from the inside to get anything you want in corporate America.

Employment Personality Tests Decoded: Crack Employment Personality Tests, Anne Hart and George Sheldon (Career Press, 2007)

This guide will tell you why corporations require these tests, give details on the most popular ones, tell you how to prepare for each and assess your score, how to ace the tests, and what employers are looking for.

How to Say It in Your Job Search: Choice Words, Phrases, Sentences and Paragraphs for Résumés, Cover Letters, and Interviews, Robbie Miller Kaplan (Prentice Hall Press, 2002)

This book gives you the power words and phrases to use that will make you stand out from the competition and provides real-life examples and samples.

I Don't Know What I Want, but I Know It's Not This: A Step-by-Step Guide to Finding Gratifying Work, Julie Jansen (Penguin Books, 2003)

This book shares the reasons that people tend to find their work unsatisfying, offers stories of people who've made successful career changes, and provides quizzes and questionnaires to help you find your most fulfilling career path.

If My Career's on the Fast Track, Where Do I Get a Road Map?: Surviving and Thriving in the Real World of Work, Anne Fisher (Harper Perennial, 2002)

Every month, hundreds of thousands of *Fortune* magazine and CNN Money.com readers turn to Anne Fisher's "Ask Annie" column for up-to-the-minute career advice. Her book is packed with insightful and engaging advice for employees at all levels of their career, from new entrants to seasoned executives. It's filled with first-rate tips on what to do after graduation, how to move your career ahead, dealing with toxic employees, how to bounce back from a failure or firing, and much more.

The Interview Rehearsal Book: 7 Steps to Job-Winning Interviews Using Acting Skills You Never Knew You Had, Deb Gottesman and Buzz Mauro (Berkeley Books, 1999)

This book shows readers how to get over job interview "stage fright," research the role, look the part, and develop effective verbal and physical communication skills.

Lifescripts: What to Say to Get What You Want in 101 of Life's Toughest Situations, Stephen M. Pollan and Mark Levine (Simon & Schuster/Macmillan, 1996)

This book provides invaluable tactics and detailed scripting on exactly what to say in stressful situations that occur during job interviews and in the workplace.

Nice Girls Don't Get the Corner Office: 101 Unconscious Mistakes Women Make That Sabotage Their Careers, Lois P. Frankel, Ph.D. (Warner Books, 2004)

This eye-opening book clearly identifies the unconscious things women do in the workplace that block their path to success. If you're wondering why you haven't received the rewards your efforts demand, read this book!

Over-40 Job-Search Guide: Ten Strategies for Making Your Age an Advantage in Your Career, Gail Geary (JIST Works, 2004)

This book gives advice on playing to your strengths, uncovering the hot sources for hiring possibilities, making great first impressions, and handling tough questions.

The Pathfinder: How to Choose or Change Your Career for a Lifetime of Satisfaction and Success, Nicholas Love (Fireside/Simon & Schuster, 1998)

Through goal setting, list making, and other techniques, this book leads readers through the process of deciding exactly what they want to do for a living and finding the best way to make it happen.

POP!: Stand Out in Any Crowd, Sam Horn (St. Martin's Press, 2006)

This fun and informative book shows you how to break out from the crowd and package your ideas to command attention. Whether you're crafting a résumé or a proposal or trying to get the attention of key clients or colleagues, this book will provide you with the insightful tools to get results.

Secrets of Six-Figure Women: Surprising Strategies to Up Your Earnings and Change Your Life, Barbara Stanny (HarperCollins, 2004)

This insider's guide to making what you're truly worth is not just for women. If you want to overcome your natural tendencies toward undervaluing your efforts and chronic underearning and learn the secrets to making top dollar, this practical and inspirational book is a must-read.

See Jane Lead: 99 Ways for Women to Take Charge at Work, Lois P. Frankel, Ph.D. (Warner Books, 2007)

This book shatters the myths surrounding female leadership and empowers women to take charge at work. It provides indispensable strategies to recognize and overcome common self-sabotaging behaviors and unleash the natural leadership skills within you. This is an essential guide for women who are ready to step up and take the reins with effectiveness and confidence.

The Right Job, Right Now: The Complete Toolkit to Finding Your Perfect Career, Susan D. Strayer, S.P.H.R. (St. Martin's Griffin, 2006)

This book effectively bridges the gap between: What do I want to do? and How do I do it? It presents a step-by-step program of self-assessment, self-marketing, and career development strategies to help you achieve lasting career satisfaction. And it teaches you how to align your skills and abilities with your needs and desired compensation to find the job that's right for you.

The 7 Habits of Highly Effective People: Powerful Lessons in Personal Change, Stephen R. Covey (Free Press, 2004)

This book continues to be a fundamental career advice guide—for a reason. I highly recommend that anyone starting a new job read it and start putting the habits into practice in his or her daily work life. If you've already read it, review it again before you start each new job to keep these habits top-of-mind.

200 Best Jobs for College Graduates, Michael Farr and Laurence Shatkin (JIST Publishing, 2006)

This book provides lists and descriptions of the jobs that offer the best pay and the fastest growth and have the most openings requiring associate's degrees and higher.

What's Holding You Back?: 30 Days to Having the Courage and Confidence to Do What You Want, Meet Whom You Want, Go Where You Want, Sam Horn (St. Martin's Press, 2000)

This book provides practical steps and advice to break through the barriers that hold you back so you can exude confidence and free yourself from your fears.

INDEX

CYNTHIA SHAPIRO, MBA, ELC, PHR

International Bestselling Author, Speaker, Career Expert

Cynthia Shapiro's fresh approach to career advice has been featured by respected news sources such as CNN, Fox News, MSNBC, PBS, *The Wall Street Journal, Fortune* magazine, and across television, radio, major magazines, and newspapers throughout the United States and around the world.

This former human-resources executive turned preeminent employee advocate and career expert has almost twenty years' experience on the front lines of human resources, personnel, labor relations, employee and executive coaching, recruiting, and hiring. Her clients include employees, managers, and executives from small start-ups to the corporations of the Fortune 100. Cynthia Shapiro's books, workshops, coaching, and speaking engagements have helped thousands of people around the world learn the insider secrets to protecting their jobs and achieving the highest levels of career success.

Cynthia Shapiro's internationally bestselling book *Corporate Confidential: 50 Secrets Your Company Doesn't Want You to Know—And What to Do About Them* (St. Martin's Griffin) is widely considered the foremost authority on the insider secrets to career protection and success. For more information, please visit corporateconfidential.com.

Cynthia Shapiro lives in Southern California.

For Cynthia Shapiro's career-consulting and job search advice, book information, articles and interviews, event schedules, free career resources, "Career Chat" discussion board, and contact information, visit CynthiaShapiro.com.